W9-AZQ-139

A
THOUSAND TIMES
MORE FAIR

ALSO BY KENJI YOSHINO

Covering:
The Hidden Assault on Our Civil Rights

A
Thousand
Times
More Fair

What Shakespeare's Plays
Teach Us About Justice

Kenji Yoshino

ecco

An Imprint of HarperCollinsPublishers

The author gratefully acknowledges the *Yale Journal of Law & the Humanities* for its permission to reproduce material published in a different form. The material originally appeared under the following titles: "The Choice of the Four Fathers: Henry IV, Falstaff, the Lord Chief Justice, and the King of France in the *Henriad*," *Yale Journal of Law & the Humanities* 22, no. 2 (2010): 463–86; "Revenge as Revenant: *Titus Andronicus* and the Rule of Law," *Yale Journal of Law & the Humanities* 21, no. 2 (2009): 203–25; and "The Lawyer of Belmont," *Yale Journal of Law & the Humanities* 9, no. 1 (1997): 183–216.

The author also gratefully acknowledges the *Cleveland State Law Review* for its permission to reproduce material initially published there under the title "On Empathy in Judgment (*Measure for Measure*)," *Cleveland State Law Review* 57, no. 4 (2010): 683–701.

A THOUSAND TIMES MORE FAIR. Copyright © 2011 by Kenji Yoshino. All rights reserved. Printed in the United States of America. No part of this book may be used or reproduced in any manner whatsoever without written permission except in the case of brief quotations embodied in critical articles and reviews. For information address HarperCollins Publishers, 10 East 53rd Street, New York, NY 10022.

HarperCollins books may be purchased for educational, business, or sales promotional use. For information please write: Special Markets Department, HarperCollins Publishers, 10 East 53rd Street, New York, NY 10022.

FIRST EDITION

Designed by Suet Yee Chong

Library of Congress Cataloging-in-Publication Data has been applied for.

ISBN 978-0-06-176910-8

11 12 13 14 15 OV/RRD 10 9 8 7 6 5 4 3 2 1

For Ron Stoneham

"Thy life's a miracle"

Contents

	Introduction	*ix*
ONE	**THE AVENGER** *Titus Andronicus*	1
TWO	**THE LAWYER** *The Merchant of Venice*	29
THREE	**THE JUDGE** *Measure for Measure*	59
FOUR	**THE FACTFINDER** *Othello*	89
FIVE	**THE SOVEREIGN** The *Henriad*	127
SIX	**THE NATURAL WORLD** *Macbeth*	159
SEVEN	**THE INTELLECTUAL** *Hamlet*	185

EIGHT   **THE MADMAN**   209
King Lear

NINE   **THE MAGICIAN**   233
The Tempest

Epilogue   259

Acknowledgments   263

Notes   267

Bibliography   291

Introduction

I INITIALLY ATTEMPTED TO WRITE ABOUT SHAKESPEARE and the law in my first year of law school, hot off an argument with my Constitutional Law professor. We were learning about stare decisis, the doctrine that legal precedents must be followed. My professor made an offhand remark about how law had a fundamentally different attitude toward originality than literature did. Put bluntly, law did not value originality. If a judge found a case essentially identical to the one he was deciding, he gained, rather than lost, authority by relying on it. In literature, he said, one did not gain authority by saying someone else had already made the point.

This contention piqued my curiosity because my major extra-curricular activity in law school was wondering why I was there. As an undergraduate English major, I had seriously considered pursuing a career as a writer or literature professor. I chose law school because I wanted to acquire the language of power, for myself and for my causes. I had not realized how narrow or dry the texts of power would be. (I am not sure what I was expecting—perhaps Prospero's grimoire, or book of magic.) So I was excited that a law professor was giving me an idea I could test against what I was sadly coming to think of as my prior literary life.

I pondered his claim for a few weeks before going to speak with him. After telling him that literary studies still felt like my native heath, I asked him if I could write a paper with him on theories of literary and legal precedent. I proposed to look at how literary works also drew strength from their canonical predecessors. A lifelong Shakespeare devotee, I had even chosen my texts. I planned to contrast the strategy Tom Stoppard used in *Rosencrantz and Guildenstern Are Dead* to revise *Hamlet* (indirect subversion in which the later play changes the meaning of the prior one without contesting any of its facts) with the strategy Aimé Césaire used in *Une Tempête* to revise *The Tempest* (direct subversion in which the later play rewrites the facts of its predecessor).

My professor attempted to dissuade me. He told me I was being trained to "think like a lawyer." Confronted with a strange new discipline, I would find it natural to cling to my old one. But doing so would delay the necessary transition. He was not unsympathetic. He had been an English major himself, but had gone into law to address— I remember his neat phrasing—"justice itself" rather than "justice represented in fiction." He was gentle about it, which I admired, not least because he had manifestly had this conversation many times before. But I received the clear message that my literary life was a thing of the past. It was time to put childish pastimes away, and to focus on my adult profession.

I do not think human beings are particularly plastic. A few weeks later, I was back in my professor's office, saying I had thought hard about his advice, but that I still wanted to write the paper. To his eternal credit, he respected the set of my jaw and agreed to let me do so. The paper was my first publication in a law review. As legal scholarship, it was a failure—I did not know enough law at the time. But it served its purpose. It fixed my conviction that I could and would always make a place for literature in my life in the law.

My focus as a law professor over the past twelve years has been on civil rights and constitutional law: "justice itself" rather than "justice represented in fiction." I have come to love the law and have never seriously regretted my decision to pursue it. Nonetheless, I have also never stopped teaching classes on law and literature. I do not regard this as a vestige of my past. To the contrary, I use this class to keep steadily visible that the law itself is a set of stories—told by legislators and judges, plaintiffs and defendants. As the late law-and-literature scholar Robert Cover put it: "for every constitution there is an epic, for each decalogue a scripture." We cannot understand the law unless we see how its formal texts are embedded in the narratives that accord them shape and meaning.

Some of my colleagues view my law-and-literature classes as soft or suspect, for many of the reasons that my original professor told me to surrender literature for law. In their view, literature is too different from law to illuminate it. Reading literature as a guide to legal decision making is, in Judge Richard Posner's memorable phrase, like "reading *Animal Farm* as a tract on farm management." Such criticism has its fiercest bite when I know the critic loves both literature and law but thinks the two practices do not enrich each other.

My students feel different. As of late, my Constitutional Law classes tend to be oversubscribed by a ratio of about two to one, but my Law and Literature classes are oversubscribed by a ratio of about six to one. These students know that literature will complete their legal educations. They get the formal legal texts every day. They miss the scriptures and the epics. I recognize my old self in their hunger, and I stand with them.

Over time, my general class on Law and Literature has morphed into a class on Justice in Shakespeare. I switched because I did not like flitting from author to author. Once I decided to focus on a single author, the choice was obvious. If I was going to teach the class under the canopy of one author's work, I wanted it to be, as Hamlet says, "fretted with golden fire" (*Hamlet*, 2.2.267). As my first student foray into law and literature suggests, nothing makes me feel as I do when I read Shakespeare. To read Shakespeare is to feel encompassed—the plays contain practically every word I know, practically every character type I have ever met, and practically every idea I have ever had.

In writing this book, I am not relying on the claim that the author of the plays was, as Mark Twain argued, a lawyer. I believe Shakespeare knew a lot about the law, but only as a by-product of knowing a lot about everything. Freud was convinced Shakespeare had anticipated most major issues in psychoanalysis. I think Shakespeare got there first with respect to issues of social justice as well.

I do not have a definition of justice. I am drawn to literature rather than to philosophy because I would rather deal with the messy, fine-grained, gloriously idiosyncratic lives of human beings than with vaulting abstractions. At the same time, I think some cases illuminate timeless principles. For this reason, I have selected plays that raise these issues, making the contemporary links explicit where appropriate. I look at how *Titus Andronicus* illuminates our current engagements in Afghanistan and Iraq because it describes how revenge cycles escalate when no credible central authority exists. I look at how the white handkerchief in *Othello* can be compared to the black glove in the O. J. Simpson trial, as both forms of "ocular proof" wrongly overwhelmed all other evidence of guilt or innocence. I look at the *Tempest* as an exemplary instance of an omnipotent ruler voluntarily surrendering power as Cincinnatus did before him and George Washington did after him, asking who is willing to do that for us today.

Even Shakespeare cannot give us all the answers. I identify with James Joyce's Leopold Bloom, who "applied to the works of William

Shakespeare more than once for the solution of difficult problems in imaginary or real life." Despite careful study, Bloom "derived imperfect conviction from the text, the answers not bearing on all points." Shakespeare himself expressed skepticism about whether justice could be achieved through beauty: "How with this rage shall beauty hold a plea, / Whose action is no stronger than a flower?" (Sonnet 65, 3–4).

At the same time, I am struck by how many contemporary issues of justice Shakespeare does illuminate. I am not alone. As word leaked out that I was working on this project, I had sudden access to the secret covens of Shakespearean "justicers" (*King Lear*, 4.2.80) who dot the globe. A group of judges and lawyers has met once a month in New York for over a decade to read Shakespeare together— they are now on their second pass through the thirty-seven plays. At the McGill Law School in Canada, a "Shakespeare moot" permits participants to draw only on Shakespeare's plays as precedents. A few months ago, I was asked for advice about the legality of Henry's actions in *Henry V* for a mock trial at the Shakespeare Theatre Company—the call I had been waiting for all my professional life.

It is not just that I have found Shakespeare to be a universal passport into profound conversation—in China as in England, in Argentina as in Hong Kong, in Italy as in Japan. It is also that his work stimulates conversations about justice that might not otherwise be possible. One reason current discussions of justice are so impoverished is that our heterogeneous society does not have many shared texts. Shakespeare's plays are among the few secular texts that remain common enough and complex enough to sustain these conversations. His answers to our dilemmas may not "bear on all points." Yet they teach us not to underestimate the action of the flower.

CHAPTER ONE

THE AVENGER

Titus Andronicus

ALTHOUGH IT PUT SHAKESPEARE ON THE MAP IN THE 1590s, critics have found *The Most Lamentable Romaine Tragedie of Titus Andronicus* "lamentable" in more ways than one. T. S. Eliot called it "one of the stupidest and most uninspired plays ever written." Harold Bloom avers he "can concede no intrinsic value" to the play, while suggesting that "perhaps it could be yet made into a musical." Others have argued that the play was not written by Shakespeare, that Shakespeare "touched up" another playwright's work, or that Shakespeare penned it when he was young and needed the money. While most critics now admit Shakespeare composed it (with coauthor George Peele), *Titus* remains the "black sheep" of the Bard's canon.

While I come to defend the play, I understand why others abhor it. Over its course, the Goth prince Alarbus is sacrificed to the gods, the Roman general Titus's son Mutius is stabbed to death, the Roman prince Bassianus is murdered, Titus's daughter Lavinia is raped and mutilated, Titus's sons Quintus and Martius are decapitated, the Goths Demetrius and Chiron are murdered and their heads are baked into a pie, their mother Tamora is served the pie before being killed, Lavinia is killed, Titus is killed, the Roman emperor Saturninus is killed, and the Goth Aaron is buried alive. When Peter Brook directed this play in 1955, he had an ambulance waiting to shuttle audience members to the hospital. Sir Laurence Olivier, who played Titus, said at least three audience members fainted every evening.

For such a lurid work, *Titus* riveted the audiences of Shakespeare's day. In 1594, *Titus* was a blockbuster success, and, as critic Jonathan Bate opines, "perhaps did more than any other play to establish its author's reputation as a dramatist." Critics explain away the play's commercial success by sniffing that *Titus* played to the popular taste for guts and gore, just as public executions and bear-baiting did. Coleridge writes that *Titus* was "obviously intended to excite vulgar audiences by its scenes of blood and horror." That view of *Titus* rose to the fore in the nineteenth century, when *Titus* was either not performed or aggressively bowdlerized.

Yet *Titus* is not Shakespeare's version of a present-day slasher film. It carries a serious message about the necessity of the rule of law. Shakespeare lived in a time without an effective police force, meaning that individuals who suffered harm had to choose whether to trust a weak state or take justice into their own hands. This put individuals in a terrible position. The natural—even rational—impulse was to turn vigilante. As modern scholars have shown, the blood feud is a common pre-modern form of justice found in societies as diverse as Iceland, the Balkans, and Italy. Yet the danger of the feud is that it inevitably escalates, eventually threatening the entire society. The only solution is to impose the rule of law, which includes giving the state a monopoly over the function of punishment. As Justice Oliver Wendell Holmes once said: "It is commonly known that the early forms of legal procedure were grounded in vengeance. Modern writers have thought that the Roman law started from the blood feud, and all the authorities agree that the German law begun in that way." *Titus* is a cautionary tale for how the rule of law must quash cycles of vengeance that would otherwise destroy society.

Recent decades have seen a revival of interest in the original, unexpurgated play. Every time a major production has been staged, it has been a runaway hit. As Bate observes: "Peter Brook's production with Laurence Olivier as Titus was one of the great theatrical experiences of the 1950s and Deborah Warner's with Brian Cox was the most highly acclaimed Shakespearean production of the 1980s." More recently, Julie Taymor's 1999 film *Titus* with Anthony Hopkins in the lead role has earned critical acclaim.

Our opinion of *Titus,* then, seems more Elizabethan than Victorian. When I ask why this play, why now, the answer is disturbingly clear. Our times are more like Shakespeare's along a crucial dimension: the fragility of the rule of law. The beginning of a fully globalized society without an overarching government puts us in the same position as Shakespeare's contemporaries. If terrorists fly planes into our buildings, we must decide whether to submit to the judgments of a weak international authority or to engage in self-help. Again, the natural impulse is to act unilaterally. But as we are coming to see, surrendering to that impulse ends in catastrophe.

It may seem fanciful to use one of Shakespeare's most obscure plays to illuminate one of our most familiar crises—our wars in Afghanistan and Iraq. But *Titus* reveals something new about these wars, which is that they are not truly wars, but vendettas. The postmodern war on terror is more like the pre-modern blood feud than either is like a conventional war. For this reason, *Titus* is not immature. It is inaugural.

TITUS STAGES AN Elizabethan anxiety about how quickly private vengeance can become unmanageable if the law does not contain it. Revenge never just evens the odds, but leads to retaliation. That retaliation triggers counter-retaliation. The mounting tit-for-tat soon becomes a full-fledged blood feud between clans. In the play, the original sacrifice of Alarbus, the Goth prince, by Titus, the Roman general, begins a cycle of violence that eventually engulfs all Goths and Romans.

Like us, Shakespeare's contemporaries were ambivalent about private vengeance. On the one hand, they lived in a society without a real police force or standing army. "Wild justice," as Sir Francis Bacon called revenge in a famous essay, was often the only kind available. The early moderns also viewed the revenge instinct to be natural. The Old Testament *lex talionis* (literally "law of retaliation") permitted, and perhaps required, such vengeance: "And if any mischief follow, then thou shalt give life for life, / Eye for eye, tooth for tooth, hand for hand, foot for foot / Burning for burning, wound for wound, stripe for stripe."

On the other hand, Elizabethans feared the way individual quarrels could spiral into blood feuds. The literary scholar Fredson Bowers writes that "private quarrels between two or three persons not infrequently spread to whole families and ended in great hurt and bloodshed." This escalation was particularly common among noble families, who held their honor dear: James I described "factions and deadly feuds" as "the motives of greate mischief in greate families."

The "deadly feuds" were sufficiently numerous that one can provide instances without straying from the author of the play. One

Shakespeare biographer believes the feud between the Montagues and the Capulets in *Romeo and Juliet* may have been based on the feud between the Long and Danvers families. The Long-Danvers feud, which dated back to the Wars of the Roses but had for some time subsided, reignited in 1594 when Sir John Danvers, a magistrate, convicted a servant of Sir Walter Long of robbery. (In *Romeo and Juliet*, a scuffle among servants rekindles hostilities.) After Sir Walter rescued the servant, Sir John put the master himself in Fleet Prison. Upon Sir Walter's release, a series of brawls erupted. Sir Walter's brother Henry wrote abusive letters to Sir John's son Charles, informing him that "wheresoever he mett him he would untie his pointes and whippe his etc. with a rodd, calling him asse, puppie, foole & boye." Charles Danvers and his brother then accosted Henry and Walter Long as they dined in an inn. Charles attacked Henry with a truncheon; Henry retaliated with his sword. Charles's brother then drew his pistol and shot Henry dead. No legal repercussions ensued—through the good offices of Henry Wriothseley, Earl of Southampton, the Danvers brothers were ushered out of the country. Shakespeare would almost certainly have been familiar with these events. Southampton is the dedicatee of Shakespeare's *Venus and Adonis* and *The Rape of Lucrece* and is widely believed to be the dedicatee ("the only begetter of these ensuing sonnets Mr. W.H.") of the sonnets.

To prevent such feuds, Christian moralists in early modern England urged people to transcend vengeful impulses. Writing in 1609, the pamphleteer Daniel Tuvil proclaimed: "Ierusalem is new erected; among her Citizens there is now no thirsting for reuenge. The law of retribution is disnuld amongst them. . . . An eie no longer for an eie: a tooth no longer for a tooth." As Tuvil's reference to the new Jerusalem suggests, the Old Testament *lex talionis* gave way to New Testament mercy. The passage in Exodus ceded to one in Romans: "Dearly beloved, avenge not yourselves, but rather give place unto wrath: for it is written, 'Vengeance is mine; I will repay, saith the Lord.'" Human beings were meant to stay their hands because God would avenge their wrongs. Bowers notes that for Catholics and Protestants alike "in the God-fearing Elizabethan age, [religion] exercised a force second to none in the constant war against the private lawlessness of the times."

The catch was that God's punishment, while certain, was often slow. Lest individuals tire of waiting, retribution was also permitted to God's agents on Earth, including the sovereign and—critically— the courts of law. The Statute of Marlbridge (1257) secured the same power for the courts as the New Testament secured for God. The statute ordained that "none from henceforth shall take any such revenge or distress of his own authority without award of our Court." This was seen less as an alternative to divine authority than a delegation of it. As Susan Jacoby writes: "The moral hierarchy was clear: God's just revenge (sometimes too slow to suit human beings but always certain); public revenge permitted to God's authorized representatives on earth (whether embodied in capital punishment, torture, or a 'just war'); private revenge forbidden to kings and commoners alike."

Delegating divine retribution to legal agents, however, was an imperfect solution, as the law could fail to provide adequate redress. In such situations, injured parties were pressed back to the original dilemma of whether to turn the other cheek or take justice into their own hands. *Titus* is representative of Elizabethan revenge tragedy in depicting "wild justice" as the natural choice, but one that necessarily dooms the avenger and his society.

TITUS BEGINS WITH the Roman general Titus Andronicus returning in triumph from his war against the Goths. During his ten-

year campaign, he has lost all but four of his twenty-five sons. Yet he
has now won a final victory, as evidenced by his prisoners—Tamora
(Queen of the Goths), her three sons, and the Moor Aaron, who is
Tamora's servant and, we later learn, her lover.

As Titus inters his dead sons in the family tomb, his eldest sur-
viving son, Lucius, reminds him to make a human sacrifice:

> Give us the proudest prisoner of the Goths,
> That we may hew his limbs and on a pile
> *Ad manes fratrum* sacrifice his flesh
> Before this earthly prison of their bones,
> That so the shadows be not unappeased,
> Nor we disturbed with prodigies on earth.
> (1.1.99–104)

The sacrifice is to be made *ad manes fratrum*—"to the shades of our
brothers"—to keep them from disturbing the Romans with "prodigies," or supernatural calamities.

Titus accordingly offers up Prince Alarbus, the highest-born
Goth male among the prisoners of war. Tamora kneels and begs for
her son's life:

> Stay, Roman brethren, gracious conqueror,
> Victorious Titus, rue the tears I shed,
> A mother's tears in passion for her son!
> And if thy sons were ever dear to thee,
> O, think my son to be as dear to me.
> Sufficeth not that we are brought to Rome
> To beautify thy triumphs, and return
> Captive to thee and to thy Roman yoke?
> But must my sons be slaughtered in the streets

For valiant doings in their country's cause?
O, if to fight for king and commonweal
Were piety in thine, it is in these.
Andronicus, stain not thy tomb with blood.
(1.1.107–19)

Tamora's plea, like many pleas for justice, rests on symmetry. The only lines with end-rhymes—"And if thy sons were ever dear to thee, / O, think my son to be as dear to me"—highlight the link between "thee" and "me," underscoring Tamora and Titus's common status as parents. Tamora then argues that the principle of proportionality has been met. Romans and Goths alike died on the battlefield. To kill more Goths after hostilities have ended is savage excess.

Titus sees the balance differently. In his view, the Roman dead cry out for retribution:

Patient yourself, madam, and pardon me.
These are their brethren whom your Goths beheld
Alive and dead, and for their brethren slain,
Religiously they ask a sacrifice.
To this your son is marked, and die he must,
T'appease their groaning shadows that are gone.
(1.1.124–29)

Titus is not meant to have our sympathies here. As Tamora recognizes, his is a "cruel, irreligious piety" (1.1.133). Tamora's son Chiron adds, "Was never Scythia half so barbarous" (1.1.134), underscoring that it is neither the Goths nor the Scythians (whom Herodotus casts as the paradigm barbarians), but the Romans who merit the designation. The question of who is "barbarous" and who is "civilized" haunts this play.

The line between the "civilized" Romans and the "barbarous" Goths is immediately blurred when the new Roman emperor
Saturninus decides to take Tamora as his wife. The reversal of fortune that marks so many of the plays—where the humble are exalted
and vice versa—occurs in the first act of this one. A woman with
grown sons, Tamora is more like a mother than a wife to the callow
emperor, promising to be "[a] loving nurse, a mother to his youth"
(1.1.337). From that position, she vows revenge on the Andronici:

> I'll find a day to massacre them all,
> And raze their faction and their family,
> The cruel father and his traitorous sons
> To whom I sued for my dear son's life,
> And make them know what 'tis to let a queen
> Kneel in the streets and beg for grace in vain.
> (1.1.455–60)

In just one scene, Tamora acquires motive and opportunity to avenge
herself on Titus. So the cycle begins.

IN A MANNER that typifies revenge cycles, Tamora's retribution
will grossly exceed the harm done her. For the death of her son at
the hands of the Andronici, she seeks to "raze their faction and their
family" (1.1.456). Even the *lex talionis*—the Old Testament rule of "an
eye for an eye"—would prohibit such amplification. Though often invoked to authorize revenge, the rule also limits it. If someone takes
my eye, I am entitled to his eye, but no more. Perhaps if Titus had
listened to her argument about proportionality and spared her son's
life, Tamora would also have adhered to that principle. But now she
explicitly forswears it.

Tamora's escalation is not just quantitative, but qualitative. *Titus* does not owe its special horror to its body count. Many of the tragedies—notably *Hamlet* and *Lear*—strew corpses across the stage. *Titus* inspires special revulsion because of *how* it writes vengeance on the body. Aaron, the puppetmaster of the Goths, exults—as do his puppets—in inflicting punishments worse than death.

Our knowledge of Aaron's plot begins when he finds Tamora's remaining sons Chiron and Demetrius vying over Titus's daughter Lavinia. He tells them they can both rape their "dainty doe" during the royal hunt the next day (1.1.617). The brothers eagerly agree. Aaron has cast a broader net: he also seeks to have Lavinia's husband, Bassianus, murdered and to frame Titus's sons, Quintus and Martius, for that crime.

On the day of the hunt, Lavinia and Bassianus happen on Tamora in a lonely part of the wood. Tamora's sons, Demetrius and Chiron, ambush the young couple there, kill Bassianus, and threaten to rape Lavinia. Lavinia asks Tamora for empathy, just as Tamora asked Titus for it. She draws on two kinds of solidarity. First, she appeals to Tamora as a woman: "O Tamora, thou bearest a woman's face" (2.2.136). Even as a supplicant, Lavinia cannot hide her contempt—she appeals to the empress as a *facsimile* of a woman. When this plea proves unavailing, Lavinia reminds Tamora that she too was recently a captive: "O let me teach thee for my father's sake, / That gave thee life when well he might have slain thee. / Be not obdurate, open thy deaf ears" (2.2.158–60). Lavinia could not have found a more dangerous argument. Tamora responds:

> Even for his sake am I pitiless.
> Remember, boys, I poured forth tears in vain
> To save your brother from the sacrifice,
> But fierce Andronicus would not relent.

Therefore away with her and use her as you will:
The worse to her, the better loved of me.
(2.2.162–67)

Naturally, Tamora remembers Titus's cruelty more than his mercy. For the death of her child, Tamora will require the death—or worse—of his.

Hearing this, Lavinia abandons hope of life: "O Tamora, be called a gentle queen, / And with thine own hands kill me in this place" (2.2.168–69). The idea that chastity is worth more than life will recur in *Measure for Measure,* with Isabella's chilly: "More than our brother is our chastity" (*Measure,* 2.4.184). Lavinia subscribes to that worldview: "'Tis present death I beg, and one thing more / That womanhood denies my tongue to tell. / O, keep me from their worse-than-killing lust" (2.2.173–75). But Tamora refuses: "So should I rob my sweet sons of their fee. / No, let them satisfy their lust on thee" (2.2.179–80).

Lavinia's rape occurs offstage. The action cuts to Titus's sons Quintus and Martius. Aaron has lured the brothers to the pit where he has stashed Bassianus's body. As in many horror films, dread is created indirectly. Martius falls into the pit. Quintus describes it: "What subtle hole is this, / Whose mouth is covered with rude-growing briers / Upon whose leaves are drops of new-shed blood?" (2.2.198–200). As critic Marjorie Garber points out, we need not be Freudians to decode this image of female sexuality. Even before Martius finds Bassianus's body, we know Lavinia has been raped.

The hapless brothers are no match for Aaron. Trying to yank Martius out of the pit, Quintus gets yanked into it. The emperor Saturninus, conducted by Aaron, discovers them there. Directly after Saturninus learns of his brother Bassianus's death, Tamora, Titus, and Lucius enter. Tamora bears a letter forged by Aaron that describes the pit and an elder tree under which the "reward" (which Aaron has planted) for the "murder" is buried. Aaron "finds" the gold. That is all Saturninus needs to convict. Turning to Titus, he says:

> Two of thy whelps, fell curs of bloody kind,
> Have here bereft my brother of his life.
> Sirs, drag them from the pit unto the prison.
> There let them bide until we have devised
> Some never-heard-of torturing pain for them.
> (2.2.281–85)

Now Titus mirrors Tamora, kneeling, weeping, and begging for the life of his children. The parallels extend to the mise-en-scène—in the original three-tiered staging, the "pit" would have occupied the same place as the tomb of the Andronici in act 1.

Law should have interrupted the vengeance cycle here. Saturninus embodies the supreme legal authority in the state. Yet his justice is peremptory in several ways. First, he assumes guilt from circumstantial evidence—when Titus questions whether the guilt of his sons has been proven, Saturninus says, "If it be proved? You see it is apparent" (2.2.292). Saturninus also refuses to let Quintus and Martius defend themselves—"Let them not speak a word: the guilt is plain" (2.2.301). Finally, he sentences them immediately to death, regretting only that the sentence is too mild: "For, by my soul, were there worse end than death / That end upon them should be executed" (2.2.302–303). His reference to a "worse end than death" echoes Lavinia's fear of Demetrius and Chiron's "worse-than-killing lust."

So we remember Lavinia. The next scene begins with this stage direction: *Enter the* Empress' Sons *with Lavinia, her hands cut off and her tongue cut out, and ravished*" (2.3.sd). Presumably, audience members start fainting here. The controlling narrative is Ovid's Philomela myth. Philomela was the sister of Procne, queen of Thrace. Procne's husband, Tereus, raped Philomela and then cut out her tongue so she could not identify him. Philomela nonetheless revealed her story to her sister by embroidering the scene into a sampler. The two sisters avenged themselves by killing Tereus's (and Procne's) son and serving him in a meal to Tereus. When Tereus asked for his son, Procne said in triumph, "The one you want is with you now—inside," and Philomela threw the child's bloody head at her rapist. Trying to vomit, Tereus took up his sword to kill the sisters, but the gods transformed them into birds. The gods returned Philomela's voice to her when she became the nightingale and captured Procne's martial spirit in the crested head of the lapwing.

Though ghastly, this story also reassures. It suggests that the gods are paying attention. In intervening in a timely way, the gods impose the closure that would later be embodied in the talionic law: one rape, one retaliation. They rehabilitate the sisters—Philomela's voice is restored and Procne is crowned. The cycle stops.

Chiron and Demetrius have learned one lesson from that story, ensuring that Lavinia will not be able to use her hands to reveal their identity. Demetrius says, "So, now go tell, and if thy tongue can speak, / Who 'twas that cut thy tongue and ravished thee" (2.3.1–2). Chiron chimes in: "Write down thy mind, bewray thy meaning so, / And if thy stumps will let thee, play the scribe" (2.3.3–4). They leave her to die.

Lavinia is the play's main horror. When I ask my students where the vengeance cycle goes berserk, they produce Lavinia's raped and mutilated body. Moral philosopher Martha Nussbaum, speaking of a recent production of *Titus* in Chicago, said it was the only time, as the member of a theater audience, that she remembers averting her eyes from a scene. Directors have struggled with how to portray it. Brook used an overly stylized Lavinia, with red ribbons trailing from her mouth and the stumps of her arms. Warner took a more literal tack, having a wild-eyed Lavinia, already catatonic with shock, holding up her stumps and bleeding from her mouth. Taymor found the middle ground by replacing Lavinia's hands with tree branches. I read this interpretation as an inversion of the Apollo and Daphne myth, in which Daphne, fleeing from the god, is turned into a laurel tree. The branches make Lavinia bearable to watch. Yet they invoke the myth only to remind us that Lavinia's transformation is only partial, her escape radically incomplete.

Lavinia's uncle Marcus finds her and must bring her to Titus. Productions often have Marcus physically obscuring Lavinia when he says, "Titus, prepare thy aged eyes to weep, / Or if not so, thy noble heart to break: / I bring consuming sorrow to thine age" (3.1.59–61). Titus welcomes death: "Will it consume me? Let me see it then" (3.1.62). Marcus reveals Lavinia: "This was thy daughter" (3.1.63). Titus says: "Why, Marcus, so she is" (3.1.64).

This line, which occurs at the play's midpoint, finally allows me to respect Titus. Lavinia has been insistently dehumanized: Aaron bestializes her as a "doe," Tamora commodifies her as a "fee," and Demetrius and Martius have raped and mutilated her. Even Lavinia's loving uncle believes her dead: "This *was* thy daughter." Titus's correction—"Why, Marcus, so she *is*"—stands as reproof. Titus has lost many sons in battle. He has presumably had living sons brought back to him maimed. So it is he, not the civilian tribune Marcus, who can see that Lavinia endures. Even Lucius, who has fought by Titus's side, falls to his knees: "Ay me, this object kills me" (3.1.65). Titus chastises him: "Faint-hearted boy, arise and look upon her" (3.1.66). In this line, Titus recovers the iambic pentameter broken by the three preceding lines. "Look more closely," Titus seems to say to his brother and son: "She is still she."

Titus's fortitude survives another test when Aaron appears to tell Titus that Saturninus will spare Titus's two sons if Titus cuts off his hand. Titus does so with a good will. But this offer is a hoax—Saturninus has said no such thing. Soon a messenger returns with the heads of Quintus and Martius as well as Titus's left hand. As if this were not enough, Titus learns that Lucius has been banished from Rome for trying to help his brothers.

Tamora has now avenged her son's death, and more. Titus has lost two sons and a son-in-law to death. His only living son—of the original twenty-five—has been banished. His daughter has been raped and mutilated, and he has lost a hand. This undoes even the stoical Marcus: "Ah, now no more will I control thy griefs: / Rend off thy silver hair, thy other hand / Gnawing with thy teeth" (3.1.260–62). Marcus wants the Andronici to die, to let "this dismal sight" lead to "[t]he closing up of our most wretched eyes" (3.1.262–63). Titus has a different idea: "Then which way shall I find Revenge's cave? / For these two heads do seem to speak to me / And threat me I shall never come to bliss / Till all these mischiefs be returned again" (3.1.271–74). When Titus says the severed heads of his sons demand revenge, he returns us to the beginning of the play. Titus must retaliate to appease the spirits of the slain. Yet at least for me, there is a difference. At the beginning of the play, I watch Titus authorize a barbaric human sacrifice with distaste. Now, when he repeats the same sentiment, I want revenge too.

Like Titus, I must wait. At this point, Titus does not know who has mutilated Lavinia. As he puzzles that out, an emotional conduit opens between father and daughter. The actress Anna Calder-Marshall, who played Lavinia in the mid-1980s, stated: "Titus has committed the most appalling deeds and it isn't until he's maimed and his daughter's maimed that he learns anything about love." She is right to focus on the symmetry of the maiming. Titus is a literal man.

When asked to be the head of Rome in act 1, he describes his own doddering head: "A better head her glorious body fits / Than his that shakes for age and feebleness" (1.1.190–91). Here, that cast of mind sharpens his perception. His own severed hand allows him to apprehend her suffering as no words could.

Aaron's plot has the unintended consequence of leading Titus into Lavinia's world. In the scene after his hand is sent back to him, Titus has returned home with Marcus and Lavinia. Watching Lavinia's response to an offer of drink, Titus utters the most powerful lines of the play:

> Hark, Marcus, what she says:
> I can interpret all her martyred signs—
> She says she drinks no other drink but tears,
> Brewed with her sorrow, mashed upon her cheeks.
> Speechless complainer, I will learn thy thought.
> In thy dumb action will I be as perfect
> As begging hermits in their holy prayers.
> Thou shalt not sigh, nor hold thy stumps to heaven,
> Nor wink, nor nod, nor kneel, nor make a sign,
> But I of these will wrest an alphabet
> And by still practice learn to know thy meaning.
> (3.2.35–45)

Anyone who has sought to understand another temporarily or permanently bereft of speech—whether that be an infant, an aged person, an invalid, a non-human animal, or here, an individual with a disability—will hear the love in these lines. To learn a language is a colossal labor, which is why we ordinarily require others to meet us on common ground. When they cannot, we must decide whether to go to them. Here, Titus shoulders that burden.

When Lavinia tries to explain what has happened, only Titus understands her. She seizes a book of Ovid that belongs to Titus's grandson and turns the pages with her stumps. Marcus, always the square, supposes she does so out of affection for the sister-in-law who originally owned the book. But Titus watches Lavinia, rather than listening to anyone else:

> Soft, so busily she turns the leaves!
> What would she find? Lavinia, shall I read?
> This is the tragic tale of Philomel,
> And treats of Tereus' treason and his rape—
> And rape, I fear, was root of thy annoy.
> (4.1.45–49)

The brothers' plot comes to light because they based it on the "plot" of the shared Ovidian story. Writing in sand with a stick held in her mouth, Lavinia reveals the names of her rapists.

This interlude convinces me that *Titus* is Shakespeare's play, because it demonstrates the complexity of revenge. We should not wish for a world in which revenge does not naturally intensify because that would be a world without love. If human beings did not form attachments, killing an individual would not result in more than the death of the perpetrator. It is because Tamora loves her son Alarbus with a mother's world-canceling love that her desire for vengeance is apocalyptic. And as love fuels vengeance, vengeance fuels love. As Judge Richard Posner says, "[v]engeance breeds intense loyalty within small, especially within family, groups, for the victim of a wrong will often be dead, weak, or otherwise incapable of revenging himself (or herself)." Vengeance teaches Titus love for his daughter.

In a move that might inform our reading of *Hamlet,* Titus feigns madness to gull his enemies. He circles the palace with petitions for justice impaled on arrows. He—and those who humor him—shoot the arrows into the sky. The petitions are addressed to the gods in the Roman pantheon. Prime among these is Astraea, the goddess of justice, who veiled her face and fled the Earth at the beginning of the Iron Age of Man. The reference is again to Ovid—*"Terras Astraea reliquit"* (4.3.4)—"Astraea has left the earth." Titus also tells his kinsmen to cast their nets and dig with spades in case Justice is in the sea or underground.

There may be an implicit criticism of the sitting sovereign Elizabeth I here. In Shakespeare's time, the queen was often represented as Astraea. She was also criticized for her "not so masterly inactivity" with respect to conflicts among her nobles. The claim that Astraea had abandoned the Earth could be seen as a dig at the quiescence of the sovereign.

Yet even as he parodies the social order, Titus, like a good Roman (or Englishman), shows his allegiance to it. He exhausts his permitted remedies—the justice of the gods and their representatives on Earth—before resorting to vendetta. When he learns that Tamora's sons raped his daughter, Titus first cries to the gods: *"Magni dominator poli, / Tam lentus audis scelera, tam lentus vides?"* (4.1.81–82) or "Ruler of the great heavens / Are you so slow to hear crimes, so slow to see?" In Shakespeare's late plays—the Romances—gods supply oracular guidance or trundle down to dance in masques. But those redemptive plays are years away: Lavinia will not turn into a nightingale. Titus then considers appealing to the sovereign, but soon recognizes the futility of any such plea. Tamora controls the emperor: "She's with the lion deeply still in league, / And lulls him whilst she playeth on her back" (4.1.98–99). Only then does he turn to self-help. Even the volley of arrows that heralds the beginning of his vendetta defers in form to the ethic that vengeance belongs to the gods.

Some of these arrows pierce Saturninus's court. The emperor is outraged, as he correctly intuits that Titus is dangerously sane. He insists Titus's sons were executed "with law" (4.4.8) or "by law" (4.4.53). This is false: Saturninus executed Quintus and Martius by fiat. In fact, the emperor has already suggested that force and law are interchangeable, stating in act 1 that he will take the throne "if Rome have law or we have power" (1.1.408). As actor and legal scholar Paul Raffield describes Saturninus's reign: "The equitable principles of common law, encapsulated by the medieval jurist Henry de Bracton in the phrase, *lex facti regem* ('law makes the king'), are rejected in favour of the civilian maxim, *quod principi placuit vigorem legis habet* ('that which pleases the prince has the force of law')." But now the emperor's "by right or might" formulation comes home: tidings arrive that Titus's banished son, Lucius, has assembled an army of Goths and is marching on his own city (foreshadowing Coriolanus in his play and Alcibiades in *Timon of Athens*). Tamora, who believes Titus's madness is genuine, comforts her husband. She promises to appear to Titus as the allegorical figure of Revenge and get him to hold a banquet for Lucius, his son. At this banquet she will find a way "[t]o pluck proud Lucius from the warlike Goths" (4.4.109).

Dressed as Revenge, Tamora takes her two sons to Titus's house. Tamora's confidence in her ability to persuade Titus may seem implausible. Yet throughout this play, Tamora and Aaron have outtalked their adversaries. The rhetorical skill of the Goths challenges their "barbarousness" in the root sense. The word "barbarous" comes from the Greek *barbaros* for those who spoke gibberish instead of Greek—"bar bar" being the onomatopoeic representation of the gabble such people supposedly spoke. In her command of language, Tamora foreshadows other eloquent outsiders in Shakespeare, such as Shylock, Othello, and Caliban.

One sign of Tamora's impending comeuppance is that, fresh

from learning Lavinia's alphabet, Titus wrests rhetorical control from the empress. When Tamora and her sons appear on his doorstep in disguise, Titus begins with guileless recognition: "I know thee well / For our proud empress, mighty Tamora. / Is not thy coming for my other hand?" (5.2.25–27). Tamora responds: "Know, thou sad man, I am not Tamora: / She is thy enemy and I thy friend. / I am Revenge, sent from th'infernal kingdom / To ease the gnawing vulture of thy mind" (5.2.28–31). Titus asks her to kill her two sons as proof: "Lo by thy side where Rape and Murder stands; / Now give some surance that thou art Revenge: / Stab them or tear them on thy chariot wheels" (5.2.45–47). (The idea that Tamora will participate in the death of her sons presages Titus's grisly plan for them.) Tamora demurs: "These are my ministers, and come with me" (5.2.60). Titus asks their names, and, put on the spot, she takes up his appellation: "Rape and Murder, therefore called so" (5.2.62). Titus then utters his cleverest line: "Good Lord, how like the empress' sons they are, / And you the empress! But we worldly men / Have miserable, mad, mistaking eyes" (5.2.64–66). Tamora tells him to invite Lucius to a banquet with the emperor, where she will help him wreak his vengeance. Titus agrees, but only on condition that "Rape" and "Murder" stay with him. His skepticism stokes her credulity: Tamora accedes.

When Saturninus and Tamora arrive for the feast, where Lucius is also present, Titus is dressed as a cook. As Titus serves up the pie, he asks Saturninus whether the centurion Virginius was right to kill his daughter after she was raped. Saturninus answers that he was, "[b]ecause the girl should not survive her shame, / And by her presence still renew his sorrows" (5.3.40–41). Titus responds:

> A reason mighty, strong, and effectual;
> A pattern, precedent, and lively warrant

For me, most wretched to perform the like.
[*Unveils Lavinia.*]
Die, die, Lavinia, and thy shame with thee,
And with thy shame thy father's sorrow die.
[*He kills her.*]
(5.3.42–46)

The language is legal—Titus takes the story of Virginius (told in Livy's *Roman History*) as a "precedent" and "warrant" for his own action.

When the horrified Saturninus asks why Titus has killed Lavinia, Titus retorts that the guilt belongs to Demetrius and Chiron because "[t]hey ravished her and cut away her tongue" (5.3.56). Saturninus asks that they be brought forth. Titus responds: "Why, there they are, both baked in this pie, / Whereof their mother daintily hath fed, / Eating the flesh that she herself hath bred. / 'Tis true, 'tis true, witness my knife's sharp point" (5.3.59–62). With these words, he kills the empress. The classical precedents rise thick and fast. Ovid's *Metamorphoses* (in which Tereus, the rapist of Philomela, consumes his own son) melds with Seneca's *Thyestes* (in which the title character is served his sons baked in a pie). Garber says, "[i]t was the staging of this scene, in Julie Taymor's film *Titus* (1999), that turned me—a lifelong meat eater—against the eating of mammal's flesh." In a Rome without laws, the only precedents to follow are the myths, which have provided the templates for Goths and Romans alike.

Titus might be said to have won. As far as we know, none of Tamora's adult relatives remains alive. But Titus's victory is Pyrrhic. He has seen too much and gone too far. My alienation begins when he kills Lavinia to put *her* out of *his* misery. I detach completely when I learn of his cannibalistic scheme. Posner describes this estrangement as a common effect of revenge literature:

We the audience start off with great sympathy for the revenger and wish him or her complete success, only to find
that as the play (or story) proceeds we cool on revenge.
The vivid picture of the revenger's wrong with which we
began fades and is replaced by an equally vivid picture of
the horrors of the revenge itself.

We should remember that our contemporary aphorism "Revenge is
sweet" clips and flips the Miltonic couplet: "Revenge, at first though
sweet, / Bitter ere long back on itself recoils." Tamora is a monster,
but Titus has become one too.

For this reason, Titus must die on our behalf. Only when he does
so can the vengeful part of us that has identified with him perish,
permitting us to gather up our belongings and return home. So immediately after Titus kills Tamora, Saturninus kills Titus, and Lucius
kills Saturninus. The stage direction says *"Uproar. The Goths protect the
Andronici, who go aloft"* (5.3.65). From that vantage, Lucius proclaims
himself the new emperor, imposing order from without. A Roman,
leading the Goths, triumphs over the Roman state with a Goth empress. The line between the barbarians and the civilized is confused
beyond repair.

The new emperor Lucius must determine what "order" entails.
Before returning to Rome, Lucius captures Aaron with the newborn
son Aaron has begotten with Tamora. In return for Lucius's promise
to spare his son, Aaron promises to confess all his sins. Forced up a
ladder to be hanged, he appropriates the makeshift gallows as a plat-
form from which he proudly declaims his misdeeds. After listening in
disgust, Lucius commands Aaron to descend. That death is too good
for him.

Lucius's punishment is that Aaron be buried up to his chest so
he can slowly starve to death. Lucius wishes Aaron a fate worse than

death, which is what Tamora wished for Lavinia, what Saturninus wished for Quintus and Martius, and what Titus wished for Tamora. Moreover, Lucius admonishes that "[i]f anyone relieves or pities him, / For the offence he dies" (5.3.180–81). As for Tamora:

> No funeral rite, nor man in mourning weed,
> No mournful bell shall ring her burial,
> But throw her forth to beasts and birds to prey:
> Her life was beastly and devoid of pity,
> And being dead, let birds on her take pity.
> (5.3.195–99)

These lines conclude the play.

Of Shakespeare's thirty-seven plays, twenty-six end with a rhyming couplet. Only one—this one—ends with a couplet with the same endwords. Even *The Comedy of Errors,* a play about twinning, rhymes "brother" with "brother" within the penultimate line, closing the last line with "another" (*Comedy,* 5.1.425–26). When we ask why *Titus* alone would click shut on one word—"pity"—we see the word redoubled to announce the absence of the quality it represents. Lucius characterizes Tamora as "devoid of pity," and, for that reason, commits her to the pity that birds of prey will give her, which is also, presumably, none. Even worse, anyone who "relieves or pities" Aaron will be put to death. Pity for Aaron is a capital crime.

I am not confident that Lucius will answer the play's final question correctly. Lucius must decide whether he will honor his promise to spare Aaron's child. He will exhibit pity at his peril. This child will grow up to learn that the Roman state tortured his father to death and desecrated his mother's corpse. The child may become an Antigone, for the end of *Titus* bears a striking resemblance to the beginning of Sophocles's play:

> But as for Polyneices, Creon has ordered
> That none shall bury him or mourn for him;
> He must be left to lie unwept, unburied
> For hungry birds of prey to swoop and feast
> On his poor body. . . .

The child's life represents both the possible end and the possible continuation of the revenge cycle. We are never told what Lucius decides.

WHEN I TEACH the Supreme Court cases dealing with the war on terror in my Constitutional Law course, I put up slides that always create trouble. These slides depict the Twin Towers of the World Trade Center in flames, with statistics about what happened on September 11, 2001. The statistics tell us that 2,819 people were killed, that only 289 bodies were found intact, and that 19,858 body parts were found. It is the body parts that enrage some of my students. One recently described my treatment as "lovingly gruesome."

For me, those body parts recall the maiming of Lavinia—the intolerable vision from which we wish to avert our eyes. The vision of the dismembered and defiled human body inspires in all but the most callous among us a primal sense of vengeance. I think my students resist the vision of the body parts because they do not want to empathize with the vengeful feelings that led to our engagements in Afghanistan and Iraq. While I understand this, I also think we cannot fully apprehend those wars unless we address these feelings. When we experience the vengeance, we see these wars for what they are—blood feuds.

As political scientist Stephen Holmes points out, this vengeance cycle began long before the September 11 attacks. Holmes contends that attributing the attacks to "religious extremism" or "radical

Islam" is far too vague. Many religious extremists have never engaged in any kind of violence against the West. While acknowledging the complexity of the motives underlying the attacks, Holmes observes that "[o]ne theme that constantly resurfaces, nevertheless, is a craving to avenge real and imagined injuries inflicted by the United States on the Muslims of the world." Holmes believes we can better understand the instigators if we look through the lens of vengeance rather than the lens of religion. We may experience ourselves as Titus mourning an unforeseen and unprovoked attack on his daughter. But the instigators see themselves in Tamora's position, exacting revenge for prior wrongs.

In other words, we begin the story in the middle, with the harm done to us. This is an entirely understandable human tendency, and I admit my own complicity in it. After the attacks, I shared the visceral outrage that made the country rally around George W. Bush, whose approval rating roared from 51 percent to 90 percent in the days after 9/11. With those on the right, I celebrated the solidarity we felt as a nation on 9/12. Again, an often overlooked aspect of revenge is that it breeds love—love of country, love of murdered innocents. I endorsed Bush's demand that the Taliban hand over Osama bin Laden and his fellow instigators. I also supported the invasion of Afghanistan for the narrow purpose of toppling the Taliban regime and anyone who would give safe haven to the perpetrators of the attack.

Yet it might be said that, even then, we were drifting from the rule of law. The Taliban was willing to hand over bin Laden, so long as the United States proved his connection to the 9/11 attacks. President Bush refused to supply that proof, in terms that echo Saturninus's peremptory claim—"If it be proved? You see it is apparent . . . their guilt is plain." As Bush said: "There's no need to discuss innocence or guilt. We know he's guilty." Bush then imposed the notion of associative guilt that lies at the core of a blood feud, observing that the Afghans "will hand over the terrorists or they will share their fate."

If the situation in Afghanistan was ambiguous, the invasion of Iraq left no doubt that the Bush administration had regressed into a blood feud. The administration justified the decision to invade Iraq in part because the president asserted a connection between Al Qaeda and Saddam Hussein. Yet as a congressional panel later decisively established, no such link existed. Claims that Iraq possessed weapons of mass destruction similarly lacked substance. The war in Iraq was motivated by something much more primitive. When asked why he had supported it, Henry Kissinger perhaps answered most honestly. He stated that it was "because Afghanistan wasn't enough. In the conflict with radical Islam, they, the Islamists, want to humiliate us. We need to humiliate them."

The idea that Muslims in Iraq were our enemies became a self-fulfilling prophecy. Prior to the United States' decision to claim over 4,000 civilian lives in Iraq, it was unclear that Al Qaeda had any foothold there. Now it clearly does. As Richard Clarke, former special advisor to the U.S. National Security Council, observed: "The pool of people who really hate us is so much greater than it was on 9/11 because of this needless and counterproductive war in Iraq. . . . The president kept saying Iraq was the central front in the war against terrorism—well, it is now."

Some will see no analogy between the blood feuds of old and the war on terror today, as the blood feuds occurred between clans, while the wars today occur among nations. But my precise point is that, with respect to the rule of law, nations today are little more than clans. The United States did not wait for the authorization of the United Nations to begin attacking Afghanistan or Iraq. This is completely unsurprising. Just as noble families did not trust the

Elizabethan state, we did not trust an international authority to give us justice.

But therein lies the tragedy—completely natural impulses can lead to completely unacceptable outcomes. My feelings about the Bush administration's actions mirror my feelings about Titus. In the beginning, I wished the avenger the best of luck. Yet as the vengeance surged, I began to detach. Certainly by the time the photographs of Abu Ghraib and the executive branch's memoranda authorizing torture surfaced, the line between the "civilized" United States and our "barbaric" enemies had been blurred. The photographs of Abu Ghraib prisoners hooded and hooked to electrodes, piled naked into pyramids, and forced into humiliating sexual positions have now become part of our nation's permanent record. The terrorists were monsters, but we had become monsters as well.

Beginning in 2004, the Supreme Court issued a quartet of opinions that mitigated the cycles of revenge by reinforcing the rule of law. It is conventional wisdom among constitutional scholars that the first of these opinions—*Hamdi v. Rumsfeld*—was a direct response to Abu Ghraib. Because the Constitution delegates war-making powers to the political branches, the Court usually defers to executive and legislative actions in this area. Yet a plurality of the Court in *Hamdi* observed that the Constitution did not provide the executive with a "blank check" to do whatever he wished. In a series of accreting decisions, the Court slowly rebuilt an edifice of minimal rights to protect detainees in the war on terror.

These technical decisions are not page-turners for the general reader. But they accomplish something crucial in their insistence that, as Justice John Paul Stevens wrote in a 2006 opinion, "the Executive is bound to comply with the rule of law." Through this opinion, some detainees received the right to defend themselves before a neutral tribunal. Saturninus's formulation of authority—"if Rome have law or we have power"—was rejected. Power was no longer an alternative ground for action, but could be exercised only within the bounds of the law.

The real solution, however, cannot come from the courts of any individual country, but must come from the rule of law imposed at the global level. Achieving that solution is much more difficult. We do not even know if it is possible to build a credible system of global governance. As we step into the international theater, we are facing at the global level what the Elizabethans faced at the national one—a weak state that tempts us to fall back into private vengeance.

Titus Andronicus instructs us that we must resist our instincts, lest the ensuing revenge cycle consume us all. But it offers no easy solutions. We are not the only culprits here—terrorism is the quintessential extra-legal activity. Yet we must recognize that we cannot dignify the "war on terror" with the name of "war" unless we constrain it with the rule of law. Otherwise, our "war on terror" is a blood feud. And we know how those end.

CHAPTER TWO

THE LAWYER

The Merchant of Venice

IT IS WITH SOME RELIEF THAT I TURN AWAY FROM *TITUS Andronicus* toward *The Merchant of Venice*. *Merchant*'s Venice is far removed from *Titus*'s Rome. It is a prosperous and stable society in which the law is stringently enforced. The existence of the rule of law permits us to shift genres from tragedy to comedy. Yet as we shall see, the rule of law is a necessary, not a sufficient, condition for the attainment of justice. Because *Merchant* fails to guarantee one of those conditions, it is properly designated a "problem comedy."

Merchant's Venice fails to ensure that those proficient in the law do not abuse it. We submit to the rule of law to quiet private vengeance, giving the state a monopoly over all violence. Yet this means we must protect ourselves against governmental abuses of power. We do so by requiring that laws be written down and applied in standardized ways—that is what it means to live under "a government of laws and not of men." But in every society, some individuals will be unusually adept at manipulating those words for their own interest. The fear and mistrust of lawyers is at heart a fear and mistrust of skillful rhetoricians.

In *Merchant,* Portia represents a lawyer so verbally proficient that no law can bind her. There are three major legal instruments in the play—the will of Portia's father, the notarized bond signed by Shylock and Antonio, and the marriage contract entered into by Portia and Bassanio. Yet Portia is able to manipulate each of these instruments to secure her own ends.

Commentators generally see one trial in the play—the formal courtroom trial of act 4. I see three. First, the Venetian gentleman Bassanio must undergo the trial of the three caskets, in which, according to the last will and testament of Portia's father, suitors of the wealthy heiress must choose among boxes made of gold, silver, and lead to win her hand. Although Portia is not permitted to divulge the right answer, she subtly guides Bassanio toward the correct casket.

The trial of the flesh bond comes next. To underwrite Bassanio's expedition to woo Portia, Bassanio's friend Antonio has entered into a deadly contract with the Jewish moneylender Shylock. Under the terms of the flesh bond, Shylock is entitled to a pound of Antonio's flesh if the merchant defaults on his loan. Immediately after Bassanio successfully woos Portia, he learns that Antonio has defaulted and that Shylock intends to collect. This results in the second, most formal trial of the play. Only through the wiles of Portia, who enters the courtroom disguised as the "doctor of laws" Balthasar, does Antonio survive.

Finally, while still disguised as Balthasar, Portia tests her new husband Bassanio's fidelity through the third trial—the trial of the rings. Directly before they are married, Portia gives Bassanio a ring, which he swears will never leave his hand. After the trial, Bassanio seeks to reward Balthasar (whom he does not recognize as his wife). Portia-as-Balthasar asks him for his ring. Bassanio's failure at this trial means that he is exposed to merciless ribbing when he returns to Belmont, where Portia lives.

While the play has a happy ending for the Venetians, it also contains a troubling message about the rule of law and the role of lawyers. In modern times, renditions of the play have become steadily more sympathetic to Shylock, as in portrayals by Patrick Stewart in a 2001 stage production and Al Pacino in a 2004 film and 2010 Shakespeare in the Park production. What I have yet to see is a correspondingly skeptical portrayal of Portia. I explore that darker vision here.

PORTIA BEGINS THE play with our sympathies. While her father's will leaves her a fortune, it also makes her vulnerable to gold diggers everywhere. It permits anyone to win Portia's hand if he chooses correctly among three caskets. As Portia laments, "so is the will of a living daughter curb'd by the will of a dead father" (1.2.23–25). Granted, fathers often chose husbands for their daughters in early modern England, as Shakespeare depicts in *A Midsummer Night's Dream* and *Timon of Athens*. But Portia's father goes a step further in commodifying his daughter. From beyond the grave, he exposes his daughter to being wooed by a series of strangers and possibly won by one of them. He has made his daughter the prize of a "lott'ry" (1.2.28).

The will imposes strict conditions on the suitors as well. Each must swear three oaths before he chooses—first, never to reveal to others which casket he chose; second, to leave immediately if he fails; and third, and most onerously, never again "[t]o woo a maid in way of marriage" (2.9.13). He is then shown the caskets—of gold, silver, and lead—each of which has an inscription on its exterior. The gold casket says, "Who chooseth me, shall gain what many men desire" (2.7.5). The silver says, "Who chooseth me, shall get as much as he deserves" (2.7.7). The lead says, "Who chooseth me, must give and hazard all he hath" (2.7.9). The caskets and their inscriptions—the matter they are made of and the matter they express—pose riddles that test each suitor's understanding of love and marriage.

The trial of the three caskets comes from the *Gesta Romanorum*, an anonymous collection of medieval stories. As Freud recognizes in his essay on *Merchant,* such trials are familiar to us from many sources, including Greek mythology (the three goddesses judged by Paris), fairy tales (the three sisters judged by the prince in "Cinderella"), and even in Shakespeare's later work (the three daughters judged by Lear). Part of the pleasure of these stories is their inexorability. The correct choice is always the last one—the goddess who speaks last, the scullery maid in the corner, the daughter who will not flatter. This is its own law—the law of the tale—that governs Shakespeare's most exquisitely plotted comedy.

The first suitor is the Prince of Morocco. Like the other Moors in Shakespeare's plays—Aaron of *Titus* and Othello—his racial difference is presented immediately: "Mislike me not for my complexion" (2.1.1) are his first words in the play. Yet while Morocco asks not to be judged on his appearance, he does so himself in choosing the gold casket as the only one worthy of Portia. The casket contains a human skull, with a scroll through its eye socket. The scroll chides: "All that glisters is not gold, / Often have you heard that told,— / Many a man his life hath sold / But my outside to behold,— / Gilded tombs do worms infold" (2.7.65–69). Morocco's interpretive failure is an overly literal cast of mind. In keeping with common Renaissance portrayals of Moors, Morocco is presented as childlike, hot-tempered, and naïve.

The second suitor is the Prince of Arragon. Unlike Morocco, Arragon is not gulled by the gold casket. He understands that "what many men desire" is superficial. Yet the amulet that saves him is worse than the danger it wards off, for, as Arragon's name suggests, it is his arrogance that makes him unwilling to "jump with common spirits" (2.9.32). He chooses the silver casket because he believes he merits Portia: "I will assume desert" (2.9.51). The silver casket contains a fool's head, usually presented as a portrait or a small puppet. The scroll reads: "Take what wife you will to bed, / I will ever be your head" (2.9.70–71). Samuel Johnson thought Shakespeare had forgotten that the failed suitors could not take wives. But I think the scroll states that Arragon does not *need* a wife: "It doesn't matter if you marry, because you're already married to your foolish self." The charge is narcissism—in assuming that he is deserving, Arragon drowns in the pool of his self-regard. Given that silver was used to make mirrors in the Renaissance, the fool's head he sees could be his own in the bottom of the casket.

Morocco and Arragon make different but related mistakes. Both look at the wrong part of the inscriptions. Consider the mottoes with the relevant verbs highlighted:

Gold: "Who chooseth me, shall *gain* what many men desire."

Silver: "Who chooseth me, shall *get* as much as he deserves."

Lead: "Who chooseth me, must *give* and *hazard* all he hath."

Morocco and Arragon focus on the last verbs: Morocco contrasts "desire" to "hazard," and Arragon contrasts "deserves" to "hazard." Yet the real contrast between the gold and silver caskets on the one hand

and the lead casket on the other can be found in the penultimate verbs. The gold casket's inscription emphasizes what the suitor will "gain," and the silver casket's motto stresses what the suitor will "get." But the lead casket's inscription underscores what the suitor must "give." In the economy of this play, giving is the secret to getting or gaining.

The way is now clear for Bassanio. Unlike the other suitors, Bassanio meets the paper requirements of this xenophobic society. Bassanio met Portia while her father was alive, and remembers receiving "fair speechless messages" from her eyes (1.1.164). In contrast to her treatment of the other suitors, Portia urges him to postpone the trial. She fears he will choose incorrectly and will then be required to leave immediately.

Bassanio, of course, chooses the correct casket. Critics dispute whether Portia helps him. I think she clearly does. Like many men in the comedies, Bassanio is not the sharpest rapier in the rack. Throughout the play, he is intellectually outclassed by practically everyone around him. Fortunately, he understands that Portia wishes to help him. Shortly before he chooses, he says: "O happy torment, when my torturer / Doth teach me answers for deliverance!" (3.2.37–38). He is counting on receiving more "speechless messages" to guide his choice.

Nor does Portia disappoint. Portia's most obvious hint is the song she has sung while Bassanio chooses, a song no other suitor gets to hear:

> Tell me where is Fancy bred,
> Or in the heart, or in the head?
> How begot, how nourished?
>
> Reply, reply.
>
> It is engend'red in the eyes,
> With gazing fed, and Fancy dies

In the cradle where it lies:
Let us all ring Fancy's knell.
I'll begin it. Ding, dong, bell.
(3.2.63–71)

It is a critical commonplace that the end words of the first stanza—
"bred," "head," and "nourished" (pronounced "nourishéd")—all
rhyme with "lead" (as does the word "fed" in the second stanza). The
song's content also suggests the lead casket in teaching that a fancy
"engend'red in the eyes" will expire "in the cradle where it lies." Bassanio gets the message. He approaches the caskets musing: "So may
the outward shows be least themselves,— / The world is still deceiv'd
with ornament" (3.2.73–74).

Other indications that Portia "cheats" are sprinkled like bread
crumbs across the play. In act 1, Portia declares to Nerissa that "a
hot temper leaps o'er a cold decree" (1.2.18–19), suggesting that her
passion will not be ruled by the dead hand of the law. In the same
scene, she jokingly tells Nerissa to mislead a drunken German suitor
by setting "a deep glass of Rhenish wine on the contrary casket"
(1.2.91–92). Portia has thought about how to guide undesirable suitors away from the correct casket, and so, presumably, about how to
guide her chosen suitor toward it. In speaking with Bassanio before
he chooses, she uses the words "hazard" (3.2.2), "venture" (3.2.10),
"peise" (3.2.22) (meaning to weigh), and "sacrifice" (3.2.57), all of
which suggest the lead casket or its inscription.

Portia's defenders bristle at the accusation that she seeks to de-
feat her father's will. Yet their entire defense is that the evidence
against her is circumstantial and that she exhibits genuine anxiety
while Bassanio chooses. Given Portia's concern with being forsworn,
it seems unlikely that she would confess her cheating to another
character. The argument about her nervousness proves nothing, as

Portia could cheat and still fear that Bassanio would miss her cues. Circumstantial though it may be, the evidence is all on one side.

I also do not fault Portia for cheating. Her father has put her in an intolerably vulnerable position. As we see throughout Shakespeare, women must use their wiles to gain agency. That is the allure of a Rosalind, a Viola, or a Portia. Unlike Rosalind or Viola, though, Portia's wiles are specifically lawyerly ones. As she herself recognizes, her challenge is to get her own "will" without breaking the terms of her father's "will." Her solution is clever—she obeys the letter of the law that says she may not tell a suitor the correct answer, but uses her rhetorical skills (in her song and speeches to Bassanio) to do everything short of that. In doing so, she violates the law's spirit. But the law of the father is so draconian that she retains my sympathies.

LIKE THE TRIAL of the caskets, the trial of the flesh bond is set up in the first act. The impecunious Bassanio goes to his friend Antonio, the merchant of the title, to borrow funds to woo Portia. Antonio has wealth, but no liquidity—his assets are tied up in ships abroad. So he and Bassanio go to the Jewish moneylender Shylock to borrow money on Antonio's credit. Shylock surprises the Christians by saying he will not charge interest for a three-month loan of 3,000 ducats. He then tells Antonio that the forfeit for default is "an equal pound / Of your fair flesh, to be cut off and taken / In what part of your body pleaseth me" (1.3.145–47). Although Shylock presents it as a joke—a "merry bond" (1.3.169)—Bassanio tells Antonio to walk away from the bargain. But Antonio reassures Bassanio that his ships will come in a month before the loan is due. Shylock seizes that moment to accuse the Christians of undue suspicion:

> Pray you tell me this,—
> If he should break his day what should I gain
> By the exaction of the forfeiture?
> A pound of man's flesh taken from a man,
> Is not so estimable, profitable neither
> As flesh of muttons, beefs, or goats,—I say
> To buy his favour, I extend this friendship,—
> If he will take it, so,—if not, adieu. . . .
> (1.3.158–65)

To be sure, if Shylock gains nothing from the "pound of flesh," he should be asked why he conditions the loan on it. But Bassanio, unlike Shylock or Portia, does not think like a lawyer. He fails to ask this question, muttering only that he "like[s] not fair terms, and a villain's mind" (1.3.175).

In the trial scene, Shylock answers his own question:

> You'll ask me why I rather choose to have
> A weight of carrion flesh, than to receive
> Three thousand ducats: I'll not answer that!
> But say it is my humor,—is it answer'd?
> What if my house be troubled with a rat,
> And I be pleas'd to give ten thousand ducats
> To have it ban'd?
> (4.1.40–46)

Shylock responds that he is entitled to assign his own value to the pound of flesh. Bassanio and Antonio were duped by his prior rhetoric, which weighed the flesh on the scales of the public market trafficking in mutton, beef, and goats. In that market, a pound of human flesh has no value. But Shylock is trading on the private market of vengeance, where the pound of flesh will "feed fat the ancient grudge" he bears Antonio. Shylock imbues Antonio's flesh with what a contract lawyer would call "idiosyncratic value," or what a layperson would call "sentimental value."

Of course, the sentiment is monstrous. But Shylock's thirst for vengeance must be understood in light of the way Jews were treated in the Renaissance. This play is set in Venice because the city was one of the few in Western Europe that did not expel the Jews. Even in Venice, Jews were forced to live in a quarter called the Ghetto, from which the modern term is derived. They were required to stay there from midnight to dawn, and forced to wear red hats when they left it.

Excluded from many occupations, Jews often turned to money-lending out of necessity. The law governing usury in Shakespeare's time was the 1571 Acte Against Usurie, which softened the preceding categorical ban on the practice. The 1571 act prohibited only usurious contracts that charged over 10 percent interest per annum. Still, violators of the act were punished by severe fines and sometimes by imprisonment. In addition, the act made wrongdoers subject to punishment by the ecclesiastical courts as well as by the common law courts, given that "all usury, being forbidden by the Law of God, is Sin and Detestable." Because Christian doctrine barred usury, Christians could not engage in the practice. In contrast, Mosaic law permitted Jews to engage in usury with strangers. Jews, then, could lend money at interest under 10 percent without violating either secular or religious law.

In this way, religious competition became enmeshed with commercial competition. The Christians resented the Jews because the Jews could engage in a trade from which Christians were barred. The Jews resented the Christians because the Christians undercut their profits. Shylock hates Antonio because "[h]e lends out money gra-

tis, and brings down / The rate of usance here with us in Venice"
(1.3.39–40). But this market subordination was just a sliver of a much
broader religious subordination. Shylock accuses Antonio of calling
him "cut-throat dog," spitting on him, and kicking him (1.3.106–
114). Far from denying these accusations, Antonio responds: "I am as
like to call thee so again, / To spet on thee again, to spurn thee too"
(1.3.125–26).

As a member of a hated minority, Shylock cannily settles on the
law as the instrument of his revenge. Knowing discretion in this
society will be used against him, Shylock chooses a legal document
seemingly immune to discretion. An international center of trade,
Venice cannot have the neutrality of its laws compromised lest for-
eigners take their commerce elsewhere. When Antonio defaults, Shylock connects the enforcement of the contract to the legitimacy of the
state. As one Venetian says, Shylock "plies the duke at morning and
at night, / And doth impeach the freedom of the state / If they deny
him justice" (3.2.276–78). Antonio himself believes the bond must
be enforced to preserve Venice's credibility. When his friend Solanio
predicts the Duke will not enforce the bargain, Antonio replies:

> The duke cannot deny the course of law:
> For the commodity that strangers have
> With us in Venice, if it be denied,
> Will much impeach the justice of the state,
> Since that the trade and profit of the city
> Consisteth of all nations.
> (3.3.26–31)

And in the famous trial scene of act 4, Shylock says of his forfeit: "If
you deny it, let the danger light / Upon your charter and your city's
freedom!" (4.1.38–39).

Shylock further shows his sophistication in ensuring that the bond is notarized. In the trial scene, he brandishes the state seal against the Christians, saying their protestations will be bootless until they can "rail the seal from off my bond" (4.1.139). He correctly states the law in Shakespeare's England. At common law—the English system of judge-made precedents dating from the medieval period—the sealed bond was virtually irresistible. The only defenses were proof of forgery or a sealed acquittance vouching that the bond had been paid.

For all his urbanity, Shylock is naïve to believe any contract is airtight. When Shakespeare wrote *Merchant,* the severity of bonds was being actively and successfully challenged. Individuals bound by such instruments were appealing to the king through the Court of Chancery. Chancery could not undo the bond, but could enter an order, known as an injunction, that prohibited the collector from enforcing it. By the 1590s, Chancery's interventions were routine.

Portia represents such an intervention—she does not contest the validity of the bond, but raises questions about its enforcement. She enters the court disguised as the "doctor of laws" Balthasar. Portia's maid Nerissa is disguised as Balthasar's male clerk. After examining the bond, Portia declares that Shylock is legally entitled to his pound of flesh. She then presents Shylock with three options familiar to any contracts lawyer—cancellation of the contract (under which he would get nothing), money damages (under which he would get the principal and some amount of interest), and specific performance of the contract (under which he would get the pound of flesh).

The trial of the flesh bond recapitulates the trial of the caskets. The three remedies Portia offers Shylock correspond to the three boxes offered to her suitors. Mercy, or forgiveness of the debt, is akin to the lead casket. It asks the person who chooses it to give without thought of recompense. The money damages correspond to the silver casket, whose inscription speaks of desert. Shylock would deserve the principal and, arguably, some amount of interest. Finally, specific performance—an extraordinary remedy that requires a party to execute the contract according to its exact terms—corresponds to the gold casket, whose inscription speaks of desire. Shylock desires the pound of flesh.

In the trial of the caskets, we are introduced to the caskets in ascending order of ostensible value. Morocco, the first suitor, examines the lead casket, then the silver, then the gold. In the trial of the flesh bond, the remedies are also presented in this order. Portia offers Shylock the options of cancellation, money damages, and, finally, specific performance.

Portia begins by telling Shylock he "must" be merciful. Shylock asks why. In one of Shakespeare's most anthologized passages, Portia replies:

> The quality of mercy is not strain'd,
> It droppeth as the gentle rain from heaven
> Upon the place beneath: it is twice blest,
> It blesseth him that gives and him that takes,
> 'Tis mightiest in the mightiest, it becomes
> The throned monarch better than his crown.
> His sceptre shows the force of temporal power,
> The attribute to awe and majesty,
> Wherein doth sit the dread and fear of kings:
> But mercy is above this sceptred sway,
> It is enthroned in the hearts of kings,
> It is an attribute to God himself;
> And earthly power doth then show likest God's
> When mercy seasons justice: therefore Jew,
> Though justice be thy plea, consider this,

That in the course of justice, none of us
Should see salvation: we do pray for mercy,
And that same prayer, doth teach us all to render
The deeds of mercy. I have spoke thus much
To mitigate the justice of thy plea,
Which if thou follow, this strict court of Venice
Must needs give sentence 'gainst the merchant there.
(4.1.180–201)

Like the lead casket, mercy requires the person who chooses it to "give" rather than to "get" or "gain."

Shylock's imperviousness to this plea may seem like the final symptom of his depravity. But parts of Portia's speech subtly guide Shylock away from mercy. The repeated reference to mercy as an attribute of the powerful would be foreign to Shylock's ears. The allusions to God and salvation would remind him that Portia is speaking from a different faith: Portia contrasts New Testament mercy to Old Testament justice through phrases like "therefore Jew, though Justice be thy plea." Portia is asking Shylock to act like a Christian rather than a Jew, which he could experience as a request for conversion. Finally, when anthologized, this speech usually ends at "the deeds of mercy." But in the real ending of the passage, Portia reminds Shylock that the law lies in his favor: "I have spoke thus much / To mitigate the justice of thy plea, / Which if thou follow, this strict court of Venice / Must needs give sentence 'gainst the merchant there" (4.1.198–201). After all her praise of the lead casket, Portia reminds him of the other two. So Shylock summarily rejects mercy: "My deeds upon my head! I crave the law" (4.1.202). In doing so, he embraces the language of desire associated with the gold casket.

Portia still staves him off, urging him to take money damages instead of the pound of flesh: "Shylock there's thrice thy money off'red thee" (4.1.223). Recall that Shylock has lent the money at no interest. When Bassanio offers Shylock 9,000 ducats, he offers liquidated damages—that is, the original 3,000 plus 6,000 for surrendering his claim to the pound of flesh. But Shylock will not take the silver casket he arguably deserves. He believes the law will requite his desire.

Portia presses no further: "A pound of that same merchant's flesh is thine, / The court awards it, and the law doth give it" (4.1.295–96). Shylock is ecstatic—the gold casket opens before him. This is an extraordinary moment in the play. It is a moment where law triumphs over power: Antonio is surrounded by a courtroom of fellow Christians, but no one can save him. He is resigned to death, and bares his breast to his enemy, a member of a usually powerless minority group. Yet it is also a moment where law triumphs over justice. Portia asks Shylock if he has scales to weigh the pound of flesh. Shylock promptly produces them. Some productions foreground the scales as a visual travesty of the scales of justice.

Portia then asks if Shylock has a surgeon by to stanch Antonio's bleeding. Shylock says he cannot discern such a condition in the contract. Portia says: "It is not so express'd, but what of that? / 'Twere good you do so much for charity" (4.1.256–7). Shylock responds, in mock puzzlement, "I cannot find it, 'tis not in the bond" (4.1.258). These often overlooked lines are critical. Shylock commits himself to a strict construction of the contract. He limits his obligation to the letter of the law, and this choice foreshadows his downfall.

For as Shylock holds the knife to Antonio's breast, Portia stays his hand:

Tarry a little, there is something else,—
This bond doth give thee here no jot of blood,
The words expressly are "a pound of flesh":
Take then thy bond, take thou thy pound of flesh,
But in the cutting it, if thou dost shed
One drop of Christian blood, thy lands and goods
Are (by the laws of Venice) confiscate
Unto the state of Venice.
(4.1.301–308)

Shylock has chosen to interpret the contract literally, saying no clause in the bond entitles Antonio to a surgeon. Portia uses the same literal mode of interpretation against him, saying no clause in the contract provides for blood. Shylock is stunned: "Is that the law?" (4.1.310). Portia responds: "Thyself shalt see the act: / For as thou urgest justice, be assur'd / Thou shalt have justice more than thou desir'st" (4.1.310–12).

Portia's gambit is rightly seen as a "wretched quibble" and a "miserable pettifogging trick." Even the strictest contract lawyer would acknowledge that if X and Y go together (as flesh and blood do), and I contract for a pound of X (a pound of flesh), then that contract includes any accompanying amount of Y (the blood spilled in acquiring the flesh). As an 1858 legal treatise on equity observed, Portia's interpretation would lead to the absurd result that "if a man contracted for leave to cut a slice of melon, he would be deprived of the benefit of his contract unless he had stipulated, in so many words, for the incidental spilling of the juice." Then as now, a party could change the default understanding, but that would be their responsibility. It was Antonio's responsibility to draft the contract to say "I give you a pound of flesh but no accompanying blood." Shylock, of course, would have rejected such a contract. In the absence of such a condition, Portia's interpretation is a shoddy technicality. But a technicality is all that is needed, given that the Christians hate the Jew.

Once he sees he is caught, Shylock bargains downward. He first returns to the remedy of money damages: "I take this offer then,— pay the bond thrice / And let the Christian go" (4.1.314–15). Bassanio has the money at the ready. Portia, however, will hear none of it: "He shall have nothing but the penalty" (4.1.318). (It is, after all, *her* money.) Shylock says he will accept the principal. But Portia remains obdurate: "He hath refus'd it in the open court; / He shall have merely justice and his bond" (4.1.334–35).

Shylock is not even permitted to choose the "merciful" option of forgiving the debt altogether. When he tries to walk out of court, Portia invokes what critics call the Alien Statute. Under this criminal law, an alien who conspires against the life of a citizen forfeits his life and property. (Notice that while Venice seeks to be neutral in its commercial law, it is more than willing to discriminate against aliens in its criminal law.) Shylock shifts from being the plaintiff in a civil action to being the defendant in a related criminal one. With this, the reversal between Shylock and Antonio is complete— Antonio's life is saved, and Shylock's is in jeopardy. The Duke and Antonio fashion a remedy that spares Shylock's life, but only if he converts to Christianity and leaves his property to his daughter, Jessica, whom he has disowned for eloping with the Christian Lorenzo. Shylock leaves the court a broken man.

Where does Portia find such an ingenious scheme to get Shylock to hang himself with his own rope? I think she inherited it from her father, re-creating the rulemaking which, by making her its sacrificial object, has most strongly etched itself on her psyche. Portia's father created a trial in which the least prepossessing of three choices contained the right answer. He ensured that once individuals stood in the place of decision, they could make no choice without enormous consequence. Finally, Portia's father was utterly unforgiving to those who chose wrongly. All these elements recur in the trial of the flesh bond.

In the casket trial, Bassanio chooses amidst music that guides him to the correct casket. In the flesh-bond trial, Shylock, like the unwanted suitors in the casket trial, must choose amidst silence, most particularly silence about his criminal liability under the Alien Statute. If Shylock had been told at the outset of the criminal liability he faced under the statute, he would have torn his bond and left the court. But he did not have the guidance of Portia's voice. Just as Portia entices Bassanio toward the correct physical casket of lead, she entices Shylock away from the correct rhetorical casket of mercy. We begin to wonder if any choice can be made in Portia's presence that is inconsistent with her will.

No sooner is Bassanio saved by Portia than he tumbles into another rhetorical trap set by his rescuer. The final trial concerns the rings Portia and Nerissa have given their husbands. After Bassanio chooses the correct casket in act 3, Portia offers him her ring, saying: "This house, these servants, and this same myself / Are yours,—my lord's!—I give them with this ring, / Which when you part from, lose, or give away, / Let it presage the ruin of your love" (3.2.170–73). Bassanio vows to guard the ring with his life. Nerissa also gives Gratiano a ring, which he also pledges to take to his grave.

Bassanio and Gratiano, however, are fickle husbands. In the courtroom scene, when Antonio's case looks hopeless, Bassanio offers up Portia as well as himself:

Antonio, I am married to a wife
Which is as dear to me as life itself,
But life itself, my wife, and all the world,
Are not with me esteem'd above thy life.
I would lose all, ay sacrifice them all
Here to this devil, to deliver you.
(4.1.278–83)

Disguised as Balthasar, Portia says: "Your wife would give you little thanks for that / If she were by to hear you make the offer" (4.1.284–85). Gratiano, always willing to go his master one worse, chimes in: "I have a wife who I protest I love,— / I would she were in heaven, so she could / Entreat some power to change this currish Jew" (4.1.286–88). Nerissa echoes her mistress: "'Tis well you offer it behind her back, / The wish would make else an unquiet house" (4.1.289–90). Shylock bemoans that his daughter, Jessica, has married one of this ilk: "These be the Christian husbands!" (4.1.291). Throughout the trial of the flesh bond, Bassanio and Gratiano fail to recognize their wives in male garb, further calling their love, or at least their perception, into question. (Male romantic imperception has been a theme for Shakespeare since at least *Love's Labour's Lost,* where the four male nobles cannot identify their masked female lovers.)

To teach her "Christian husband" a lesson, Portia devises a final trial. As Balthasar, Portia asks Bassanio for the ring on his finger as a reward for saving Antonio's life. Bassanio has at least learned a little about sentimental value from the trial of the flesh bond. He recognizes "[t]here's more depends on this than on the value" (4.1.430), and promises Portia "[t]he dearest ring in Venice" (4.1.431) instead.

Yet Bassanio has not learned his lesson well enough. Like Shylock, Portia successfully rewrites his distinction between public and private value:

> That scuse serves many men to save their gifts,—
> And if your wife be not a mad-woman,
> And know how well I have deserv'd this ring,
> She would not hold out enemy for ever
> For giving it to me: well, peace be with you!
> (4.1.440–44)

Portia rhetorically removes the ring from the private realm. She emphasizes that "many men" use sentimental value as an excuse to save their goods from the public market. She also stresses the "unreasonable" aspects of sentimental value by saying only a "mad-woman" would condemn the transaction. Moreover, like Shylock, she presents the transaction in take-it-or-leave-it terms, not allowing the discussion that would reveal the flaws in her argument. When Shylock says, "If he will take it, so, if not, adieu," and when Portia says, "well, peace be with you!" their percussive monosyllables signal impending departure and a refusal to dicker. Antonio, as taken in by Portia as he was by Shylock, says, "My Lord Bassanio, let him have the ring, / Let his deservings and my love withal / Be valued 'gainst your wife's commandment" (4.1.445–47). Bassanio surrenders the ring. Soon thereafter, Nerissa wheedles her ring from Gratiano.

Like Shylock, Portia later points out the shortcomings in her own argument. When she confronts Bassanio, this time as his wife, she asks:

> What man is there so much unreasonable
> (If you had pleas'd to have defended it
> With any terms of zeal):—wanted the modesty
> To urge the thing held as a ceremony?
> (5.1.203–206)

Now it is not Bassanio's wife who is a madwoman, but Bassanio's lawyer who is a potential madman. Poor Bassanio is utterly outclassed by an adversary who can make arguments of perfect symmetry that catch him coming and going. Nerissa, of course, chastens Gratiano in the same way.

The three caskets and the three legal remedies teach us to look for three rings. The third ring belongs to Shylock. In act 3, Shylock's kinsman Tubal reports that he met a man who sold a monkey to Jessica for a turquoise ring. Shylock is distraught: "Out upon her!—thou torturest me Tubal,—it was my turquoise, I had it of Leah when I was a bachelor: I would not have given it for a wilderness of monkeys" (3.1.110–13). Shylock's ring is a relatively humble turquoise, but the mythical quality of this "Oriental," or Middle Eastern, stone was that it created amity between husband and wife. Monkeys, on the other hand, were a symbol of avarice. Like the Christian husbands, Jessica is unable to keep her ring off the market.

The ring sequence shows the positive side of Shylock's resistance to commodification. Shylock will not part with the pound of flesh for any sum. This confuses the other characters in the play, not just because they are Christians who would not draft such contracts, but also because they are Venetians who cannot believe anything is off the market. Here Shylock articulates the same principle of non-commodification in a more sympathetic light. He knows how to keep his keepsakes.

The three rings also recall the three caskets. Shylock's ring, like the lead casket, represents love, for which Shylock is willing to give and hazard all he has—however comically that plenty is expressed as a "wilderness of monkeys." Bassanio's and Gratiano's rings, in contrast, are like the gold and silver caskets (we learn in act 5 that Gratiano's ring is made of gold). Portia claims Bassanio's ring through the familiar arguments from desire and desert. She uses the language of desire when she says "I will have nothing else but only this" (4.1.428), and the language of desert when she speaks of "how well I have deserv'd this ring" (4.1.442). Gratiano faithfully reports this later when he says "My Lord Bassanio gave his ring away / Unto the judge that begg'd it, and indeed / Deserv'd it too" (5.1.179–81). And while Nerissa claims Gratiano's ring offstage, Gratiano says she made a similar pair of claims on him—"and then the boy (his clerk) / That took some pains in writing, he begg'd mine" (5.1.181–82). Although Bassanio has been taught not to make the claims of desire and desert, he has not been taught to resist them. In contrast to the Christian husbands he derides, Shylock is able to do so. Only he is not at fault for losing his ring.

When Portia produces the ring, it is an early assertion of her dominance in the relationship. Throughout the play, she has persuaded Bassanio to do her bidding. We know she will continue to do so throughout their marriage.

FOR MANY CENTURIES, Portia has been held up as an emblem of a good lawyer. The first law school for women, which would later become the New England School of Law, was called the Portia Law School. After Justice Sandra Day O'Connor ascended to the high court, Justice John Paul Stevens once referred to her as the "Portia who now graces our Court." He meant it as a compliment.

But we should take a more skeptical look at Portia. It is a commonplace to state that people hate lawyers—as law professor Ann Althouse has observed, lawyers may be the only group of people about whom it is still acceptable to say that it would be better if we were all dead. Much of the animus against lawyers arises from the idea that we are mouths for hire, using our rhetorical skills to secure happiness and safety for the Belmonts in which we live, ignoring the consequences for those outside that magic circle. When lawyers do *not* have this attribute, like Mahatma Gandhi or Nelson Mandela, the public tends to forget these figures were lawyers at all.

As we reflect on the three trials superintended by Portia, her rhetorical skill should inspire misgiving. Only Shylock approaches her skill. Shylock is eloquent enough to hoodwink Antonio and Bassanio into entering the infamous flesh bond. But Shylock is decisively out-lawyered by Portia in the famous trial scene in the play. I initially admire Portia because only she can stop Shylock. By the play's end, I wonder who can stop *her.*

The three trials in this play are attempts by law to bind the human beings who live under it. Each is based on a legal document—the father's will, the merchant's contract, and the marriage bond. But ultimately Portia is not bound by any of these documents. She always finds a way to get her will.

In doing so, Portia becomes a figure for the lawyer. When she appears in court as the "doctor of laws," the costume is less a disguise than a revelation of the role she has been playing all along. As Bassanio notes: "In law, what plea so tainted and corrupt, / But being season'd with a gracious voice, / Obscures the show of evil?" (3.2.75–77). Portia is the one we fear for her ability to season everything with a gracious voice, and thereby shape our realities against our better judgments.

This concern about the rhetorical skill of lawyers both predates and postdates Portia. It stretches back to the original lawyers, the Sophists of antiquity, who took pride in using rhetoric to make "the weaker argument appear the stronger." And it reaches forward to speak in our times, when lawyers are feared and hated for our sophistry. Law professor Marc Galanter observes that the case against lawyers has always contained the charge that we "corrupt discourse." I wish to argue that this concern about the sophistry of lawyers is vigorously alive today, by looking at a modern example of a super-lawyer.

OF ALL THE hairsplitting legalisms of our time, perhaps the most famous was uttered in 1998 by President Bill Clinton during the Monica Lewinsky scandal: "It depends on what the meaning of the word 'is' is." Clinton was, of course, a lawyer, and his capacity to parse texts in legalistic ways was on display throughout the scandal.

The Lewinsky affair achieved legal significance because Paula Jones, an employee of the state of Arkansas, had sued Clinton for sexual harassment. As is common in sexual harassment suits, Jones's lawyers sought to find other women with whom President Clinton might have had an inappropriate relationship. That dragnet swept up Lewinsky, a former intern in the White House. In his Paula Jones deposition of January 17, 1998, President Clinton swore: "I have never had sexual relations with Monica Lewinsky. I've never had an affair with her." This statement dovetailed with an affidavit submitted by Lewinsky ten days earlier, which asserted: "I have never had a sexual relationship with the president." When questioned about the Lewinsky affidavit, Clinton affirmed it was "absolutely true." Clinton also remained silent as his lawyer, Robert Bennett, stated to the judge that Lewinsky had filed an affidavit "saying that there is absolutely no sex of any kind in any manner, shape or form, with President Clinton." At a White House press conference on January 26, 1998, Clinton reiterated: "I'm going to say this again: I did not have sexual relations with that woman, Miss Lewinsky. I never told anybody to lie, not a single time; never."

As it turned out, a staggering amount of evidence substantiated a liaison between Clinton and Lewinsky, including a navy blue dress stained with Clinton's semen. Independent Counsel Kenneth Starr opened his grand jury probe into the Lewinsky allegations the day after Clinton's White House press conference. On August 17, 1998, President Clinton testified to the Lewinsky grand jury. In this appearance, Clinton finally admitted to having had an "improper intimate relationship" with Lewinsky. He continued to insist, however, that he had not committed perjury in his January deposition.

How could this be? First, Clinton distinguished between an "intimate relationship" and a "sexual relationship." He observed that he and Lewinsky had not had a "sexual relationship" because they had never had sexual intercourse. As the president put it:

> If you said Jane and Harry have a sexual relationship, and you're not talking about people being drawn into a lawsuit and being given definitions, and then a great effort to trick them in some way, but you are just talking about people in ordinary conversations, I'll bet the grand jurors, if they were talking about two people they know, and said they have a sexual relationship, they meant they were sleeping together; they meant they were having intercourse together.

Clinton's first appeal was to the common-sense meaning of the phrase "sexual relations" as used in ordinary language. While the president declined to state the exact nature of his physical relationship with Lewinsky, he insisted they had never had intercourse.

Unfortunately for Clinton, a specific definition of sexual relations *was* adopted in the *Jones* deposition. Under that definition, "a person engages in 'sexual relations' when the person knowingly engages in or causes . . . contact with the genitalia, anus, groin, breast, inner thigh, or buttocks of any person with an intent to arouse or gratify the sexual desire of any person." The president had an answer for this one as well: "[I]f the deponent is the person who has oral sex performed on him, then the contact is with—not with anything on that list, but with the lips of another person. It seems to be self-evident that that's what it is." Clinton's follow-up seemed superfluous: "Let me remind you, sir, I read this carefully."

Of course he read it carefully—he was a lawyer. He saw the word "lips" was missing from the listed body parts. This created a loophole in the definition of "sexual relations" for receptive oral sex. As *The Starr Report* observed, this meant that if Lewinsky performed oral sex on Clinton, she was having "sexual relations" with him, but he was not having "sexual relations" with her. Faced with a legal definition of "sexual relations," Clinton responded with a legalism. His appeal was now not to "Harry and Jane," but to the "reasonable person" so often invoked in the law. In fact, he shifted subtly from one to the other, noting in his grand jury testimony that "any person, any *reasonable* person" would recognize the validity of his distinction.

Yet Clinton still had some explaining to do. He had sat by in silence as his attorney in the Paula Jones deposition maintained that Lewinsky had filed an affidavit in which she said "there is absolutely no sex of any kind in any manner, shape or form, with President Clinton." This statement would seem to be framed broadly enough to be irrefutably false, whether one took a layperson's or a lawyer's view.

Asked whether the statement was false, Clinton produced his coup de grâce: "It depends on what the meaning of the word 'is' is. If the—if he—if 'is' means is and never has been, that is not—that is one thing. If it means there is none, that was a completely true statement." Clinton was relying on the tense of the verb "to be." As he elaborated: "Now, if someone had asked me on that day, are you having any kind of sexual relations with Ms. Lewinsky, that is, asked me a question in the present tense, I would have said no. And it would have been completely true."

This was the statement that would go viral (a 2010 Internet search of the eleven words generates more than half a million hits). To be sure, this quotation sounds more absurd shorn of context. Standing alone, "[i]t depends on what the meaning of the word 'is' is," does not seem like a defense based on present versus past tense. Rather, as conservative columnist George Will observed, it sounds like a post-modern attack on reality.

Strangely enough, I believe the phrase better captured what was going on without context than with it. The great constitutional law scholar Thomas Reed Powell once said: "If you think you can think about something which is attached to something else without thinking about what it is attached to, then you have what is called a legal mind." Portia displays her legal mind when she separates the "pound of flesh" from the blood with which it is inextricably combined. Clinton displayed his legal mind even during his first campaign for the presidency. Asked whether he had ever violated international law, he stated that he had experimented with marijuana while in England. But, he said, "I didn't inhale." So it should be no surprise that he was able to distinguish between an "intimate relationship" and a "sexual relationship," between "oral sex" and "sexual relations," and, finally, between "is" and "is."

Portia's sophistry extends beyond her hairsplitting legalisms, to her capacity to persuade others to behave badly while minimizing her own exposure. She evades the strictures of her father's will by slyly dropping hints to Bassanio, persuades Shylock to self-destruct, and later entraps Bassanio into surrendering his ring. Clinton similarly used his persuasive skills to endanger others while protecting his interests. Lewinsky stated that the president never "explicitly" told her to lie. However, she testified that he encouraged her to use "cover stories." For instance, Clinton allegedly said: "You know, you can always say you were coming to see [his assistant] Betty [Currie] or that you were bringing me letters."

Clinton also endangered Betty Currie, who was drawn unwillingly into the scandal. Currie testified that she sought to avoid learning any details of the relationship between Lewinsky and the president. When Lewinsky tried to confide in her, Currie responded: "Don't want to hear it. Don't say any more. I don't want to hear any more." Nonetheless, because she sat directly outside the Oval Office, Currie inevitably came to know about the liaison between Lewinsky and the president. Both parties used her as an intermediary for gifts and notes. After Lewinsky received a subpoena, Currie was tasked with picking up a box of gifts that Clinton had given to Lewinsky. Currie did not open this box, but kept it under her bed in her residence until she was forced to surrender it during the grand jury proceedings.

When he became aware that Currie had been called to testify, Clinton confronted her with a series of rapid-fire statements:

> "You were always there when she was there, right? We
>   were never really alone."
> "You could see and hear everything."
> "Monica came on to me, and I never touched her, right?"
> "She wanted to have sex with me, and I can't do that."

Currie believed the president wanted her to agree with these statements and, at the time, she indicated her agreement. While testifying before the grand jury, however, she made the right decision. She admitted that she knew the president and Lewinsky had in fact been alone in the Oval Office and that she could not see or hear them when they were alone. Unlike Lewinsky, Currie could not be persuaded to lie under oath. But this was not for any lack of trying on Clinton's part. Clinton was willing to have her commit perjury, while framing his words carefully enough to maintain plausible deniability. And deny he did, explaining that he was running over the chain of events in his mind, rather than attempting to influence her testimony.

Unlike Portia, Clinton was called to account. He was impeached on charges of perjury and obstruction of justice. Though acquitted by the Senate of these charges, he was disbarred by both the state of Arkansas and the Supreme Court Bar. But this distinction between Clinton and Portia may be more contingent than principled. After all, Portia misrepresented herself as a lawyer in the flesh-bond trial. If she could not be disbarred, it was only because she was not a lawyer to start with. At a recent moot court exercise, Judge Richard Posner, sitting on a fictional appeal from *Shylock v. Antonio,* was asked if Portia should be sanctioned. The answer, of course, was yes.

CHAPTER THREE

THE JUDGE

Measure for Measure

ON THE FIRST DAY OF CONFIRMATION HEARINGS FOR NOW-Justice Sonia Sotomayor in the summer of 2009, I sat in a freezing television studio. As a longtime supporter, I had resolved to give her my all. This meant granting all media requests, such as this one to sit for hours in a studio waiting for a break in the action that would permit commentary. The anchor sitting next to me cheerfully expressed her hope that one of the senators would not use up his or her allotted ten minutes. I shot her a pitying look.

Since 1987, when Judge Robert Bork "borked" himself by actually answering questions, the value of confirmation hearings as "get-to-know-you" events has plummeted. The incentive in these hearings is for the senators to say as much, and for the nominees to say as little, as possible. In 1993, Justice Ruth Bader Ginsburg stated the rule that has come to bear her name. With the circumspection that has marked her career, she said she planned to give "no hints, no forecasts, no previews."

What the confirmation hearings *do* provide is an opportunity for us to reflect as a nation on the judge's role. The battle lines were starkly drawn. President Barack Obama stated that he would look for the quality of "empathy" in nominating judges. This claim inflamed many conservatives. Senator Jeff Sessions, the ranking Republican on the Senate Judiciary Committee, characterized the empathy standard as a dangerous departure from the rule of law. Empathy for some, he noted, was always prejudice toward others.

What I found troubling about this conversation is that many individuals behaved as if we were having it for the first time. In fact, we have been having it for centuries, if not millennia. We cycle through three conceptions of judging—one that values empathy too much, leading to the erosion of the rule of law; one that errs in the opposite direction, asking for "strict construction" of the "letter of the law"; and, finally, one that realizes that judging is much messier than either extreme would indicate.

Measure for Measure presents these models by brilliantly playing off three senses of the title. The first sense of "measure for measure" is the Christian one, coming from the Sermon on the Mount:

> Judge not, that ye be not judged. For with what judgment ye judge, ye shall be judged: and with what measure ye mete, it shall be measured to you again. And why beholdest thou the mote that is in thy brother's eye, but considerest not the beam that is in thine own eye? Or how wilt thou say to thy brother, Let me pull out the mote out of thine eye; and, behold, a beam is in thine own eye? Thou

hypocrite, first cast out the beam out of thine own eye; and then shalt thou see clearly to cast out the mote out of thy brother's eye.

I love this passage because it so cleverly uses an organ of judgment—the eye—as its instance of an object of judgment. If I judge the mote in your eye, I am implicitly assuming that my own eye has nothing in it that would impede my vision. Yet my own perspective may be just as partial, if not more so. Ordinary judgment—sight alone—will not reveal my error, as I, after all, have a beam in my eye that will prevent me from seeing it. What is needed is not sight, but insight—I need to look at your visual "impairment" and infer that my own impairment might be the same or worse. I need to empathize rather than judge. The ethic of judgment such empathy engenders is an ethic of non-judgment, recalling the idea that because we are all sinners, none of us should cast the first stone. We should instead suspend or defer our judgment—"Judge not lest ye be judged." Vincentio, Duke of Vienna, originally stands for this ethic in the play.

The second sense of "measure for measure" is the Old Testament ethic of commensurability, in which the punishment fits the crime. This is the talionic law, explored in both *Titus Andronicus* and *The Merchant of Venice*. As it says in Exodus: "And if any mischief follow, thou shalt give life for life, eye for eye, tooth for tooth, hand for hand, foot for foot, burning for burning, wound for wound, stripe for stripe." This principle of retribution stands at the opposite extreme from the Duke's conception of forgiveness. Angelo, the Duke's deputy, stands for it in the play.

The final sense of "measure for measure" is pagan, flowing from antiquity. This is the sense of judging "with measure," guided by Aristotelian temperance or the Archimedean mean. This justice leads to less conclusive results than the other two, requiring more human agency and discretion. It is represented by Escalus, the wise older advisor whose name means "scales."

The play persuasively presents the third model—the via media—as the best. It demonstrates that no sane person would wish to live in a society governed solely by empathy or by the letter of the law. As usual, Shakespeare got there first. This play's insight should inform contemporary conversations about judging. It instructs us to eliminate the extreme positions at the outset. We are never dealing solely with "empathy" or "the rule of law," but competing values that must each be honored. Perhaps against intuition, good judgment requires militant moderation.

ALTHOUGH NOT THE most prominent or sympathetic character in *Measure,* the young gentleman Claudio drives the action of the play. Claudio has broken Vienna's law against fornication (sex outside marriage) with his fiancée, Juliet, resulting in an out-of-wedlock pregnancy. Ordinarily, this would not be a problem, given that the laws against fornication—or any of Vienna's laws, for that matter—have long gone unenforced under Duke Vincentio. However, Vincentio has left Vienna for a time in the hands of his young deputy Lord Angelo. Angelo begins zealously to enforce all the laws in the city, and Claudio is sentenced to death.

Claudio sends his friend Lucio, a pimp, to his sister Isabella, a novice in a convent. Though appalled by what her brother has done, Isabella is equally appalled by the state's brutal punishment. She goes to plead with Lord Angelo for Claudio's life. Angelo successfully defends the importance of upholding the letter of the law against pleas for mercy. Emotionally, however, Angelo recognizes himself in Isabella's chilly rectitude and falls in love, or lust, with her. He promises that he will save her brother's life if she will sleep with him. Isabella informs her brother of the proposition. Claudio initially tells her not to accede, but then, to her horror, begins to waver.

Luckily for Isabella, Duke Vincentio has only pretended to have left Vienna. Disguised as a friar, he suggests to Isabella that she trick Angelo. Angelo has broken an engagement with the gentlewoman Mariana, solely because she lost her dowry in a shipwreck. Vincentio tells Isabella to accept Angelo's proposition, but to have Mariana keep the assignation under cover of night. The plan goes off with only one hitch—after Angelo sleeps with Mariana, thinking she is Isabella, he does not keep his end of the bargain. Fearing that Claudio will avenge his sister, he orders the young man executed.

The play culminates with the "return" of the Duke to the city. Isabella goes to the Duke to ask for justice. It is a classic case of sexual harassment, insofar as it is Angelo's word against Isabella's. Given Angelo's prior record and position of power, Isabella is at first deemed insane. However, at the denouement of the play, the Duke reveals that he has been in Vienna all along and knows exactly what has transpired. Angelo wishes to be put to death, but Mariana asks that he be permitted to live. The Duke tests Isabella's virtue by putting the matter into her hands without revealing that he has secretly prevented Claudio's execution. Isabella pleads for Angelo's life. Moved by this, the Duke doles out pardons. He reveals that Claudio is still alive and pardons him; he pardons Angelo so he can marry Mariana; and he even pardons the pander Lucio, who has slandered him, so long as Lucio marries the woman he has gotten pregnant. In the final lines of the play, Vincentio asks Isabella to marry him.

Isabella does not answer his proposal. Her silence stands for the absence of answers to many of the play's questions. The Duke's clemency has resulted in a happy ending, but it risks replicating the problem with which we began the play—the problem of lawless Vienna. But if the Duke is too lenient a judge, Angelo is so harsh that he cannot comply with his own judgments. The question is how to find one's way between the two extremes. Escalus, the elder statesman in the background of the play, offers an answer.

MEASURE BEGINS WITH Duke Vincentio lamenting that he has let Vienna slip into anarchy through mistaken kindheartedness. The central problem with Vienna's laws is that they are overly harsh—one act of sex outside marriage, for instance, is punished with death. One wonders why the Duke has not agitated to amend these laws, as the real problem is legislative. But the play takes the laws to be immutable. Consequently, the Duke has used his powers to prevent any of the laws from being enforced for some indeterminate period of time: the young gentleman Claudio says nineteen years (1.2.157) while the Duke puts it at fourteen (1.3.21). Critics attribute the discrepancy to authorial oversight. At the risk of bardolatry, I think it is deliberate. One symptom of a confused state is the absence of a sense of when it began to fall apart.

What is beyond dispute is that Vienna is in chaos. As the Duke says:

> We have strict statutes and most biting laws,
> The needful bits and curbs to headstrong jades,
> Which for this fourteen years we have let slip;
> Even like an o'er-grown lion in a cave
> That goes not out to prey. Now, as fond fathers,
> Having bound up the threatening twigs of birch,
> Only to stick it in their children's sight
> For terror, not to use, in time the rod
> Becomes more mock'd than fear'd: so our decrees,

Dead to infliction, to themselves are dead,
And Liberty plucks Justice by the nose,
The baby beats the nurse, and quite athwart
Goes all decorum.
(1.3.19–31)

The unenforced laws are variously compared to bridles that have slipped off their horses, a lion too fat to leave its cave, and, finally, the spared rod that spoils the child. With the last image, Vincentio introduces a subtler problem with unenforced laws than simple inefficacy—unenforced laws diminish the credibility of government because "the rod / Becomes more mock'd than fear'd." Albert Einstein opposed Prohibition for this reason—he feared unenforced laws would lower "the prestige of government." In this sense, an unenforced law is worse than no law at all.

The obvious solution would be for the Duke to announce a new era of enforcement. The Friar whom the Duke addresses says as much: "It rested in your Grace / To unloose this tied-up justice when you pleas'd; / And it in you more dreadful would have seem'd / Than in Lord Angelo" (1.3.31–34). The Duke, however, fears being a hypocrite and (less to his credit) being *seen* as a hypocrite. So he pretends to leave the city, assigning the task of reform to Angelo. The Duke makes a poor first impression—he has not only let the state break down, but wants someone else to fix it.

The Duke chooses his deputy with care. He first summons Escalus, the elder of his two advisors, and rightly praises Escalus's knowledge of statecraft. Yet after meting out this praise, the Duke makes Angelo, the younger advisor, his deputy. Angelo is the true mirror image of the Duke, as rigid as the Duke has been lax. He is repeatedly characterized by others as super- or subhuman. We discern that the Duke is using him, rather than the more reasonable Escalus, to press the state to the other extreme. The Duke also suspects Angelo of not being as pure as he appears.

After the Duke takes his ostensible leave, we experience Vienna's lawlessness directly when Angelo and Escalus hear a case. The constable Elbow hauls the pimp Pompey and the bartender Froth into court. Elbow, whose name suggests a kink or crookedness, is the archetype of the lowly constable who served without pay in English villages, following other incompetent Shakespearean policemen like Dull in *Love's Labour's Lost* and Dogberry and Verges in *Much Ado About Nothing*. He cannot get his words straight: "I am the poor Duke's constable, and my name is Elbow. I do lean upon justice, sir, and do bring in here before your good honour two notorious benefactors" (2.1.47–50). He means "the Duke's poor constable," and "two notorious malefactors," but the judges need time to stitch this together. When Pompey protests his innocence, Elbow says, "Prove it before these varlets here, thou honourable man, prove it" (2.1.85–86). Escalus cottons on: "Do you hear how he misplaces?" (2.1.87). Angelo has already lost patience. He stalks out of the court, hoping Escalus will "find good cause to whip them all" (2.1.136).

Pompey begins to bait the hapless constable. Elbow uses "respected" for "suspected" in saying that Pompey's "mistress is a respected woman" (2.1.160–61). Pompey retorts that Elbow's "wife is a more respected person than any of us all" (2.1.162–63). The outraged Elbow cries out: "Thou liest, wicked varlet! The time is yet to come that she was ever respected with man, woman, or child" (2.1.164–66). Escalus sadly asks: "Which is the wiser here, Justice or Iniquity?" (2.1.169). Escalus is referring to medieval morality plays, in which Justice and Iniquity were personified. Justice always triumphed in those pageants, but her victory in Vienna is less assured. By riffing off Elbow's malapropisms, Pompey not only evades judgment but tricks the constable into insulting himself and his wife.

Elbow's mistakes are funny, but, on reflection, no laughing matter. Law is language with violent consequences. This violence is easier to see in *Merchant,* where Portia's and Shylock's competing interpretations of the flesh bond are a matter of life and death. Yet when Elbow confuses legal terms—as he muddles "battery" and "slander"—we see that the constable's misuse of legal language could have effects as dire as a more sophisticated person's manipulation of it. In Vienna, the law has become crooked at the primal level.

Whether viewed from the highest or lowest level, Duke Vincentio's lax reign has failed. In depicting the dangers of such a lawless world, *Measure* reveals itself to be a more complex play than *Merchant.* For all its problems, *Merchant* resolves into the comfortable message that all human beings should be more merciful. Portia should have been more merciful to Shylock, who should have been more merciful to Antonio. Anyone who thinks this message through, however, will become suspicious of it. A society with too much mercy, and too little law, is a society in which no one would wish to live. *Measure,* written eight years after *Merchant,* is in this regard a more mature and surprising play.

Put differently, the Sermon on the Mount is a good guide for individuals, but not for states. Machiavelli points out in *The Prince* that rulers must be cruel to be kind: "if a ruler can keep his subjects united and loyal, he should not worry about incurring a reputation for cruelty; for by punishing a very few he will really be more merciful than those who overindulgently permit disorders to develop, with resultant killings and plunderings." Shakespeare was certainly familiar with Machiavelli's work—he has Richard of Gloucester vow that he will "set the murderous Machiavel to school" (*Henry VI, Part 3,* 3.2.193). Regardless of whether he was drawing on Machiavelli here, Shakespeare shows his understanding that rulers cannot be too kind. The Duke adheres to the Sermon on the Mount, but his Christ-like failure to judge has led to a disintegration of the state. In *Titus*, the rule of law fails because of pagan vengeance. In *Measure*, it fails because of Christian charity.

ANGELO'S ASCENSION MARKS the stern return of law. Angelo proclaims that the brothels in the city will be pulled down. He expedites the criminal docket, as we see when a prisoner who has languished in prison for nine years is sentenced to death. Most important, he condemns Claudio to death for fornication with his fiancée, Juliet. As the madam Mistress Overdone exclaims: "here's a change indeed in the commonwealth!" (1.2.96–97).

With respect to Claudio, the sense of injustice is extreme. I imagine the Vienna of this play as the middle panel of Hieronymus Bosch's *The Garden of Earthly Delights* (c. 1503)—a panorama of fantastical debauchery. Yet unlike the hardened bawds in the play, Claudio is married to Juliet in all but name. As Claudio protests to Lucio: "You know the lady; she is fast my wife, / Save that we do the denunciation lack / Of outward order" (1.2.136–38). The couple has entered into the *sponsalia de praesenti*, a mutual recognition of each other as husband and wife. They have not formally married because they are waiting for her dowry.

Moreover, the statute they have violated—like the other statutes in Vienna—has not been enforced for at least fourteen years. Even if the couple were aware of this law, they were not on notice that "the drowsy and neglected act" (1.2.159) would be enforced against them. Under Roman law, courts could invalidate statutes that had been unenforced for long periods under the doctrine of "desuetude," which recognized the unfairness of resurrecting dead letters. To add insult to injury, the anti-fornication statute is draconian, mandating death within three days. But in Angelo's puritanical worldview, the punishment fits the crime.

Angelo's enforcement of Vienna's sex laws could be described as Puritanical in the literal sense. Known for standing on the letter of the law, the Puritans were often pejoratively called "precisians" or "precisemen." The adjective "precise" shadows Angelo throughout the play—Vincentio says, "Lord Angelo is precise" (1.3.50), and Claudio calls him "[t]he precise Angelo" (3.1.93). Like Angelo, the Puritans in early modern England recommended the death penalty for fornication. Shakespeare had reason to take this recommendation personally, as his wife, Anne Hathaway, gave birth to their daughter Susanna six months after their marriage. In the source material for *Measure,* Claudio's counterpart is prosecuted for rape. By changing Claudio's crime to fornication, Shakespeare makes the young man's circumstance his own.

Yet the play is no simple screed against moralism, as Claudio's sister Isabella is the real moralist of the play. We first meet Isabella at the convent, where she is about to become a nun. In five lines, Shakespeare establishes her character:

ISABELLA.
And have you nuns no farther privileges?

NUN.
Are these not large enough?

ISABELLA.
Yes, truly; I speak not as desiring more,
But rather wishing a more strict restraint
Upon the sisters stood, the votarists of Saint Clare.
(1.4.1–5)

The order of Saint Clare was famously strict—its members became known as the "Poor Clares" for taking their vows of poverty so seriously. Isabella's wish for more restraint seems priggish.

If we imagine Isabella's life in Vienna, however, we might look on her with kinder eyes. We meet four other women in this play: the "fornicatress" Juliet, the abandoned Mariana, the madam Mistress Overdone, and the nun Francisca. With these models of womanhood in lawless Vienna, a frightened girl might well wish to enter a nunnery, and the strictest one in town. As we understand today, one of the costs of a lawless society is that its public spaces become unsafe. Recall, for instance, New York City in the mid-1980s, where the subways had grown so dangerous that "subway vigilante" Bernhard Goetz was celebrated for gunning down four muggers. Peace in this play is found in enclosures—Isabella's nunnery, Mariana's moated grange, Angelo's house "circummur'd with brick" (4.1.28).

Whatever we make of Isabella, she is the perfect foil for Angelo. Their first exchange is comically brief because they efficiently conclude that Claudio's sin is execrable and that the rule of law must be upheld. Isabella faintheartedly asks Angelo if the law is not a trifle harsh. Angelo curtly disagrees. This is enough for Isabella: "O just but severe law! / I had a brother, then: heaven keep your honour" (2.2.41–42). I like Northrop Frye's summary: "Isabella: 'I understand you're going to cut my brother's head off.' Angelo: 'Yes, that is the idea.' Isabella: 'Well I just thought I'd ask. I have to go now; I have a date with a prayer.'"

The outraged Lucio persuades Isabella to try again. Her second, more impassioned plea unmistakably echoes Portia's famous "quality of mercy" speech from *Merchant*. Here is Portia again:

> The quality of mercy is not strain'd,
> It droppeth as the gentle rain from heaven

Upon the place beneath: it is twice blest,
It blesseth him that gives and him that takes,
'Tis mightiest in the mightiest, it becomes
The throned monarch better than his crown.
His sceptre shows the force of temporal power,
The attribute to awe and majesty,
Wherein doth sit the dread and fear of kings:
But mercy is above this sceptred sway,
It is enthroned in the hearts of kings,
It is an attribute to God himself;
And earthly power doth then show likest God's
When mercy seasons justice: therefore Jew,
Though justice be thy plea, consider this,
That in the course of justice, none of us
Should see salvation: we do pray for mercy,
And that same prayer, doth teach us all to render
The deeds of mercy.
(4.1.180–198)

Isabella articulates the identical sentiments to Angelo:

No ceremony that to great ones longs,
Not the king's crown, nor the deputed sword,
The marshal's truncheon, nor the judge's robe,
Become them with one half so good a grace
As mercy does. . . .

Why, all the souls that were, were forfeit once,
And He that might the vantage best have took
Found out the remedy. How would you be
If He, which is the top of judgment, should

But judge you as you are? O, think on that,
And mercy then will breathe within your lips,
Like man new made.
(2.2.59–63, 73–79)

These matched pleas form a portal between the plays, inviting us to compare them. Both express the New Testament ethic of "judge not lest ye be judged." God could have condemned us all, but chose to show us mercy, teaching us by example to show mercy to our fellow sinners.

In *Merchant*, Shylock does not engage Portia's arguments, but simply stands on his bond. Shylock's inability to respond may reflect his status as a private citizen. Under the early modern worldview, individuals were always supposed to show mercy. Yet unlike Shylock, Angelo is a ruler. So Shakespeare allows Angelo to answer Isabella's plea for mercy with devastating cogency.

Angelo also begins his case by standing on the law: "It is the law, not I, condemn your brother" (2.2.80). Later, he will also describe himself as "the voice of the recorded law" (2.4.61). His role as magistrate is not to judge the laws, but merely to apply them. If Vincentio can be seen as the "activist judge" who refuses to apply laws he does not like, Angelo is the opposite—the "restrained" jurist so lauded by conservatives today. Moreover, Angelo understands this strict application to be consistent with mercy: "I show [pity] most of all when I show justice; / For then I pity those I do not know" (2.2.101–102).

This is a powerful point. We often think of legal proceedings as concerning only the people involved in them. This is not the case. Any special accommodation we make to particular defendants constitutes bias against the rest of the world. The play has already suggested this danger. Escalus pleads for Claudio's life in part because

Claudio comes from a good family: "Alas, this gentleman, / Whom I would save, had a most noble father" (2.1.6–7). But if Claudio were pardoned on that ground, it would be a grave injustice to individuals not lucky enough to travel in the same circles as the sovereign.

Indeed, Supreme Court Justice Stephen Breyer has embraced Angelo's line with glad recognition. At a conference on "Shakespeare and the Law" at the University of Chicago (where he also played the part of Hamlet Sr.'s ghost), Justice Breyer marveled at the aptness of Angelo's line. "We're speaking to the 298 million Americans who aren't in the courtroom," said Breyer. "How often I've used that line. And how often I justify all kinds of things by it. And there it is, right there, in *Measure for Measure*."

Perhaps most powerfully, Angelo refutes the core contention (made by Vincentio, Isabella, and Escalus throughout the play) that he, as a sinner himself, cannot judge others. He finds a way to judge while evading the charge of hypocrisy loaded into the New Testament sense of "measure for measure." As he says to Escalus:

> I not deny
> The jury passing on the prisoner's life
> May in the sworn twelve have a thief, or two,
> Guiltier than him they try. What's open made to justice,
> That justice seizes. What knows the laws
> That thieves do pass on thieves? 'Tis very pregnant,
> The jewel that we find, we stoop and take't,
> Because we see it; but what we do not see,
> We tread upon, and never think of it.
> You may not so extenuate his offence
> For I have had such faults; but rather tell me,
> When I that censure him do so offend,

Let mine own judgement pattern out my death,
And nothing come in partial. Sir, he must die.
(2.1.18–31)

Angelo's distinction between God's justice and human justice is marked by an appealing humility. Justice can only judge what it sees. Unlike God, humans cannot see everything. So purveyors of human justice admit, as they must, that the guilty sometimes try the guilty. But this does not mean human beings who judge each other are necessarily compromised, so long as they submit themselves to the same laws.

Angelo might have found a worthy adversary in Portia. Isabella is certainly not up to besting him in debate. She concedes that her love for her brother has made her speak insincerely: "O pardon me, my lord; it oft falls out / To have what we would have, we speak not what we mean. / I something do excuse the thing I hate / For his advantage that I dearly love" (2.4.117–20).

Yet Shakespeare permits Angelo only an intermediate victory. As the Duke (watching in disguise) points out, everything depends on whether Angelo can live up to his ideals: "If his own life answer the straitness of his proceeding, it shall become him well: wherein if he chance to fail, he hath sentenced himself" (3.2.249–51). Angelo should be careful in what measure he metes, because that measure will be meted unto him. What is fascinating—and chilling—about Angelo is his confidence in his own rectitude.

Angelo's lack of self-knowledge is his Achilles' heel. In this play, as in all of Shakespeare, self-knowledge is a predicate to knowing anything else. The Duke rises in our estimation when Escalus states that Vincentio has "above all other strifes, contended especially to know himself" (3.2.226)—though significantly, Escalus never says Vincentio has succeeded in that endeavor! In contrast, we know Lear is a flawed ruler when Regan describes her father as someone who "hath ever but slenderly known himself" (*Lear*, 1.1.294–95). The link between governing the self and governing the state is as old as Plato, and recurs throughout the Shakespearean corpus. Self-knowledge in the plays is always a necessary, though never a sufficient, prerequisite of good governance.

Angelo believes himself to be in perfect control of self and, therefore, of state. The Duke intuits this when he says, "Lord Angelo is precise; / Stands at a guard with Envy; scarce confesses / That his blood flows" (1.3.50–52). Lucio concurs that Angelo is "a man whose blood / Is very snow-broth; one who never feels / The wanton stings and motions of the sense" (1.4.57–59). Lucio links Angelo's cold-bloodedness to a lack of sexual desire. He speculates that Angelo "was begot between two stockfishes" (3.2.105), or two dried fish, and that Angelo himself is "ungenitured" (3.2.167–68), or lacking genitals. Brought into the world through asexual reproduction, Angelo is sexless himself.

Almost all the laws treated in the play are sex laws—laws against brothels, procuring, prostitution, and fornication. Sexuality in this play stands for natural sin, following the biblical idea that Adam and Eve fell through sexual knowledge. The two "saints" of the play—Isabella and Angelo—seem immune to sexual temptation. But this, in Shakespeare as in life, is an illusion.

Isabella is a case study of sexual repression. When arguing with Angelo about the importance of her chastity, she says: "Th'impression of keen whips I'd wear as rubies, / And strip myself to death as to a bed / That longing have been sick for, ere I'd yield / My body up to shame" (2.4.101–104). As Harold Bloom says, "Had the Marquis de Sade been able to write so well, he might have hoped to compete with that."

Like a magnet, Isabella's barely repressed sexuality draws out Angelo's. In pleading for Claudio, she asks him:

Go to your bosom,

Knock there, and ask your heart what it doth know

That's like my brother's fault. If it confess

A natural guiltiness, such as is his,

Let it not sound a thought upon your tongue

Against my brother's life.

(2.2.137–42)

Isabella has made this argument—unsuccessfully—before. Yet this time she addresses Angelo's body: "[g]o to your bosom." When questioned whether he feels lust, Angelo must acknowledge he feels it for his questioner: "She speaks and 'tis such sense / That my sense breeds with it" (2.2.142–43). The two meanings of "sense"—reason and sensuality—merge here. What attracts Angelo to Isabella is their mutual coldness: his lust burns like ice.

No one is more startled than Angelo when he feels his desire for Isabella: "Ever till now / When men were fond, I smil'd, and wonder'd how" (2.2.186–87). I love the ruefulness of this line, which evokes a vision of him shaking his head in wonderment at his own frailty. When he marvels, "Blood, thou art blood" (2.4.15), the line is saved from tautology by expressing his new knowledge that his blood is not "snow broth," but human blood.

Unfortunately, Angelo is not humanized by his desire, but plummets from angelic heights to diabolical depths. Floodgates open: "I have begun / And now I give my sensual race the rein" (2.4.158–59). He threatens Isabella that if she does not sleep with him, he will not only kill Claudio but torture him before doing so. Shakespeare understood that the intensely private realm of sexuality is particularly likely to result in public hypocrisy, as we see on both sides of the political aisle today. To take but two examples, Republican Senator John Ensign of Nevada, who criticized President Clinton for adultery, himself recently confessed to adultery; Democratic Governor Eliot Spitzer of New York, who led a crackdown on sex trafficking, himself regularly frequented prostitutes. Now as then, it is dangerous not to know the welter behind one's internal walls.

Angelo's flaws do not surprise the Duke. Vincentio has put Angelo in charge in part to test him: "Hence shall we see / If power change purpose, what our seemers be" (1.3.53–54). The Duke's suspicions of Angelo's bad character arise from his knowledge of Angelo's relationship with the Viennese gentlewoman Mariana. As the Duke informs Isabella, Angelo was engaged to Mariana through a "pre-contract" known as the *sponsalia per verba de futuro,* or a promise to marry in the future. Angelo broke off this engagement because Mariana's dowry was lost in a shipwreck. This engagement brings Angelo's situation closer to Claudio's, with two key distinctions. Legally, Angelo is less culpable than Claudio, because Angelo has not had sex with his fiancée. Morally, Angelo is more culpable because he has been motivated by money, not love. In addition, Angelo has shown himself a "seemer"—while he broke the engagement because of the disappearance of the dowry, he has spread the rumor that he did so because he has learned something negative about Mariana's reputation.

Unfortunately for Angelo, the Duke has remained in Vienna. Disguised as a friar, he offers Isabella counsel. The Duke suggests that Isabella accede to Angelo's demands, but that Mariana keep the assignation. This "bed trick" was a common conceit of the theater of this period, and also figures in *All's Well That Ends Well.* It turned on the legal notion that sexual relations were enough to transform a *sponsalia per verba de futuro* into a marriage. The plan is successful—Angelo believes Isabella has kept her side of the bargain. But Angelo further reveals his perfidy when he fails to uphold his end, ordering Claudio's death. The busy Duke intercepts the order and has the head of a pirate, Ragozine, substituted for Claudio's. To test her virtue, the Duke, still disguised, tells Isabella that Angelo has executed Claudio, and that she should sue for justice when the Duke returns.

Like *Merchant, Measure* culminates in a public trial. When the Duke appears at the city gates, Isabella demands justice. Angelo accuses her of insanity. The Duke initially seems to credit Angelo's account. But then the Duke reveals that he has been in Vienna in disguise, and Angelo realizes he has been observed all along.

The Duke asks Angelo if he has anything left to say for himself. Angelo does not—he longs only for death. The Duke agrees easily to this, saying Angelo should marry Mariana to restore her honor, and then be executed. As Vincentio says:

> The very mercy of the law cries out
> Most audible even from his proper tongue:
> "An Angelo for Claudio; death for death.
> Haste still pays haste, and leisure answers leisure;
> Like doth quit like, and Measure still for Measure."
> (5.1.405–409)

Like Shylock, Angelo is hanged with his own rope. He has eschewed a New Testament ethic of mercy for an Old Testament ethic of retribution of an eye for an eye. This too is recognized as a form of "measure for measure"—"An Angelo for Claudio; death for death." The Duke mimics Angelo's own earlier line about how he shows pity "most of all when [he] show[s] justice" (2.2.101). In the Duke's keen phrasing, it is not the "justice" of the law, but the "mercy" of the law that cries out for retribution—death to Angelo now is the only way of showing mercy to Claudio. Hypocritical as he has been, Angelo understands this—he wishes to die.

Mariana intercedes on her fiancé's behalf, asking that she not be mocked with a husband: "They say best men are moulded out of faults, / And, for the most, become much more the better / For being a little bad. So may my husband" (5.1.437–39). This is a bit much. Angelo is more than a "little bad." As Isabella has pointed out, he is "a murderer," "[a]n adulterous thief," "an hypocrite," and "a virgin-violator" (5.1.41–43). So in the end, only Isabella can plead for Angelo. Acknowledging this, Mariana asks her to kneel beside her.

Isabella, unlike Portia, shows herself capable not only of speaking about mercy, but of giving it. Although she still believes Angelo has caused the death of her brother, she asks the Duke to spare Angelo's life:

> Most bounteous sir:
> Look, if it please you, on this man condemn'd
> As if my brother liv'd. I partly think
> A due sincerity govern'd his deeds
> Till he did look on me. Since it is so,
> Let him not die.
> (5.1.441–446)

The Duke accepts her plea, pardoning Angelo so he can marry Mariana. He then dispenses pardons all around. He reveals that Claudio is alive, and pardons him so he can marry his fiancée, Juliet. In less than ten lines, he sentences Lucio to death for slandering him, then pardons him so he can marry the woman he has impregnated. Finally, and most controversially for critics, he asks Isabella to marry him. She does not answer.

The last act of the play is too quick, lurching toward happy endings for everyone. The pendulum has swung wide. The lawless Vienna of the play's inception has become a polity in which the laws have been remorselessly enforced. Yet once the problems of the other extreme are exposed, the Duke reverts to type. Vienna seems poised to sink back into lawlessness.

SHAKESPEARE DOES OFFER a solution, though it lurks in the shadows of the play. The solution finds a middle ground, focusing on the word "measure" in "measure for measure." This notion of temperance, or the via media, falls less obviously within the Judeo-Christian tradition than within the teachings of antiquity. This solution is embodied in the figure of Escalus. He is not a major character in the play, but he deserves our close attention.

Escalus is manifestly meant to be an iconic figure. His name is the first word of the play. In the initial scene, the Duke lauds his political wisdom:

> The nature of our people,
> Our city's institutions, and the terms
> For common justice, y'are as pregnant in
> As art and practice hath enriched any
> That we remember.
> (1.1.9–13)

This paean poses the riddle of why Vincentio passes over Escalus to choose Angelo as deputy: "Old Escalus / Though first in question, is thy secondary" (1.1.45–46). The answer is that Angelo's inflexibility will only highlight Escalus's worth.

The play shows Vincentio's praise of Escalus to be richly deserved. Escalus's great virtue is that he is not doctrinaire. With respect to the Duke's laxity, he muses that "Mercy is not itself, that oft looks so; / Pardon is still the nurse of second woe" (2.1.280–81). Yet Angelo's rigid justice is not to his liking either. He urges temperance: "Let us be keen, and rather cut a little, / Than fall, and bruise to death" (2.1.5–6).

Perhaps most important, Escalus imposes his own conception of proportionality on the law. As noted, the real problem with Vienna is a legislative problem—its "strict statutes and most biting laws" (1.3.19) impose punishments grossly out of proportion to their crimes. This presses judges to choose between two evils—the evil of non-enforcement with the attendant harm to the state's credibility, or the evil of enforcement with its attendant harm to the state's justice. Vincentio chooses the former evil, Angelo chooses the latter. Escalus finds a middle way.

To see how, it is instructive to compare Escalus's choice with Angelo's. Angelo does not look to the substantive fairness of the law produced by the legislature. In his exchange with Isabella, he says, "It is the law, not I, condemn your brother" (2.2.80), relying on the idea that he is a mechanical engine of the law. He does not ask if the law is a good law or a bad law, or whether the punishment is proportioned to the crime. His sense of "measure for measure" goes only to the procedural fairness of the law's administration. So long as he would submit to the law if convicted, he can enforce it without compunction.

In contrast, Escalus rejects this passivity as unjust. He resists the idea that Claudio should be put to death for a single act of fornication. When he has discretion himself, we see him use it wisely. The first time Pompey comes before him, Escalus lets him off with a warning, which seems reasonable given that the laws are being newly enforced. The second time, however, he punishes him. Similarly, we hear that after "[d]ouble and treble admonition" (3.2.187) he has also punished the madam Mistress Overdone.

The three judges of the play can be seen as three aspects of the sitting sovereign, King James I. Like Vincentio, James acknowledged that he had been too lax at the beginning of his rule. Like Angelo, he engaged in practices viewed to be overzealous, such as pulling down the brothels in the suburbs of London. But the ultimate wisdom he bequeathed to his son in the *Basilicon Doron* (the "Kingly Gift") of 1599 was to find, like Escalus, the middle way.

> I neede not to trouble you with the particular discourse of the foure Cardinall vertues, it is so troden a path: but I will shortly say vnto you, make one of them, which is Temperance, Queene of all the rest within you. . . . Vse Iustice, but with such moderation, as it turn not into tyrannie: otherwaies *summum ius* is *summa iniuria*. . . . And as I said of Iustice, so say I of Clemencie, Magnanimitie, Liberalitie, Constancie, Humilitie, and all other Princelie vertues: *Nam in medio stat virtus*. And it is but the craft of the Diuell that falselie coloureth the two vices that are on either side thereof, with the borrowed titles of it, albeit in very deede they haue no affinitie therewith: and the two extremities themselues, although they seeme contrarie, yet growing to the height, runnes euer both in one. For *in infinitis omnia concurrunt;* and what difference is betwixt extreame tyrannie, delighting to destroy all mankinde, and extreame slackness of punishment, permitting euery man to tyrannize ouer his companion?

James's insight is that the ends of the continuum—tyranny and extreme mercy—have more in common with each other than either does with the middle of the spectrum. Tyranny permits the state to destroy citizens, while anarchy allows citizens to destroy each other. So the king rules the state, but Temperance should be the "queene" over the king.

The most hopeful sign in the Duke's last soliloquy is that he recognizes and rewards Escalus: "Thanks, good friend Escalus, for thy much goodness; / There's more behind that is more gratulate" (5.1.525–26). The old advisor is not flashy. But this is often true of good judges.

LET ME NOW return to the Sotomayor confirmation hearings. My motive here is not to focus on the particulars of her confirmation, which have already been eclipsed by her work as a justice. Rather, I seek to underscore how the hearings drew out a timeless conflict between alternative visions of judging.

The first model was that of the empathetic judge presented by the president who nominated Sotomayor. President Obama's adherence to this model dates back to his days as a senator. In opposing the confirmation of now–Chief Justice John Roberts, he began by observing that "adherence to legal precedent and rules of statutory or constitutional construction will dispose of 95 percent of cases that come before a court, so that both a Scalia and a Ginsburg will arrive at the same place most of the time on those 95 percent of the cases." But he continued:

> [W]hat matters on the Supreme Court is those 5 percent of cases that are truly difficult. In those cases, adherence to precedent and rules of construction and interpretation will only get you through the 25th mile of the marathon. That last mile can only be determined on the basis of one's deepest values, one's core concerns, one's broader perspectives on how the world works, and the depth and breadth of one's empathy.

Obama would repeatedly return to the importance of empathy in judging. He used similar language to oppose the confirmation of now-Justice Samuel Alito. When asked during his presidential campaign how he would select his justices, he repeatedly adverted to the "empathy" standard.

President Obama's empathy standard was predictably controversial. Karl Rove called it the new "code word for judicial activism." He was joined by Senator Sessions and a host of other politicians and commentators who believed that empathy was a threat to the rule of law. The president's opponents produced a countermodel, embodied in the nominee whom Obama had criticized. In his opening remarks during his 2005 confirmation hearings, Roberts compared his job to that of an umpire. "Judges are like umpires," then-Judge Roberts said. "Umpires don't make the rules; they apply them. The role of an umpire and a judge is critical. They make sure everybody plays by the rules. But it is a limited role."

Throughout the entire confirmation process, Sotomayor's opponents painted her as an "empathetic" judge who would be biased toward those with whom she identified. They brandished a thirty-three-word sentence as support for this proposition. In a 2001 speech at Berkeley, then-Judge Sotomayor said: "I would hope that a wise Latina woman with the richness of her experiences would more often than not reach a better conclusion than a white male who hasn't lived that life." The "wise Latina" comment was repeated ad nauseam as evidence that Sotomayor was biased at best and racist at worst.

I find that *Measure,* Shakespeare's deepest meditation on the role of a judge, illuminates this controversy. Sessions could be understood to be playing Angelo to Obama's Vincentio. Sessions characterized Obama's "empathy" standard as encouraging bias—"Empathy for one party is always prejudice against another." This claim echoes Angelo's claim that he shows mercy most when he shows justice—"[f]or then I pity those I do not know" (2.2.102).

Yet we must also remember that Angelo falls in the play because his position is untenable. In attacking Sotomayor's "wise Latina" comment, Sessions appeared to believe that pure neutrality was possible. Like Angelo, he believed that judgment could be a relatively mechanical enterprise, like being an umpire. This in turn suggested that a judge's experiences as a Caucasian would not "color" his judgment. But of course, all of a judge's experiences will to some extent affect his or her judgments.

In defending Sotomayor in the media, I found it useful to raise the instance of a case in which she held that individuals had due process rights before the state could impound their cars. In this opinion, she observed that for many residents of New York, one's car was one's primary asset and one's means of getting to work to earn a livelihood. She argued that an asset of such importance could not be taken away by the state without notice and an opportunity to be heard. I think many would trace the vehemence of this opinion to her background as someone who had grown up as a less-than-affluent New Yorker. However, no one ever brought up this case as an instance of bias, treating it, if they treated it at all, as an instance of her life experience.

Judges, it seems, can use their *experience* to decide cases, but not their empathy. Yet it is difficult to discern where the line between these two lies. Sometimes neither will be necessary. Certain terms of the Constitution are relatively precise, like the one that the president "shall hold his Office during the Term of four Years." These provisions are not debated, even among liberals who supposedly ignore the text. The phrases in the Constitution that engender debate are more abstract, like "due process," "privileges or immunities," "equal protection," and "freedom of speech." In giving these majestic phrases content, both progressives and conservatives must draw on their own experience, and their empathetic engagement with their fellow citizens. In so doing, neither side is detecting a right with predetermined metes and bounds. Neither side is inventing a right out of nothing.

Sotomayor ultimately prevailed over Sessions, but on his terms. Sotomayor characterized the "wise Latina" comment as a "rhetorical flourish that fell flat," while the White House stated that she would probably have "chosen her words differently" if given the opportunity. Sotomayor also insisted that she disagreed with the president that a judge should follow his or her "heart," observing that there was "one law" and that the judge's job was to apply it.

Her recantation of the claim that experience could affect judgment was probably the most politic thing she could do. It preserved a fantasy about how Americans wish to perceive the law. I do not fault her for making a strategic decision when the stakes were so high. I fault those who pressured her to do so. Placed in context, these thirty-three words are clearly a rejoinder to the claim made by the first woman to serve on the U.S. Supreme Court, Justice Sandra Day O'Connor. Asked whether being a woman made a difference to how she judged, Justice O'Connor stated that she believed "A wise old man and a wise old woman will reach the same conclusion in deciding cases." Again, this was the most diplomatic thing for Justice O'Connor to say. But after she ascended to the bench, Justice O'Connor did not walk this talk. In a 1994 case concerning women on juries, for instance, she observed that "[a] plethora of studies make clear that in rape cases, for example, female jurors are somewhat more likely to vote to convict than male jurors." She continued that "though there have been no similarly definitive studies regarding, for example, sexual harassment, child custody, or spousal or child abuse, one need not be a sexist to share the intuition that in certain cases a person's gender and resulting life experience will be relevant to his or her view of the case."

In making her "wise Latina" comment, then-Judge Sotomayor

was describing what Justice O'Connor was doing on the bench. As should be obvious, Justice O'Connor's opinions did not lead to the breakdown of the rule of law. As President Obama might say, in 95 percent (or much more) of Supreme Court cases, I doubt that it would be possible to guess whether an opinion was written by a woman or a man. But in some cases, life experience as a woman—or man—will matter.

Viewed in this light, President Obama's "empathy" standard makes him look more like Escalus than like Vincentio. He was careful to say that when the law was clear, judges should apply it. What he had the temerity to do was to puncture the fiction that judges could be the "voice of the recorded law." But Angelo's model of judgment is pure fantasy, as evidenced by the chief justice himself. As some of the Democrats on the Judiciary Committee pointed out, Chief Justice Roberts, who claimed only to be an umpire, has in fact been an active player in many cases that have come before him. For instance, Roberts wrote a 2007 opinion that invalidated voluntary school integration programs on the basis of *Brown v. Board of Education,* the landmark case mandating racial integration in public schools. Whether one agrees or disagrees with the opinion, it is patently not a simple call of a "ball" or a "strike."

The president has never advocated a model of pure empathy devoid of law. The converse statement could not be made of some of his opponents. After Justice Sotomayor was successfully confirmed, Senator Sessions stated that he was at least convinced Obama would no longer use the word "empathy." It seemed that Sessions wanted a law that was entirely devoid of that quality.

My problem with confirmation hearings is not that they engender heated debate about the judge's role. To the contrary, I welcome such debate. My problem is that these conversations focus so much on extreme models of judging that should be eliminated before the debate begins. Shakespeare understood that judges could not choose either pure empathy or pure law. From its inception, judging has concerned the question of how fairly to apply general rules to particular circumstances. We have had a long time to struggle with the competing principles that make this a timeless predicament. Like Escalus, we should find the middle way. It is time to become more passionate about temperance.

Chapter Four

The Factfinder

Othello

The great eighteenth-century legal commentator William Blackstone maintained that for every case that turned on an issue of law, over a hundred turned on an issue of fact. To live in such a world—as we always have and will—means justice will be driven by those who determine what happened. Law calls such personages "factfinders."

In Shakespeare's England, a long transition from supernatural to human factfinding was nearing completion. Through much of the Middle Ages, the dominant factfinder was God, who revealed facts in various narrowly prescribed ways. Starting at least with the Fourth Lateran Council of 1215, however, a public movement away from supernatural proofs toward human ones gained momentum. By Shakespeare's time, the jury's ascendancy as the primary finder of fact was secure. This legacy can be seen in seventeenth-century charters of the New England colonies, which contained the guarantee of trial by jury. Ultimately, those guarantees were enshrined in the U.S. Constitution.

Shakespeare's plays contain both supernatural and human factfinding. Viewed as a whole, the corpus appears to contain more nostalgia for supernatural factfinding and more anxiety about human factfinding than we might expect of an early modern author. Shakespeare richly depicts and defends the wager by battle. At first glance, he provides no similar exploration of human factfinding.

This chapter reads *Othello* as that exploration. Othello is a Venetian general who also happens to be a Moor. At the beginning of the play, he has eloped with the white gentlewoman Desdemona. Although her father strenuously objects to the marriage on racial grounds, Othello manages to get the Venetian duke's blessing, not least because the duke needs Othello to head off a Turkish invasion of Cyprus (then a Venetian possession). By the time Othello and Desdemona arrive on Cyprus, however, the Turks have already been dispatched by a storm. Othello's ensign Iago uses their idle time on the island to make Othello believe Desdemona has cheated on him with Othello's lieutenant Cassio. Initially skeptical, Othello becomes convinced of his wife's infidelity when Iago, through his wife, Emilia, acquires the handkerchief that Othello gave to Desdemona as his first gift. Othello murders the innocent Desdemona in her wedding bed. Matters get sorted out only when the Venetian nobles assemble on the island. After he realizes he has been deceived, Othello first attempts unsuccessfully to kill Iago, and then commits suicide.

The play contrasts two forms of human factfinding—one communal and rational, as practiced by the Venetian nobles, and one isolated and impassioned, as practiced by Othello. It leaves no doubt about the superior form, as the tragedy of the play is Othello's chronic inability to find the facts. In particular, Othello is grossly prone to a form of bias that takes physical evidence (Desdemona's handkerchief) to be definitive proof of a metaphysical trait (Desdemona's fidelity). The play portrays the bias as problematic but natural and depicts the collective, rational factfinding of the Venetian nobles as the corrective.

We live in a time when human factfinding has triumphed decisively over supernatural factfinding: we trust judges or juries to find the facts rather than requiring parties to carry hot coals or to battle their accusers. I therefore ask whether a tragedy like Othello's could happen in our time. Of course it can and does.

To show this, I compare *Othello* and the 1995 trial of O. J. Simpson. The analogy has little to do with race. It relies instead on the ability of ocular proof—hard physical evidence—to overwhelm all other forms of evidence. In the Simpson trial, the distracting object was not a white handkerchief "spotted with strawberries," but a black glove spotted with blood. By exonerating Simpson, the jury showed that even collective human factfinding is vulnerable to what I will call ocular proof bias.

This vulnerability raises the question of whether the jury is really as much of an antidote to such ocular proof bias as it seems to be. Recently, much has been made of the putative "CSI [*Crime Scene Investigation*] effect," in which forensic science television shows like CSI ostensibly cause juries to fixate obsessively on physical evidence. Although both the cause and extent of the CSI effect have been questioned, juries do seem at least as susceptible as ever to ocular proof bias.

My point is not that we should abandon the jury system, but that we should understand better why we continue to use it. As legal historian George Fisher points out, we use the jury not because it is an infallible factfinder, but because it gives us closure in a world in which infallible factfinders do not exist. The jury permits us to evade the inherent difficulties of factfinding, because, like God, the jury need not respond to questions or justify its results. But if so, we have not traveled as far from the supernatural proofs as we may think. *Othello* helps us grapple with the question of whether human factfinding is a triumphal step away from supernatural factfinding, or simply a different way of letting an inscrutable but definitive authority help us negotiate a world that is, and will remain, largely opaque to human apprehension.

To a certain point, medieval legal process seems familiar. Litigation began when one party or the state publicly accused an individual; a court would hear both sides and render judgment. Critically, however, the judgment would relate not to guilt or innocence but to how guilt or innocence would be established. The three dominant methods all relied on God to sort out the facts. These were the "supernatural proofs": trial by ordeal (in which individuals were burned with irons or submerged in water), trial by compurgation (in which defendants, along with their allies, swore their innocence before God), or trial by battle (in which defendants dueled with their accusers).

Perhaps the most familiar supernatural proof was the ordeal, such as the ordeals of fire and water. The ordeal by fire forced the accused to carry a hot iron for a prescribed distance. The burns would be bandaged for several days and then inspected. Healing wounds bespoke the suspect's innocence; festering ones her guilt. In the ordeal by cold water, the accused was trussed and immersed in sanctified water. If he sank, he was deemed innocent because the purity of the water had accepted him. If he floated, he was deemed guilty and executed. (The pronouns here are deliberate—trial by fire was more often used for women, perhaps because it was understood even then that, on average, women were more likely to float than men because their body mass had more fat.) The ordeals were reserved for cases in which the offense was grave or the party's word was deemed unreliable.

For less serious crimes, judges would often choose trial by compurgation, also called "wager of law." In this procedure, the accused would swear his innocence supported by others who would do the same. Although they originally swore to the innocence of the accused, over time "oath-helpers" testified only to his good character. Compurgation assumed individuals would not jeopardize their eternal salvation by bearing false witness. As befit a lesser offense, this was a much lighter burden of proof: as legal historian John Baker observes, the accused could swear "in very general terms and without possibility of cross-examination."

The third supernatural proof was trial by battle, also called wager of battle, which came to England after the Norman Conquest. Trial by battle pitted the accused against his accuser under the assumption that God would strengthen the arms of the just. Originally available for all disputes, wager of battle was later limited to the most serious crimes. It was the Norman alternative to the ordeal. On the Continent, felonies would generally be tried by the ordeals. In England, however, the party seeking redress for a felony would use the "trial by battle as the presumptive mode of proof."

The overriding benefit of all three supernatural proofs was their divine legitimacy. To structure a world where facts could be hard to find, an omniscient God revealed them. As medieval historian Robert Bartlett nicely summarizes the ordeal: "It was a device for dealing with situations in which certain knowledge was impossible but uncertainty was intolerable." And, as Baker adds, "Supernatural proofs and the oaths which they tested were absolute and inscrutable; no legal questions were asked, no reasons given, no facts found, no rules declared." The supernatural proofs gave decisive social closure.

Yet what was comforting about the proofs was also troubling. The proofs represented a paradoxical stance of humility and hubris toward divine authority. On the one hand, human beings were submitting to God's judgment. On the other, they were requiring God to "sit in" on all human trials, rather than remitting individuals to the ordinary laws of nature. The supernatural proofs demonstrated human arrogance in assuming that God was always at the beck and call of human beings who wanted answers to their questions.

The ordeal was particularly susceptible to this charge because the church's involvement was so pervasive. A priest determined how far the accused carried the iron, how hot the iron was, and whether the wound had "healed" or "festered." A priest sanctified the water, checked the knots, and decided whether the accused had "floated" or "sunk." Even during its heyday (from about 800 to 1200), the ordeal was used only when other forms of proof, such as witnesses or a confession, could not be acquired. Last resorts are first to go: the Catholic Church prohibited clergy from participating in the ordeals in the Fourth Lateran Council of 1215. Stripped of its divine imprimatur, the ordeal soon died out in Western Europe.

While the other supernatural proofs survived, they, too, were riddled with problems. Compurgation aroused a healthy skepticism about the trustworthiness of individuals or their oath-helpers. As historian Leonard Levy observes, it "had become too easy a proof, almost a certain success for the party, however culpable or liable, who was lucky enough to be awarded the right to resort to his oath with the support of oath-helpers." Compurgation was in decline even before 1600. The trial by battle had also lost trust. It became routine for individuals to hire others to fight for them. Levy notes: "Champions were hired to do battle on behalf of a litigant whenever one of the parties was unable, for reasons of age, sex, or physical infirmity, to represent himself." Sovereigns also worried about the effect of the death toll on the nobility. Astonishingly, the wager by battle was abolished only in 1818, but this malingering is attributable to its lack of use in the intervening centuries.

The decline of the supernatural proofs meant human beings had to shoulder the burden of factfinding. One stark shift was away from the ordeal toward the confession. While the confession had always been a means of determining guilt, its importance increased as faith in the other proofs declined. The Fourth Lateran Council that abolished the ordeals created the requirement of annual confession by the faithful. In England, the confession came to be seen as the "queen of proofs."

The problem remained of suspects who did not confess. The Continent and England adopted dramatically different solutions. The Continent's inquisitorial model depended on torture to secure confessions. In contrast, the English moved to a jury system, under which an impartial body of individuals served as factfinders. Fisher draws a direct causal link between the demise of the ordeal in 1215 and the first "true" criminal jury in England, which sat in Westminster in 1220.

The shift away from these supernatural proofs toward human proofs was glacial. Historian John Langbein suggests the reason: "It is almost impossible for us to imagine how difficult it must have been for the ordinary people of that age to accept that substitution. The question that springs to the lips is: 'you, who are merely another mortal like me, who are you to sit in judgment upon me?'" Angelo takes up this concern in *Measure for Measure* when he considers "the laws / That thieves do pass on thieves" (2.1.22–23). The question of how fallible human beings, rather than God, would discover the facts remained a critical issue at the time Shakespeare was writing.

The plays stage ambivalence about this shift from divine to human factfinding. There are no instances of ordeal or compurgation in Shakespeare. Wager of battle, however, figures prominently in *Henry VI, Part 2; Richard II*; and, if one stretches, *King Lear*. The trial by battle receives its fullest treatment in *Henry VI, Part 2*, where the armorer's apprentice Peter Thump is forced into such a trial by his master, who accuses him of treason. It seems impossible to all, particularly to poor Peter himself, that he could prevail. Yet he does, because his master indulges in drink before the battle. The armorer confesses on his deathbed that his accusation was false, thus vindicating the trial procedure. In *Richard II*, the king interrupts the battle at Coventry between the Dukes of Hereford and Norfolk by throwing down his warder, or baton. In doing so, he articulates the contemporary concern that sovereigns had over the havoc such wagers could cause among the nobles: "And grating shock of wrathful iron arms, / Might from our quiet confines fright fair peace, / And make us wade even in our kindred's blood" (*Richard II*, 1.3.136–38). In *Lear*, Edgar defeats Edmund, though the conditions here are less formal than those attending a proper wager (which is perhaps not surprising given that the historical Lear reigned in the ninth century B.C.)!

Despite the prevalence of trials by battle, the plays should not be read as categorical defenses of the wager. They represent historical periods before the time in which they were written. The faith placed in the wager could be compared to the faith placed in the oracle in *The Winter's Tale*—as representations of a bygone system, rather than an endorsement of a current one. Moreover, such trials were innately dramatic, lending themselves to the stage. For all these caveats, none of the plays depicts the wager by battle as fallible.

Just as the plays stage some confidence in trial by battle, they stage some anxiety about human factfinding, such as the trial by jury. In *Measure*, Angelo admits that: "The jury passing on the prisoner's life / May in the sworn twelve have a thief, or two, / Guiltier than him they try" (*Measure*, 2.1.19–21). In *Henry VIII*, a play representing a time close to Shakespeare's own, the Earl of Surrey accuses Cardinal Wolsey of engineering the political fall of Buckingham, and Wolsey hides behind the "noble jury" that convicted him (*Henry VIII*, 3.2.269).

At first glance, no Shakespeare play makes an explicit defense of human factfinding. *Othello*, however, can be read as an exploration of both the strengths and weaknesses of such factfinding. *Othello* is a play about epistemology—about the question of how we know what we know. The play powerfully juxtaposes two forms of human factfinding. One, represented by the Venetian nobles, proceeds in a collective, rational manner, leading to a *veredictum*—a true saying. The other, represented by Othello, moves in an isolated, impassioned manner, leading tragically to error.

LIKE *MEASURE, OTHELLO* is largely based on a story from Giraldi Cinthio's *Hecatommithi* (1565). Most of the action of act 1 of *Othello*, however, has no precursor in Cinthio's novella. Shakespeare's decision to base this single act in Venice, rather than on the military garrison of Cyprus, could be explained as the imposition of the familiar court-country-court framework Shakespeare uses in so many plays (although in *Othello*, the final reversion has the "court" coming to Cyprus). Venice, in *Othello* as in *Merchant*, stands for law and order. The Senator Brabantio cries out to Roderigo in act 1, "What tell'st thou me of robbing? This is Venice: / My house is not a grange" (1.1.104–105).

Venice's "civilized" nature displays itself in how its leaders think in an emergency. We meet the Duke and some senators in a late-night council convened to assess reports that a Turkish fleet is "bearing up" (1.3.8) on Cyprus. The reports of the number of ships range wildly from 107 to 200 (1.3.3–5). The Duke says that "[t]here is no composition in these news / That gives them credit" (1.3.1–2). But the Second Senator reminds him that while the numbers "jump not on a just account— / As in these cases, where the aim reports, / 'Tis oft with difference" (1.3.5–7). When estimating the boats in a fleet (especially given the technology of the times), some variation is to be expected. Moreover, the Senator says this disagreement should not obscure uniform agreement that a Turkish fleet is moving on Cyprus. The Duke responds rationally that "the main article I do approve / In fearful sense" (1.3.11–12).

In a potentially confusing development, a sailor enters to announce that the Turks are headed for Rhodes, not Cyprus. The Duke canvasses his colleagues. The First Senator rejects this red herring: "This cannot be, / By no assay of reason: 'tis a pageant / To keep us in false gaze" (1.3.18–20). An "assay" was another word for a trial, and in this "assay of reason," such fabrications are swiftly exposed. It makes no sense for the Turks to be sailing toward Rhodes, which is better fortified and less strategically important than Cyprus: "We must not think the Turk is so unskilful / To leave that latest which concerns him first, / Neglecting an attempt of ease and gain / To wake and wage a danger profitless" (1.3.28–31). The trial's conclusion is promptly vindicated—word arrives that the Turks are heading toward Cyprus.

This war-room tribunal inspires confidence for several reasons. First, it is collective, relying on more than one individual to determine the facts. The Second Senator corrects the Duke's erroneous surmise; the First Senator dismisses the sailor's misleading report. Second, it is rational—despite exigent circumstances, reports are calmly tested through "assay[s] of reason." Finally, it is nonhierarchical—the more forceful argument, rather than the more forceful person, prevails.

These values are distinct but related—the nonhierarchical nature of the proceedings means senators may correct the Duke.

The tribunal soon passes another test. Another senator, Brabantio, storms in accusing the general Othello of having bewitched his daughter, Desdemona. Brabantio's objection to the marriage is that Othello is a Moor and Desdemona is white. But that is not his legal charge. Interracial marriage was generally legal at English common law. Instead, the charge is that Othello has used witchcraft to seduce Desdemona.

If asked which Shakespeare play begins with a witch trial, I think most readers of Shakespeare would not guess *Othello*. Race overwhelms witchcraft as a theme in the play. Yet the two themes are intertwined, as Brabantio thinks interracial marriage to be so unnatural only witchcraft could have produced it. Brabantio first raises the possibility that Othello has bewitched Desdemona to the youth Roderigo: "Is there not charms / By which the property of youth and maidhood / May be abused?" (1.1.169–71). By the time he gets to the Duke's tribunal, Brabantio's question has matured into a charge. As he rants to Othello:

> O thou foul thief, where hast thou stowed my daughter?
> Damned as thou art, thou hast enchanted her,
> For I'll refer me to all things of sense,
> If she in chains of magic were not bound,
> Whether a maid so tender, fair and happy,
> So opposite to marriage that she shunned
> The wealthy, curled darlings of our nation,
> Would ever have, t'incur a general mock,
> Run from her guardage to the sooty bosom
> Of such a thing as thou?
> (1.2.62–71)

The Senator repeats his suspicion of witchcraft in two other speeches (1.3.60–65, 100–107), always insisting that no sane white woman would take up with a Moor. Brabantio is seized by an idée fixe, just as the man he accuses will later be so seized.

The Duke receives mixed marks as the judge. His first reaction is to assume that Brabantio, as a powerful senator, is correct in his accusation:

> Whoe'er he be, that in this foul proceeding
> Hath thus beguiled your daughter of herself,
> And you of her, the bloody book of law
> You shall yourself read, in the bitter letter,
> After your own sense, yea, though our proper son
> Stood in your action.
> (1.3.66–71)

The Duke's assertion that he will let the law work impartially even on his own son inspires confidence in the rule of law. At the same time, he delivers the "bloody book of law" to Brabantio to read after his "own sense," which permits Brabantio to be the judge in his own case. (This is consistent with early modern practice, in which individuals of higher status were formally deemed to have more credibility than individuals of lower status.) Only when the Duke realizes Brabantio is accusing Othello—a general indispensable to the Venetian state—does the Duke subject Brabantio's allegation to higher scrutiny: "To vouch this is no proof, / Without more certain and more overt test / Than these thin habits and poor likelihoods" (1.3.107–109).

Once the statuses of accuser and accused cancel each other out, a recognizably modern trial occurs. Just as the Duke ultimately recognizes that the rumor of the Turks going to Rhodes is a "pageant to

keep us in false gaze," he recognizes that "thin habits and poor likelihoods" are "no proof." The tribunal is also procedurally fastidious.
Unlike, for instance, the imperial fiat with which Saturninus sentences Titus's sons, the Duke permits the accused Othello to speak
for himself and to call a witness, Desdemona.

One can hardly imagine a world in which Othello was not permitted to speak, as his celebrated account of how he courted Desdemona is now canon. The Moor immediately undercuts his claim that
he is "[r]ude . . . in . . . speech" (1.3.82) with what G. Wilson Knight
has dubbed "the Othello music":

> Her father loved me, oft invited me,
> Still questioned me the story of my life
> From year to year—the battles, sieges, fortunes
> That I have passed.
> I ran it through, even from my boyish days
> To th' very moment that he bade me tell it,
> Wherein I spake of most disastrous chances,
> Of moving accidents by flood and field,
> Of hair-breadth scapes i'th' imminent deadly breach,
> Of being taken by the insolent foe
> And sold to slavery; of my redemption thence
> And portance in my travailous history;
> Wherein of antres vast and deserts idle,
> Rough quarries, rocks and hills whose heads touch
>   heaven
> It was my hint to speak—such was my process—
> And of the cannibals that each other eat,
> The Anthropophagi, and men whose heads
> Do grow beneath their shoulders. This to hear
> Would Desdemona seriously incline,

But still the house affairs would draw her thence,
Which ever as she could with haste dispatch
She'd come again, and with a greedy ear
Devour up my discourse; which I, observing,
Took once a pliant hour and found good means
To draw from her a prayer of earnest heart
That I would all my pilgrimage dilate,
Whereof by parcels she had something heard
But not intentively. I did consent,
And often did beguile her of her tears
When I did speak of some distressful stroke
That my youth suffered. My story being done
She gave me for my pains a world of sighs,
She swore in faith 'twas strange, 'twas passing strange,
'Twas pitiful, 'twas wondrous pitiful;
She wished she had not heard it, yet she wished
That heaven had made her such a man. She thanked me
And bade me, if I had a friend that loved her,
I should but teach him how to tell my story
And that would woo her. Upon this hint I spake:
She loved me for the dangers I had passed
And I loved her that she did pity them.
This only is the witchcraft I have used. . . .
(1.3.129–170)

This speech seems irresistible. By its end, the Duke (perhaps apply-ing a "reasonable daughter" test) says: "I think this tale would win my daughter too" (1.3.172). Placed on the defensive, Brabantio says he will withdraw the charge of witchcraft if Desdemona corroborates "she was half the wooer" (1.3.176).

When Desdemona arrives, Brabantio calls: "Come hither, gentle mistress: / Do you perceive, in all this noble company, / Where most you owe obedience?" (1.3.178–180). Shakespeare is practicing here for *Lear:* as E. A. J. Honigmann points out, "gentle mistress" is "not how a father normally addressed his daughter." The widower Brabantio greets his only daughter more as wife than child. Desdemona's answer makes the painfully necessary adjustment:

> My noble father,
> I do perceive here a divided duty.
> To you I am bound for life and education:
> My life and education both do learn me
> How to respect you; you are the lord of duty,
> I am hitherto your daughter. But here's my husband:
> And so much duty as my mother showed
> To you, preferring you before her father,
> So much I challenge that I may profess
> Due to the Moor my lord.
> (1.3.180–89)

This speech presages how Cordelia addresses Lear when placed in a similar predicament (*Lear*, 1.1.95–104). And just as Lear responds to Cordelia, Brabantio effectively disowns his daughter.

While not perfect, the Venetian tribunal sets a benchmark against which other factfinders will be measured. It exposes the "false pageant" of the Turks as a ruse to hide the truth of their movement on Cyprus. Similarly, it pierces the "appearance" that Othello has used witchcraft and concludes that he has fairly wooed and won Desdemona. Brabantio may be right that lawless action cannot happen in the Venice of this play. And so the action moves to Cyprus.

*   *   *

IN *OTHELLO*, CYPRUS contrasts with Venice in several ways. It is an outpost of civilization rather than the center of it. It is a military garrison rather than a civilian city. As the birthplace of Venus, the goddess of love, it is also a place where rationality is allegorically suspended. As many have commented, love—and lovemaking—are outside Othello's portfolio of competence. He is a fighter, not a lover.

Moreover, by the time Othello arrives at Cyprus, fighters are no longer needed. The Turks have been annihilated by a storm, much as the Spanish Armada was demolished in 1588. While Othello waits until act 3 to lament "Othello's occupation's gone" (3.3.360), he is obsolete before he sets foot on the island.

So it is on Cyprus that Iago's plot against Othello gains traction. Iago first sets Othello against his lieutenant Michael Cassio. Knowing the lieutenant has "unhappy brains for drinking" (2.3.31), Iago gets him inebriated, which leads Cassio to start a brawl with Montano, the erstwhile governor of Cyprus. The fracas spawns another late-night factfinding exercise. Othello intervenes to break up the fight:

> Why, how now, ho? From whence ariseth this?
> Are we turned Turks? and to ourselves do that
> Which heaven hath forbid the Ottomites?
> For Christian shame, put by this barbarous brawl;
> He that stirs next, to carve for his own rage,
> Holds his soul light: he dies upon his motion.
> Silence that dreadful bell, it frights the isle
> From her propriety. What is the matter, masters?
> Honest Iago, that look'st dead with grieving,
> Speak: who began this? on thy love I charge thee.
> (2.3.165–74)

Othello claims the Christian and civilized ground here. In act 1, Iago called Othello "a Barbary horse" (1.1.110) to Brabantio, seeking to depict Othello as Berber and Moor, bestial and barbarous. But here Othello appropriates the word "barbarous" and deploys it against the white Venetians. No one experiences his use as ironic. Othello represents civilization on this wild isle.

The trial at the end of the first act asks: "Did Othello use witchcraft to beguile Desdemona?" The Venetian tribunal correctly answers: "No." The trial at the beginning of the second act asks: "Who started the brawl on Cyprus?" The Cypriot tribunal, consisting only of Othello, answers "Cassio," which is at least partially correct.

We should not be too hard on Othello. Even the Venetian council might not have been able to ferret out Iago's agency in the brawl. Successful factfinding depends not just on the integrity of the tribunal, but also on the difficulty of the question. Moreover, Othello exhibits procedural care, giving all parties a chance to speak. It is not Othello's fault that Montano is too injured, and Cassio is too ashamed (or drunk), to bear witness.

But Othello's factfinding cleaves from, as well as to, that of the Venetian council. Othello does not permit collective decision making—he sits as a solitary judge. He does not see that "honest" Iago might have a motive to incriminate Cassio, even though Iago sought Cassio's job. Nor does he wait for the incapacitated witnesses to regain their ability to speak before rendering judgment. Worst of all, he gets angry:

> Now, by heaven,
> My blood begins my safer guides to rule
> And passion, having my best judgement collied,
> Assays to lead the way. Zounds, if I once stir,

Or do but lift this arm, the best of you

Shall sink in my rebuke.

(2.3.200–205)

In contrast to the Venetian council's "assay of reason," Othello's is an "assay of passion."

By his own admission, Othello's passion "collies" his "best judgment," making it—and perhaps him—more stereotypically "black." The likely historical trigger for the composition of *Othello* was the visit of an ambassador from the King of Barbary, who arrived in England for a six-month stay in London in August 1600. Later that year, John Pory published a translation of John Leo's *A Geographical Historie of Africa,* which made reference to the ambassador. Leo, himself a Moor, wrote at length about his countrymen:

> Most honest people they are, and destitute of all fraud
> and guile, very proud and high-minded, and wonderfully
> addicted unto wrath. . . . Their wits are but meane, and
> they are so credulous, that they will beleeue matters im-
> possible, which are told them. . . . No nation in the world
> is so subject unto jealousie; for they will rather leese their
> lives than put up any disgrace in the behalfe of their
> women.

Critic Geoffrey Bullough's claim that Shakespeare "almost certainly consulted" this account finds support in the striking correspondence between Leo's discussion of the typical Moor and Othello. Like the "typical" Moor, Othello is honest and free of "all fraud and guile." Perhaps relatedly, he is unable to see guile in others, meaning he is "so credulous, that [he] will beleeue matters impossible." And as we see in his first test as factfinder, he is prone to anger, which does not bode well for his ability to answer the play's next question: "Is Desdemona faithful?"

Iago builds his case for Desdemona's infidelity through a stream of innuendo. In the first round of insinuation, Iago (1) characterizes Cassio as "steal[ing] away" (3.3.39) from a private conversation with Desdemona when Othello approaches; (2) forces Othello to admit that when Othello was courting Desdemona, Cassio "went between [them] very oft" (3.3.100); (3) refuses to share his thoughts with Othello, making Othello think "there were some monster in thy thought / Too hideous to be shown" (3.3.110–11); (4) reminds Othello that Desdemona "did deceive her father, marrying you" (3.3.209); and (5) perhaps most chillingly to a present-day audience, presses Othello to admit that their marriage is "unnatural" on racial grounds (3.3.232–42).

Othello is not the simpleton he is often portrayed to be. Although stirred by Iago's allegations, he, like the Duke, sees that "to vouch this is no proof." Like the Duke, he insists on proof:

> Villain, be sure thou prove my love a whore,
> Be sure of it, give me the ocular proof,
> *Catching hold of him*
> Or by the worth of man's eternal soul
> Thou hadst been better have been born a dog
> Than answer my waked wrath!
> (3.3.362–66)

Othello is angry again. This time, his anger has found its proper object. But it is hard to read this moment as a defense of "assays of passion," because his anger again "collies" his judgment.

Much—perhaps too much—has been made of Othello's race in this play. But the general's race might influence the way he sees reality. Because Othello is constantly judged by the "ocular proof" of his skin color, he may be particularly susceptible to judging based on such proof. Widening the lens, we recall that all three Moors in the Shakespearean corpus have been judged according to their skin color. In *Titus,* Aaron the Moor has his mixed-race child deemed a "black and sorrowful issue" (*Titus,* 4.2.68). In *Merchant,* the Prince of Morocco introduces himself to Portia by saying, "Mislike me not for my complexion" (*Merchant,* 2.1.1). And in *Othello,* Brabantio uses Othello's race as "ocular proof" that he engaged in witchcraft.

While Othello may be particularly prone to trusting his eyes, this tendency was broadly shared by Shakespeare's contemporaries. Langbein describes how the demise of the supernatural proofs originally meant that only "full proof"—the testimony of two eyewitnesses or a confession—could result in a conviction. But, as he says, the jurists who devised this system "solved one problem by creating another." Their system worked for the easy cases of overt crime, but not for the hard cases of covert crime where no eyewitnesses or confession materialized. Those hard cases still needed to be dealt with, for "[n]o society will long tolerate a legal system in which there is no prospect of convicting unrepentant persons who commit clandestine crimes." On the Continent, torture produced the requisite confessions. In England, which formally eschewed torture, a jury had to weigh circumstantial evidence.

Iago's response to Othello's demand for proof cunningly tracks the historical dilemma that for clandestine crimes, full proof was vanishingly unlikely. How, he asks, will Othello be "satisfied" (3.3.397)? By seeing Desdemona "topped" (3.3.399)? With a mock seriousness as cruel as it is officious, he muses aloud on the difficulty of providing "full proof":

> It were a tedious difficulty, I think,
> To bring them to that prospect. Damn them then

If ever mortal eyes do see them bolster
More than their own. What then? how then?
What shall I say? where's satisfaction?
It is impossible you should see this
Were they as prime as goats, as hot as monkeys,
As salt as wolves in pride, and fools as gross
As ignorance made drunk.
(3.3.400–408)

Iago has an extraordinary ability to conjure word-pictures. In act 1, he supplies Desdemona's father, Brabantio, with the unforgettable picture of "the beast with two backs" (1.1.115). While he claims now to Othello that "ocular proof" of Desdemona's infidelity will be impossible to secure, he also provides a close facsimile in this passage. Some of his images are so vivid one feels one *has* seen them. We know Iago has made an impression because Othello later echoes the imagery Iago has fed him ("Were they as prime as goats, as hot as monkeys") in his oath "Goats and monkeys!" (4.1.263). Iago's demonic gift of insinuation is that he seems to echo others—Othello says "thou echo'st me" (3.3.109)—while making others echo him.

After establishing the difficulty of producing "full proof," Iago states that he can produce circumstantial evidence, which, *faute de mieux,* will lead Othello to the truth: "But yet, I say, / If imputation and strong circumstances / Which lead directly to the door of truth / Will give you satisfaction, you may have't" (3.3.408–11). Othello is all too eager to hear the second round of innuendo. Iago attests that he (1) has heard Cassio cry out Desdemona's name in his sleep; (2) has seen Cassio wipe his beard with Desdemona's handkerchief; and (3) knows of the existence of "other proofs" he does not name. Crucially, between his first and second barrages, Iago has had a windfall. His wife, Emilia, according to his instructions, has filched Desdemona's handkerchief, which was Othello's first gift to her. Iago has planted this handkerchief in Cassio's room. The handkerchief is not "ocular proof" in the sense Othello originally meant (direct observation of the crime). It is nonetheless circumstantial evidence that, unlike Iago's other "proofs," can be touched and seen.

By act 4, all "proofs" but the physical one have evaporated. Iago ensures this by focusing on the relationship between Desdemona's honor and the handkerchief: "Her honour is an essence that's not seen, / They have it very oft that have it not. / But for the handkerchief—" (4.1.16–18). In other words, a person's honor is difficult to ascertain. But whether someone has given away a handkerchief is not. The metaphysical question of guilt or innocence has been reduced to the empirical question of whether Desdemona has lost her handkerchief.

Othello miserably says: "By heaven, I would most gladly have forgot it! / Thou said'st—O, it comes o'er my memory / As doth the raven o'er the infectious house / Boding to all—he had my handkerchief" (4.1.19–22). Iago then tells Othello that Cassio has confessed to Iago that he slept with Desdemona. This literally shorts out Othello's brain, triggering an epileptic fit: "Handkerchief! confessions! handkerchief!—To confess, and be hanged for his labour! . . . Confess! handkerchief! O devil!—[H]e falls in a trance" (4.1.37–38, 43). In becoming the inarticulate "barbarian" he is cast to be, Othello equates the lost handkerchief with a confession, which would constitute "full proof" of Desdemona's adultery.

Even after he awakens from his trance, Othello never regains his faculties of speech in this act. In another piece of luck for Iago, Othello sees Cassio in possession of the handkerchief. Iago engages Cassio in conversation out of earshot of Othello. Poor Othello is so far gone that he convicts on the basis of a "confession" he can see only in pantomime. There is no question of giving Cassio or Desdemona a chance to explain or rebut. Othello has declined from the calm general to the frantic animal his racist detractors have cast him to be. He has, in his mind, become a cuckold, and given that cuckolds were thought to have horns growing from their heads, a beast: "A horned man's a monster, and a beast" (4.1.62). We see this transmutation from man to beast in his loss of language. Compare the self-possessed lyricism of his line in act 1 when he was accosted by Brabantio's mob: "Keep up your bright swords, for the dew will rust them" (1.2.59) with his response now: "I will chop her into messes! Cuckold me!" (4.1.197). It is that "monster," that "beast," who kills Desdemona in her wedding bed.

No SHAKESPEARE PLAY is pure tragedy, because none ends without some promise that order will be made of chaos. Marjorie Garber describes the pattern well:

> The characteristic Shakespearean triple pattern (court-country-court) always includes a return from the enchanted place, whether that place is called a green world, a second world, a place of "anti-structure" or of carnival. The middle place is often identified with imagination, art, wonder, and dream (if the play is a comedy or romance), or with wilderness, danger, and madness (if the play is a tragedy). In almost all cases it brings with it an element of disguise and of (temporary) social leveling. There is always a return from this middle place, at least for most of the characters in the play; but those who return often return transformed.

In *Othello*, the inevitable Shakespearean "return from this middle place" is a return from the intermediate world of madness to the world of rationality represented by Venice. Yet in this play, the mountain comes to Muhammad, given that Venice—in the form of the nobles Lodovico and Desdemona's uncle Gratiano—comes to Othello.

The denouement of the play is a final factfinding exercise, supervised by some combination of Gratiano, Lodovico, and Montano. The question is: "Who killed Desdemona?" Like the earlier question that Othello had to answer—"Who started the brawl on Cyprus?"—this question has two answers. Cassio is the immediate cause of the brawl, but Iago is the ultimate one. Similarly, Othello is the immediate cause of Desdemona's death, but again, Iago is the ultimate one. Unlike Othello, the Italian tribunal apprehends Iago, both figuratively and literally. It does so by following the collective, rational procedures adopted by the Duke's tribunal in act I.

The factfinders—here consisting of Montano and Gratiano—are in danger of holding Othello alone liable, as Othello held Cassio alone liable for the brawl. Othello has confessed his guilt to Emilia, just as Cassio confessed his guilt to Othello. Fortunately, however, Emilia is on the scene to negate this "full proof." She accuses Iago of telling Othello that Desdemona was untrue to him. This charge in itself does not bring Iago's villainy to light, as Iago could have believed in Desdemona's infidelity in good faith. Nonetheless, I sense that Iago feels his danger for the first time. He insists on Emilia's silence: "Go to, charm your tongue" (5.2.179). But Emilia has begun to see her husband's true nature: "Villainy, villainy, villainy! / I think upon't, I think I smell't, O villainy! / I thought so then: I'll kill myself for grief! / O villainy, villainy!" (5.2.187–90). Iago commands her to leave the room, as a husband at the time had the right to do: "What, are you mad? I charge you, get you home" (5.2.191). Emilia refuses, taking an appeal from domestic male authority to its public counterpart: "Good gentlemen, let me have leave to speak. / 'Tis proper I obey him—but not now. / Perchance, Iago, I will ne'er go home" (5.2.192–94).

Imagine if at this moment the tribunal had refused her permission to speak. That possibility is all the more chilling because we have just endured a scene where Othello, as judge, jury, and executioner, has not given Desdemona that chance. But this tribunal will hear her out, no matter how many times the increasingly desperate Iago attempts to silence her.

It is not just Iago, but Othello, who fears what Emilia has to say. Emilia's attempt to testify is interrupted this time by the general:

> O! O! O!
> *Othello falls on the bed*
> (5.2.195)

"O" is the letter in Shakespeare most pregnant in meaning, standing variously for the world, the crown, female genitalia, nothingness, and the theater. The letter "O" can be read as a concrete poem, for many of its meanings derive from its shape. Cleopatra refers to "the little O, the earth" (*Antony and Cleopatra*, 5.2.80). The "O" is also a symbol for the vagina, also known in early modern England as an "O-thing," which is what gives *Much Ado About Nothing*, a play that turns on a young woman's virginity, its double entendre. Hamlet also says to Ophelia that a "nothing" is "a fair thought to lie between maids' legs" (*Hamlet*, 3.2.111–12). "O" also meant "nothing" in the sense of "zero," as when Lear gives "[n]othing" (*Lear*, 1.1.247) to Cordelia, a sense heightened when Ian McKellen's Lear screams the word through the circle of a coronet in the 2009 film adaptation. Finally, the "O" was a symbol of the theater—as in the Chorus's mention of "this wooden O" (*Henry V*, Prologue, 13) into which the action of *Henry V* must be crammed.

Othello, the only Shakespeare play to begin with that letter, threads its way through these "O"s. Othello begins as a commander of the Venetian world. He is brought down by his obsession with his wife's sexual fidelity. At the end of the play, he is reduced to nothing, falling on the wedding bed that operates in the mise en scène as a stage upon a stage. Othello's cri de coeur—"O! O! O!"—succinctly summarizes the play.

Because Othello fears to confront the truth, Iago can still escape it. Othello insists that Desdemona was "foul" and piteously offers his "ocular proof"—"that recognizance and pledge of love / Which I first gave her: I saw it in [Cassio's] hand, / It was a handkerchief, an antique token / My father gave my mother" (5.2.212–15).

Now the handkerchief operates properly as proof—proof of Iago's guilt in Emilia's eyes, rather than proof of Desdemona's guilt in Othello's. When the handkerchief is mentioned, Emilia understands all, including her own complicity in Iago's scheme: "O God, O heavenly God!" (5.2.216). Iago tries to silence her yet again, showing sincere emotion for the first time in the play—"Zounds, hold your peace!" (5.2.216). But Emilia cannot be silenced now: "'Twill out, 'twill out! I peace? / No, I will speak as liberal as the north. / Let heaven and men and devils, let them all, / All, all cry shame against me, yet I'll speak" (5.2.217–20). No hierarchy—of husband over wife, or even God over mortal—will stop her. Iago tries to send her home again, but she will not go. Finally showing his hand, Iago tries to stab her to death. The Italians are horrified: "Fie! Your sword upon a woman?" (5.2.222). Protected by them, Emilia utters the five lines that expose her husband:

> O thou dull Moor, that handkerchief thou speak'st of
> I found by fortune and did give my husband,
> For often, with a solemn earnestness
> —More than indeed belonged to such a trifle—
> He begged of me to steal't.
> (5.2.223–27)

Othello, instantly recognizing the truth, makes an unsuccessful run to kill Iago. Iago, with greater success, stabs his wife to death.

This tribunal is much more like the Duke's tribunal than Othello's. First, it is nonhierarchical—just as the senators were able to contradict the Duke, Emilia is not silenced or sent home. Second, it is rational—although emotions are again running high here, the Italians govern their rage rather than being governed by it. When Gratiano says: "Fie! Your sword upon a woman?" (5.2.222), we hear the strong indignant voice of justice, not irrational fury. Finally, the tribunal is collective—the Italians form a large enough bloc that Iago cannot silence Emilia.

Othello recognizes the superiority of the Venetian state when he sentences himself:

> Soft you, a word or two before you go.
> I have done the state some service, and they know't:
> No more of that. I pray you, in your letters,
> When you shall these unlucky deeds relate,
> Speak of me as I am. Nothing extenuate,
> Nor set down aught in malice. . . .
> . . . . Set you down this,
> And say besides that in Aleppo once,
> Where a malignant and a turbanned Turk
> Beat a Venetian and traduced the state,
> I took by th' throat the circumcised dog
> And smote him—thus!
> *He stabs himself*
> (5.2.336–41, 49–54)

Othello is on both sides of this dagger. He allies the hand that wields the dagger to Venice by comparing it to the hand that defended the honor of the state. He allies the body that receives the mortal blow to the barbaric body of the "turbanned Turk" and "circumcised dog." In this formulation, the act is less a suicide than a homicide, and less a homicide than a state-sanctioned execution. The speech acknowledges the superiority of the civilized Italians, not least in their ability to find the fact of the matter.

IN ANGLO-AMERICAN LAW, human factfinding has decisively triumphed over divine factfinding. Within human factfinding, collective factfinding has generally trumped individual factfinding. As a result, the paradigmatic factfinder in this country today is the jury, constitutionally required for almost all criminal cases and constitutionally available for almost all federal civil cases. Appellate courts are required to give findings of fact by a jury massive deference.

The question arises of how much comfort we should take in this development. On the one hand, *Othello* suggests we should take a great deal of comfort from the collective, rational, and democratic Venetian tribunal. But this is only in comparison to the individual and paranoid factfinding in which *Othello* engages. It is not an absolute claim that collective deliberative bodies like juries will always be free of biases like the ocular proof bias that ensnared Othello.

The O. J. Simpson murder trial of 1995 underscores this point. To be clear, my interest in the Simpson trial does not stem from the fact that Simpson was an African-American man accused of killing his white wife, though others have made this comparison to *Othello*. Rather, my comparison relies on how a form of circumstantial ocular proof overwhelmed the factfinding process in both cases. In *Othello*, the ocular proof is the white handkerchief "spotted with strawberries" that gets lost; in the Simpson trial, it was the black glove spotted with blood that did not fit. At least at a surface level, the Simpson trial undercuts *Othello*'s confidence in the jury. It seems that groups, as well as individuals, have an overwhelming bias toward physical evidence.

In developing the analogy, I propose six points of comparison. First, the handkerchief and the glove were originally love tokens, tragically inverted in their symbolism. As both Othello and Emilia tell us, the handkerchief was Othello's first gift to Desdemona. Desdemona accordingly cherishes it. Although Iago has asked Emilia repeatedly to steal it, she has found this difficult because Desdemona "so loves the token / . . . That she reserves it evermore about her / To kiss and talk to" (3.3.297–300). Emilia predicts that Desdemona will be distraught when she cannot find the handkerchief, and she is. Part of the irony of the play is that the handkerchief, originally a treasured token, ultimately becomes a damning one—Desdemona will soon exclaim "would to God that I had never seen't!" (3.4.79).

Nicole Brown Simpson bought two pairs of Aris Light gloves at Bloomingdale's in Manhattan in December 1990. She gave these gloves to her husband for Christmas that year. The prosecution produced photographs of Simpson wearing Aris Light gloves at various events beginning on December 19, 1990, and extending as late as 1994. As *Newsweek* would comment, it was a "tragic irony" that Nicole had bought the gloves that figured in her murder.

Second, the handkerchief and glove, while seemingly everyday objects, were imbued with mystical significance. When introduced in act 3, the handkerchief is described simply as a "napkin" (3.3.291). After Othello begins to suspect Desdemona of having given the handkerchief to Cassio, he provides a much more vivid vision of its provenance. Othello tells his wife that the handkerchief was given to his mother by an Egyptian charmer who said it would preserve love between spouses. (In its "Oriental" mysticism, this takes us back to

Shylock's turquoise ring, as turquoise was also seen to be an exotic Middle Eastern stone that promoted marital harmony.) Othello may be fabricating this history to increase Desdemona's guilt for having lost it. Regardless, his description is unforgettable:

> 'Tis true, there's magic in the web of it.
> A sibyl that had numbered in the world
> The sun to course two hundred compasses,
> In her prophetic fury sewed the work;
> The worms were hallowed that did breed the silk,
> And it was dyed in mummy, which the skilful
> Conserved of maidens' hearts.
> (3.4.71–77)

Previously in the play the handkerchief is described as "[s]potted with strawberries" (3.3.438). If Othello's account is to be believed, those strawberries are made of the blood of virgins. The handkerchief stained with blood mimics the wedding sheets spotted with blood that signified that the bride came to the marriage as a virgin. The loss of the handkerchief can be read as a metaphorical loss of these sheets, which would also represent the loss of Desdemona's reputation for chastity.

As the *New York Times* reported, the jurors in the Simpson trial were "treated to a highly technical discussion about everyday objects" when the gloves were discussed. "Glove expert" Richard Rubin, a former executive at the high-end glove manufacturer Aris Isotoner, testified for two days about the distinctive features of the bloody gloves. The jury learned that the model number of the gloves was 70263, and that only about 10,000 of these gloves were sold in the country in size extra-large. Scrutiny imbues any object with significance. But as the *Times* summarized Rubin's testimony, the gloves were revealed to be special in their own right: "There was the intricate 'Brasser stitching'—22 to 24 stitches per inch—made by Singer sewing machines long out of production, which only a few craftsmen can operate; a palm vent; a blind hem by the wrist; decorative 'silking' on their back made by a particular configuration of needles." While Rubin did not testify that the Singer sewing machines were operated with prophetic enthusiasm by 200-year-old sibyls, neither did he foreclose that possibility.

Third, the handkerchief and glove were found in incriminating places, which would evidence guilt unless they were planted. In response to Othello's demand for "ocular proof," Iago says he saw Cassio "wipe his beard" with the handkerchief. This is a rank falsehood, but even the image of Cassio in possession of the handkerchief sends Othello into a jealous frenzy. That image later comes to life when Othello sees the prostitute Bianca tossing the handkerchief in Cassio's face. Othello comes to believe that Cassio has received the handkerchief from Desdemona, but that Cassio cares so little for Desdemona that he has in turn given the token away to Bianca.

The conclusion Othello draws from the handkerchief's placement is not unreasonable. But we know it is unwarranted because the handkerchief has been planted by Iago in Cassio's bedchamber. After finding it, Cassio gives the handkerchief to Bianca because he wants Bianca to copy its pattern before its rightful owner asks for its return. An innocent explanation exists for the handkerchief's placement.

In the Simpson case, a left-handed bloodstained glove was found at the scene of the double murder, outside Nicole Simpson's condominium complex in Brentwood. Its mate, also bloodstained, was found at Simpson's estate in Rockingham. The placement of the right-hand glove also strongly suggested Simpson's guilt. As prosecutor Marcia Clark put it:

So what do we find on the Rockingham glove, the one he drops? We find everything. Everything.

We find fibers consistent with Ron Goldman's shirt. We find the hair of Ron. We find the hair of Nicole. We find the blood of Ron Goldman. We find the blood of Nicole Brown. And we find the blood of the defendant. And we find Bronco fiber from the defendant's Bronco. We find blue black cotton fibers just like those found on the shirt of Ron Goldman and on the socks of the defendant in his bedroom.

The prosecution argued from this evidence that Simpson killed Brown and Goldman, drove home to his Rockingham estate, and dropped the glove entering the house.

The defense team did not, and could not, argue that the murderer was not wearing the gloves. Rather, they argued that the right-handed glove was taken from the scene of the murder and planted on Simpson's Rockingham estate to frame him for the murder. That would require an Iago figure. The defense team cast Mark Fuhrman, a police officer who had repeatedly made racist remarks in the past, in that role.

Fourth, in the assessment of guilt or innocence, the handkerchief and the glove played an inordinately large role. In *Othello,* the question of whether Desdemona is guilty of adultery comes to depend to a staggering degree on whether she has the handkerchief. Thomas Rymer criticized this aspect of the play in 1693:

> So much ado, so much stress, so much passion and repetition about an Handkerchief! Why was this not call'd the *Tragedy of the Handkerchief?* . . . Had it been *Desdemona's* Garter, the Sagacious Moor might have smelt a Rat: but the

> Handkerchief is so remote a trifle, no Booby, on this side
> *Mauritania*, cou'd make any consequence from it.

Rymer's complaint here is that a play's MacGuffin must at least be something of consequence. The handkerchief is what jurists call "gossamer evidence," both literally, insofar as it is described as a "web," and figuratively, insofar as it is such an insubstantial form of proof.

Indeed, as we have seen, the handkerchief is but one of many pieces of circumstantial evidence that Iago adduces to prove Desdemona's guilt. The others include: (1) Cassio has been seen having a private conversation with Desdemona; (2) Cassio functioned as the go-between when Othello was wooing Desdemona; (3) Desdemona deceived her father, and could therefore be deceiving Othello; (4) Desdemona, who is white, is likely to revert to type and take a white lover; and (5) Cassio has cried out Desdemona's name in his sleep. Yet all of these other pieces of circumstantial evidence are eclipsed by the white handkerchief. If Desdemona has lost the handkerchief, she is guilty.

In the Simpson trial, the question of Simpson's guilt rested unduly on whether the bloody gloves belonged to him. As legal commentator Vincent Bugliosi observes: "Many feel it was the pivotal point in the trial, from which the prosecution never recovered." The prosecution's willingness to allow the glove demonstration was criticized as a world-historical bungle. The glove would clearly have shrunk owing to the blood and dew in which it had been steeped. Moreover, Simpson had to wear a latex glove underneath the bloody glove so it would not be compromised as evidence. Nonetheless, once the demonstration had occurred, the damage was done. In his closing arguments, defense attorney Johnnie Cochran stated: "We may all live to be 100 years old, and I hope we do, but you'll always remember that those gloves, when [prosecutor Christopher] Darden asked him to try them on, didn't fit. They know they didn't fit and no matter what they do, they can't make them fit." At least three of the jurors said that they voted to acquit on this ground. "In plain English," one juror stated after the trial, "the glove didn't fit."

Again, the emphasis on the glove was irrational because the prosecution adduced many other pieces of evidence against Simpson, including the following: (1) a history of arrests of Simpson for domestic abuse of Nicole Simpson; (2) hair belonging to Simpson found on Ron Goldman's shirt; (3) blood at Brentwood of the same type as Simpson's (which would match only 0.5 percent of the rest of the population); (4) blood on Simpson's socks that matched Nicole's blood; (5) footprints at the crime scene made with a pair of size 12 Bruno Magli shoes, which is the size that Simpson wore.

Fifth, the emphasis placed on ocular proof is understandable as a form of human cognitive bias. While in hindsight we know it to be undue, such emphasis should also seem familiar. It is a common human tendency to overvalue the concrete over the abstract—when we cannot measure what is important, we make important what we can measure. Iago does all he can to capitalize on this human tendency when he says to Othello: "Her honour is an essence that's not seen, / They have it very oft that have it not. / But for the handkerchief—" (4.1.16–18).

Like Desdemona's honor, Simpson's guilt was impossible to measure directly. But like the whereabouts of the handkerchief, the fit of the glove was a different matter. As Cochran said: "I don't think he could 'act' the size of his hands. He would be a great actor if he could 'act' his hands larger." The public was all too willing to follow Cochran from the abstract to the concrete. Many misquoted Cochran's famous jingle "If it doesn't fit, you must acquit" as "If the glove doesn't fit, you must acquit." But Cochran's quotation was not about the glove, but about the prosecution's case in general.

Sixth and finally, a purpose of the factfinding process should be to correct such forms of human error, making the prominence of both handkerchief and glove emblematic of a failed process. Although framed as a natural form of bias, Othello's undue emphasis on the handkerchief is also a problem. In the play, the solution is the Italian tribunal, which sifts the evidence in act 5 and quickly ascertains the truth. This would seem to suggest that larger groups tend to be harder to fool than individuals, especially if they engage in rational dialogue.

The Simpson case may seem to challenge that view. The jury in that case concluded that Simpson was not guilty, a verdict that I believe was clearly erroneous. At least some of the jurors were swayed by the "ocular proof" of the glove that did not fit. So having a jury will not, in and of itself, cure the human cognitive bias toward the concrete over the abstract.

Nor is the Simpson case idiosyncratic. Recent years have led to a renewed anxiety about the jury's inability to overcome ocular proof bias owing to the so-called *CSI* effect. Supporters of the *CSI* effect posit that the wild popularity of television shows depicting the use of forensic science, like *CSI,* has led juries to place excessive value on scientific evidence. Although empirical investigation into this effect is still nascent, the few empirical studies that have been done show no statistically significant link between these television shows and the higher demand for forensic evidence. Nonetheless, some scholars have posited that, owing to the general proliferation of technology in society, juries may in fact be demanding more scientific evidence than they have historically. The so-called *CSI* effect, they contend, is actually just a "tech effect." Regardless of the cause, jurors appear to place inordinate emphasis on "hard" or "physical" evidence.

* * *

MY GENERAL MALAISE about human factfinding should not be understood as a blanket indictment of the modern jury. Collective, deliberative factfinding is infinitely superior to individual, impassioned factfinding. I only wish to point out that the jury is not a panacea, and may still be prone to particular forms of cognitive bias, such as the ocular proof bias.

In a sly way, *Othello* itself points out the fallibility of collective human factfinding. While the Venetian nobles inside the play do well with issues of fact, we as the audience outside the play generally do not. Most audience members and readers do not realize that we ourselves have been duped about the timing of the play. When Bianca talks to Cassio, she refers to the fact that he has kept "a week away," suggesting that he has been on Cyprus for that amount of time. However, the play represents only three days—the first day in Venice, the second day of revelry on Cyprus, and the third day that contains the remainder of the action. Any complacency we have about our own omniscience should be appropriately modified by what critics have called the "double time" problem in the play.

Given this, it strikes me that the best defense of the jury cannot lie solely in the capacity of collective bodies to find the truth. Other values must be at stake, such as articulating the values of the community. This, in fact, may be an alternative way of understanding what happened in the Simpson trial. As legal scholar Paul Butler has argued, the Simpson jury may have been so outraged at Mark Fuhrman's racism that it engaged in a form of jury nullification. Under this interpretation, the jury may not have been misled by the facts at all. It may have chosen deliberately to disregard them.

We will never know the answer to that question, and this brings me to the final point about the value served by the jury. Juries are black boxes—they cannot be forced to explain their reasons or justify their decisions. As Fisher points out, this aspect of juries is a crucial one because it gives a closure to cases that would otherwise be hard to achieve. This makes the jury the proper human analog to God—inscrutable, unquestionable, final. Recall that Bartlett stated that the divine ordeal "was a device for dealing with situations in which certain knowledge was impossible but uncertainty was intolerable." In a world that has moved away from divine to human proof, the jury may serve as that device.

But this brings us full circle to the divine proofs. We rejected the divine proofs because they were too mystical and irrational. We sought instead to perfect human factfinding. But given that this is impossible, we hide the imperfection so we can move on with our lives. We do not live with the facts as they are, but as they are given to us, from a body of peers that speaks from a black box. This may be why Shakespeare seems to have been so skeptical about the shift from divine to human proof. Then as now, it was not so great a shift.

CHAPTER FIVE

THE SOVEREIGN

The Henriad

To speak of justice in Shakespeare's plays without speaking of the sovereign would be like playing *Hamlet* without the prince. In Shakespeare's time, the sovereign was the ultimate symbolic source of justice. Shakespeare's deepest meditation on how a ruler establishes legitimacy lies in the four plays scholars have dubbed the *Henriad* (*Richard II; Henry IV, Part 1; Henry IV, Part 2;* and *Henry V*). In these plays, we follow the development of the dissolute youth Prince Hal as he matures into the legendary King Henry V.

The *Henriad*—whose name draws on the *Iliad* to mark its epic sweep—tells the tale of three successive sovereigns. Richard II is a tyrant deposed by Henry Bolingbroke, who becomes Henry IV. Henry IV finds little solace in the crown, as he feels immense guilt for having seized it from an anointed sovereign. He also worries about his successor: his oldest son, Prince Hal, is reckless, spending all his time in the tavern world of Eastcheap. Hal's surrogate father figure in the tavern is one of Shakespeare's most glorious creations, Falstaff. Yet Hal knows he must someday leave that demimonde to assume the throne. After Henry IV dies, Hal becomes Henry V. Delighted at this turn of events, Falstaff rides to London to collect the perks of cronyism. But Hal cuts him dead, saying, "I know thee not, old man" (*Henry IV, Part 2,* 5.5.47), and embraces Falstaff's old nemesis, the Lord Chief Justice. Falstaff dies offstage of a broken heart in *Henry V.* In that play, the new King Henry V conquers France in the fabled Battle of Agincourt.

I read the *Henriad* as a choice the young Hal makes among three fathers—his biological father, Henry IV; his tavern "father," Falstaff; and his legal "father," the Chief Justice. At the beginning of the *Henriad,* Hal rejects his biological father, Henry IV, for Falstaff. He then rejects Falstaff in favor of the Lord Chief Justice, who represents incorruptible virtue. Yet by the time we reach the final play of the sequence—*Henry V*—the Lord Chief Justice has silently been replaced by the unscrupulous Archbishop of Canterbury. Henry V, then, ends up rejecting all three fathers because none can give him the authority he needs.

Shakespeare here anticipates the great sociologist Max Weber, who, in his 1919 lecture "Politics as a Vocation," describes three paths through which a leader can establish authority. First, there is feudal authority, which he calls the "authority of the 'eternal past,'" exercised by the "patriarchs and patriarchal rulers." Second, there is the authority of charisma, the cult of personality that can equally be exercised by the "elected ruler" or "the great demagogue." Finally, there is legal authority exercised by the "servant of the state." Henry IV, Falstaff, and the Chief Justice represent each type. Yet Weber contends that actual authority usually combines these forms. What we see at the end of the *Henriad* is that Henry V has absorbed traits from each father he has rejected. The product is nothing less than awe-inspiring. Henry V has an instinctive ability to cycle among these three sources to consolidate his power.

At the same time, Henry V's pursuit of power is opportunistic, calculating, and ruthless. As literary scholar Stephen Greenblatt shows, he self-consciously views statecraft to be a form of stagecraft, caring more about the appearance of legitimacy than legitimacy itself. Shakespeare shows us how Henry V projects the persona of a just ruler almost as if he were revealing a magician's trick. He does not claim that Henry V is a just ruler, only that he excels at giving that impression.

In doing so, Shakespeare raises disturbing questions about the possibility of just rule. Henry V receives the most positive portrayal of any sitting sovereign in a Shakespeare history play. The contestability of Henry's authority, then, raises the fear that just rule is nothing more than what power calls itself. And to the extent that Shakespeare's world is meant to represent our own, we should question whether we believe in legitimate authority today.

During his presidency, George W. Bush was insistently compared to a Prince Hal who had matured into a Henry V. Bush achieved the highest approval rating of any president in the history of the Gallup poll in the wake of 9/11. That popularity slowly dwindled, quieting the chorus of those linking Bush and Henry. But the connection between Bush and Henry V may still hold. Bush may illuminate Henry more than Henry illuminates Bush, helping us understand Shakespeare's deep suspicion about legitimate authority.

HAL'S MOST OBVIOUS male role model is his biological father. Even leaving aside the natural rebelliousness of sons, Hal has reason to distrust Henry IV. While Richard II was tyrannical, he was also legitimate. In wresting the crown away from its natural, divinely sanctioned line, Henry IV arguably committed treason.

Shakespeare maintains steady pressure on this problem of legitimacy. While still king, Richard makes a dire prophecy about Bolingbroke's fate if he usurps the crown:

> But ere the crown he looks for live in peace,
> Ten thousand bloody crowns of mothers' sons
> Shall ill become the flower of England's face,
> Change the complexion of her maid-pale peace
> To scarlet indignation, and bedew
> Her pastor's grass with faithful English blood.
> (*Richard II*, 3.3.95–100)

Richard's ally the Bishop of Carlisle concurs: "And if you crown him, let me prophesy / The blood of English shall manure the ground, / And future ages groan for this foul act" (4.1.137–39).

Richard's prophecy comes to pass. After usurping the crown, Henry IV spends the rest of his life putting down rebellions. Even in the first line of *Henry IV, Part 1*, we see a formerly energetic man transformed into a fatigued and embattled king: "So shaken as we are, so wan with care" (*Henry IV, Part 1*, 1.1.1). In that play, Henry must postpone his trip to the Holy Land to quash a rebellion led by the Percy family. He successfully defeats the insurgency at the Battle of Shrewsbury, but the play ends with work to be done.

In *Henry IV, Part 2*, Henry IV decisively subdues the remaining rebels but continues to decline. At its midpoint, we see him suffering from insomnia and envying commoners their sleep. He ruefully recollects Richard's prophecy "[f]oretelling this same time's condition, / And the division of our amity" (*Henry IV, Part 2*, 3.1.78–79). On his deathbed, he confesses the illegitimacy of his usurpation to Prince Hal: "God knows, my son, / By what by-paths and indirect crook'd ways / I met this crown, and I myself know well / How troublesome it sat upon my head" (4.5.183–86). He notes that his reign has been consumed by the struggle to justify his legitimacy: "For all my reign hath been but as a scene / Acting that argument" (4.5.197–98). Because he cannot get his own country in order, Henry never makes it to the Crusades. In his final hours, he puzzles out a seemingly hopeful prophecy that he will die in Jerusalem when informed that the palace room where he first "did swoon" is known as the "Jerusalem Chamber" (4.5.233–34).

While he does not possess feudal authority, Henry IV believes he can pass it to Hal: "for what in me was purchas'd / Falls upon thee in a more fairer sort; / So thou the garland wear'st successively" (4.5.199–201). With more than a tinge of envy, Henry IV states: "thou stand'st more sure than I could do" (4.5.202). Yet simply because Henry IV bequeaths the crown does not necessarily mean that Prince Hal possesses it legitimately. If an individual steals property, his son does not rightfully own it just because he acquires it through inheritance. Henry V is well aware of this infirmity. Before the Battle of Agincourt, he asks God to ignore his father's usurpation: "Not today, O Lord, / O not today, think not upon the fault / My father made in compassing the crown" (Henry V, 4.1.289–91). Because he deposed a legitimate ruler, Henry IV is a tainted source of feudal authority.

Henry IV is also an extremely unfriendly source of authority for Hal. In Henry IV, Part 1, King Henry IV publicly states that he envies Northumberland for having Harry Percy, known as Hotspur, as his son:

> Yea, there thou mak'st me sad and mak'st me sin
> In envy that my lord Northumberland

Should be the father to so blest a son,
A son who is the theme of honour's tongue,
Amongst a grove the very straightest plant,
Who is sweet Fortune's minion and her pride;
Whilst I, by looking on the praise of him,
See riot and dishonour stain the brow
Of my young Harry. O, that it could be proved
That some night-tripping fairy had exchanged
In cradle clothes our children where they lay,
And called mine "Percy", his "Plantagenet";
Then would I have his Harry, and he mine.
(*Henry IV, Part 1*, 1.1.77–89)

Shakespeare drastically alters Hotspur's age to make him a contemporary of Hal (the historical Hotspur was in fact a contemporary of the historical Henry IV). This revision makes Hotspur into Hal's foil throughout the *Henriad*. It sets Hal up for the harshest rebuke a parent can offer a child—that he wishes a mix-up had occurred in the nursery.

Henry IV repeats this rebuke to Hal's face, observing that Hotspur has a better claim to the throne: "Now by my sceptre, and my soul to boot, / He hath more worthy interest to the state / Than thou, the shadow of succession" (3.2.97–99). Hotspur's claim of "worthy interest" trumps Prince Hal's claim of succession, which has become shadowy through disrepute. The charge is uncomfortably familiar. Henry IV identifies Hal with Richard II, in that they are legitimate but undeserving, "[a]s thou art to this hour was Richard then" (3.2.94). He also identifies himself and Hotspur—"And even as I was then is Percy now" (3.2.96). Henry IV effectively says, "You are more like the king I deposed, and I am more like the man I wish were my son." It is no wonder Hal rejects the court for the tavern world and his chilly biological father for the gargantuan warmth of Falstaff.

FALSTAFF IS MADE of charisma. Charisma, which derives from the Greek word for "divine favor," is hard to define. I use it here to mean personal magnetism that arouses ardent devotion in others. Harold Bloom, a famous devotee of Falstaff, guesses that the character "ran away from the role originally intended for him." Even this epic cannot contain him. He is featured again in *The Merry Wives of Windsor,* allegedly at Queen Elizabeth's request that Shakespeare write a play showing Falstaff in love.

Falstaff's charisma, though, is that of the "great demagogue" rather than that of the ruler. When Falstaff is first introduced, he is asking Prince Hal for the time: "Now, Hal, what time of day is it, lad?" (1.2.1). Hal scornfully asks why the fat knight, who is stirring from a drunken stupor, would need to know the time. Falstaff's unabashed response is that he can thieve only at night. He immediately ties his thievery to Hal's future status as king:

> [B]ut I prithee, sweet wag, shall there be gallows stand-
> ing in England when thou art king? And resolution thus
> fubbed as it is with the rusty curb of old Father Antic
> the law? Do not thou, when thou art king, hang a thief.
> (1.2.55–59)

This early exchange reveals much. Falstaff expresses fatherly familiarity with his "lad" and "sweet wag" Hal (not Harry, much less Henry). Falstaff genuinely loves Hal. At the same time, Falstaff is introduced as a quintessentially anti-legal figure. He wishes for a topsy-turvy world in which "old Father Antic the law" will not curb thieves. Far from being hanged, thieves in Falstaff's world will be knighted as "Diana's foresters, gentlemen of the shade, minions of the moon" (1.2.24–25). Most dangerously for Hal, Falstaff wishes to use the prince to bring his anarchic world into being.

Initially, the threat posed by Falstaff seems weak. Falstaff's immediate excursion into outlawry is a proposed robbery at Gad's Hill. Falstaff decides to waylay some travelers and steal their gold. Hal falls in with this plot only because Hal's friend Poins sees an opportunity to trick Falstaff. Poins plans to let Falstaff and his three cronies commit the crime and then rob the robbers.

Falstaff successfully executes his plan. As he does so, he cries out: "You are grand-jurors, are ye? We'll jure ye, faith" (2.2.88–89). He calls the travelers "grand-jurors" because, at the time, only those with property could perform that office. In saying that he will judge ("jure") the jurors, Falstaff again inverts law's ordinary structure. Thieves judge jurors. Falstaff not only robs, but uses the rhetoric of the law while doing so. Hal indirectly restores the law by robbing the robbers. Disguised in buckram suits, he and Poins set on Falstaff and his accomplices, who run howling into the night.

Falstaff's outlawry extends to his speech. He breaks the iambic pentameter spoken by the high characters in the *Henriad*. This is not strictly a class distinction, for "Sir John Falstaff" is a knight. Falstaff has the education of a gentleman, as we see from his frequent learned references to classical mythology ("Diana's foresters" [1.2.24]), religion ("slaves as ragged as Lazarus" [4.2.24–25]), and medicine ("I have read the cause of his effects in Galen" [*Henry IV, Part 2*, 1.2.115–16]). If we forget this, it is only because Falstaff's learning is eclipsed by his native intelligence, in particular his sublime alertness to the possibilities in language. Falstaff could no more speak iambic pentameter than the stilted Henry IV could speak prose. Form follows substance—Falstaff breaks the rules of meter, overflows those rules, and expects not just to be forgiven, but to be loved for this excess. And his audiences—inside and outside the play—do love him.

Hal delights in Falstaff. He understands Falstaff to be a verbal Proteus who can wriggle out of any fetters. The sharp pleasure Hal feels at Gad's Hill is not so much in thwarting Falstaff, but in the expected lies Falstaff will tell to cover up his failure. As Poins observes, "[t]he virtue of this jest will be the incomprehensible lies that this same fat rogue will tell us when we meet at supper: how thirty at least he fought with, what wards, what blows, what extremities he endured; and in the reproof of this lives the jest" (*Henry IV, Part 1*, 1.2.176–80). Falstaff delivers. As he recounts the event back at the tavern, his embellishments are as brazen as they are transparent. He initially says he was set on by two men, then by four, seven, nine, and eleven. He has hacked notches in his sword with his dagger to provide "ocular proof" of the fight. When Hal and Poins confront him with the truth, Falstaff remains unfazed. He now states he must have known all along that it was Hal who accosted him. Falstaff's "instinct" (2.4.264) kept him from killing the heir apparent. Falstaff cannot be shamed—as Freud observes, "the demands of morality and honour must rebound from so fat a stomach."

This tomfoolery is relatively unconcerning. Yet Bloom, whose identification with Falstaff is extreme, overreaches when he says Falstaff "harms no one" in the play. This may be true before civil war erupts. Once war comes, Falstaff does immense harm. Hal puts Falstaff in charge of raising and leading a regiment. Falstaff admits he has "misused the King's press damnably" (4.2.12–13). He has permitted the wealthy to buy themselves out of the draft, pocketing "three hundred and odd pounds" (4.2.14) for himself. He describes the remaining soldiers as "slaves as ragged as Lazarus in the painted cloth where the glutton's dogs licked his sores—and such as indeed were never soldiers, but discarded unjust servingmen, younger sons to younger brothers, revolted tapsters and ostlers trade-fallen" (4.2.24–29). Hal observes: "I did never see such pitiful rascals" (4.2.63). Falstaff responds: "Tut, tut, good enough to toss; food for powder, food for powder. They'll fill a pit as well as better. Tush, man, mortal men, mortal men" (4.2.64–66). We hope he is joking, but his callousness extends into battle. At Shrewsbury, he reports: "I have led my ragamuffins where they are peppered; there's not three of my hundred and fifty left alive, and they are for the town's end to beg during life" (5.3.35–38).

Unlike sentimental critics, Hal takes his friend's measure from the start. In the second act, King Henry IV summons Hal. Both Hal and Falstaff know this will be a paternal audit. They prepare for it by playacting, with Hal taking his father's part, and Falstaff taking Hal's. Playing Hal, Falstaff defends himself:

> No, my good lord, banish Peto, banish Bardoll, banish
> Poins, but for sweet Jack Falstaff, kind Jack Falstaff, true
> Jack Falstaff, valiant Jack Falstaff, and therefore more
> valiant being, as he is old Jack Falstaff, banish not him
> thy Harry's company, banish not him thy Harry's com-
> pany. Banish plump Jack and banish all the world.
> (2.4.461–67)

Playing his father, Hal says: "I do, I will" (2.4.468). This is the sharpest, most scythe-like comma in literature. Hal speaks "I do" in jest, but "I will" in deadly earnest; he speaks "I do" as Henry IV, but "I will" as Henry V, the king he will become.

Hal's sense of his predicament can be seen in the ruse he plays on the "drawer," or bartender, Francis. Hal has Poins go into another room of the tavern and repeatedly call Francis's name. In the meantime, Hal engages Francis in conversation. Francis becomes increasingly agitated. He cannot leave the prince, but he must take care of his customers. The ruse ends when both Hal and Poins call "Francis!" at the same time. As the stage action notes: *"Here they both call him. The Drawer stands amazed, not knowing which way to go"* (2.4.77).

Critics call Hal's jape petty. We can pity Francis's discomfiture without ceding that Hal is driven only by cruelty. Hal dramatizes his own dilemma. He, like the Drawer, is called simultaneously by court and tavern. Hal represents the voice of the court here, as he does while playacting with Falstaff. Yet his identification is with the Drawer, immobilized by equal opposing forces. The voice of the court is frosty and powerful. The voice of the tavern is warm and degenerate.

The dilemma seemingly dissipates at the end of *Henry IV, Part 1*. After Hal saves his father's life at Shrewsbury, Henry IV and Hal reconcile. Their amity does not last. In *Henry IV, Part 2*, it is as if the rapprochement had never occurred. Yet this play produces the character who, it seems, can truly help Hal.

ALTHOUGH HE IS the embodiment of legal authority in the *Henriad*, the Lord Chief Justice is easily ignored. He appears in only one of the four plays—*Henry IV, Part 2*—and is never given a name. It took a practicing lawyer to see that he represents something distinctive in Shakespeare. Daniel Kornstein observes that in the Chief Justice, "Shakespeare gives us the most unqualifiedly, unmistakably complimentary portrait of a sober, solid, fair-minded lawyer figure in all the canon." The Chief Justice is originally Hal's enemy—Hal is banished from the Privy Council before the action of *Henry IV* begins because he has struck the Chief Justice. By the end of *Henry IV, Part 2*, Henry embraces the Chief Justice against all expectation.

Falstaff and the Chief Justice are natural enemies and recognize

each other as such. Falstaff wins the early rounds. In the first act of
Henry IV, Part 2, the Chief Justice confronts Falstaff. The Justice re-
bukes the knight for ignoring a court summons for the robbery on
Gad's Hill: "I sent for you when there were matters against you for
your life, to come speak with me" (*Henry IV, Part 2,* 1.2.131–32). Falstaff
easily parries: "As I was then advised by my learned counsel in the
laws of this land-service, I did not come" (1.2.133–34). Falstaff hides
behind his military service, which immunizes him from civilian law.

The Chief Justice acknowledges this excuse and even credits Falstaff's service: "Well, I am loath to gall a new-healed wound. Your
day's service at Shrewsbury hath a little gilded over your night's ex-
ploit on Gad's Hill. You may thank th'unquiet time for your quiet
o'er-posting that action" (1.2.146–50). The Lord Chief Justice is bal-
anced, even in his rhetoric—the "day" at Shrewsbury outweighs the
"night" on Gad's Hill; the "unquiet" time of civil war justifies the
"quiet" passing over of Falstaff's crime.

Even after withdrawing the summons, the Chief Justice tries moral
exhortation. Falstaff repeatedly outsmarts him, making this scene
come to the modern ear like a vaudeville act.

CHIEF JUSTICE:
Your means are very slender, and your waste is great.

FALSTAFF:
... I would my means were greater and my waist slenderer.
(1.2.139–42)

CHIEF JUSTICE:
There is not a white hair in your face but should have his
effect of gravity.

FALSTAFF:

His effect of gravy, gravy, gravy.

(1.2.159–61)

CHIEF JUSTICE:

Well, God send the Prince a better companion!

FALSTAFF:

God send the companion a better prince! I cannot rid my hands of him.

(1.2.199–201)

We might ask, with Escalus of *Measure for Measure,* "Which is the wiser here, Justice or Iniquity?" (*Measure,* 2.1.169). Like Constable Elbow in *Measure,* some Justices in the *Henriad* reflect their names. Justice Silence says almost nothing; Justice Shallow is Falstaff's gull. In contrast, the Chief Justice is truly wiser than the iniquitous Falstaff. But Falstaff has three potent safeguards—the protection of the heir apparent, the confusion in the state created by the rebellion, and his rollicking charisma.

We see Falstaff use all his advantages in the next act, when the Hostess of the tavern has Falstaff arrested for chronic nonpayment of debt. When the Chief Justice intervenes, Falstaff states:

> My lord, this is a poor mad soul, and she says up and down the town that her eldest son is like you. She hath been in good case, and the truth is, poverty hath distracted her. But for these foolish officers, I beseech you I may have redress against them.
>
> (*Henry IV, Part 2,* 2.1.102–106)

Falstaff slanders the Hostess by saying that she has alleged that the Chief Justice is the father of her oldest child. Falstaff excuses her because of her poverty and insanity, but seeks to sue the officers who have arrested him. Falstaff now seeks to "jure" the "grand jurors1" in an even more literal fashion.

The Chief Justice answers with commendable calm. He does not get distracted either by the preposterous claim that he has sired the Hostess's child or by Falstaff's claim of governmental misconduct. To the contrary, he observes that Falstaff's rhetorical moves are all too familiar:

> Sir John, Sir John, I am well acquainted with your manner of wrenching the true cause the false way. It is not a confident brow, nor the throng of words that come with such more than impudent sauciness from you, can thrust me from a level consideration. You have, as it appears to me, practised upon the easy-yielding spirit of this woman, and made her serve your uses both in purse and in person. (2.1.107–15)

The clear-eyed Chief Justice apprehends all. Rhetoric is not reality; audacity not authority. Falstaff's habit of "wrenching the true cause the false way" will not prevent the Chief Justice from giving a "level consideration," a phrase that recalls the scales of justice.

Falstaff then plays his other aces, observing that he must be freed so he can follow royal orders:

> My lord, I will not undergo this sneap without reply. You call honourable boldness impudent sauciness; if a man will make curtsy and say nothing, he is virtuous. No, my lord, my humble duty remembered, I will not be your

suitor. I say to you I do desire deliverance from these officers, being upon hasty employment in the King's affairs.
(2.1.121–27)

The Chief Justice is stymied. He cannot send Falstaff to jail without
depriving the king of a military leader (such as he is). So he sends
Falstaff to the war. For all his claims of haste, Falstaff invites a friend
to lunch the moment he is freed.

When Falstaff learns that King Henry IV is dead and that Hal
has become king, he immediately seeks revenge for the "sneap" (snub)
he has received from the Chief Justice:

> Boot, boot, Master Shallow! I know the young King is
> sick for me. Let us take any man's horses—the laws of
> England are at my commandment. Blessed are they that
> have been my friends, and woe to my Lord Chief Justice!
> (5.3.130–34)

It is always dangerous when any individual claims the law of the land
as his or her own. We see this earlier in Shakespeare's corpus when
the rebel Jack Cade says: "Away, burn all the records of the realm, my
mouth shall be the parliament of England" (*Henry VI, Part 2,* 4.7.11–
13). We see it later when *Lear*'s Goneril says, "[T]he laws are mine"
(*Lear,* 5.3.156). Falstaff has long wished to declare victory over "old
father Antic the law," and now he believes he has achieved it.

When the Chief Justice learns of Henry IV's death, he similarly
fears that the king's demise has left him "open to all injuries" (*Henry
IV, Part 2,* 5.2.8). Lord Warwick concurs that he thinks "the young King
loves you not" (5.2.9). The Chief Justice replies: "I know he doth not,
and do arm myself / To welcome the condition of the time, / Which cannot look more hideously upon me / Than I have drawn it in my fantasy"

(5.2.10–13). Shakespeare reveals the humanity of the Chief Justice here. We see him not as an abstract embodiment of justice, but as a human being who has an imagination, and who is afraid. The nobles around him sympathize with his plight. Lancaster says: "You stand in coldest expectation. / I am the sorrier; would 'twere otherwise" (5.2.31–32).

The predicted downfall of the Chief Justice is specifically tied to the predicted ascension of Falstaff. The Duke of Clarence states: "Well, you must now speak Sir John Falstaff fair, / Which swims against your stream of quality" (5.2.33–34). This brings out the best in the Chief Justice:

> Sweet Princes, what I did I did in honour,
> Led by th'impartial conduct of my soul.
> And never shall you see that I will beg
> A ragged and forestall'd remission.
> If truth and upright innocency fail me,
> I'll to the King my master that is dead,
> And tell him who hath sent me after him.
> (5.2.35–41)

The Chief Justice would rather follow his old master Henry IV into death than submit to the Lord of Misrule.

At the end of *Henry IV, Part 2,* Hal does call the Chief Justice to account for sending him to prison: "How might a prince of my great hopes forget / So great indignities you laid upon me? / What! rate, rebuke, and roughly send to prison / Th'immediate heir of England?" (5.2.68–71). The Chief Justice answers with dignity and integrity. In Henry V's time, as well as in Shakespeare's time, the judiciary was not independent of the executive. To the contrary, the Chief Justice was an agent of the king. The Chief Justice emphasizes this point in his speech: "I then did use the person of your father; / The image of his power lay then in me" (5.2.73–74). He elaborates that he punished Hal not because Hal struck him as an individual, but because Hal struck him as Henry IV's representative: "Your Highness pleased to forget my place, / The majesty and power of law and justice, / The image of the King whom I presented, / And struck me in my very seat of judgment" (5.2.77–80).

But the Chief Justice was Henry IV's representative at the time only because Henry IV was king. The two men interacted in their official capacities, not as individuals. Now that Hal has become Henry V, the Chief Justice can represent him. So the Chief Justice asks Henry V what he would want if his own son were "to spurn at [his] most royal image, / And mock [his] workings in a second body" (5.2.89–90). "If the deed were ill, / Be you contented, wearing now the garland, / To have a son set your decrees at naught?" (5.2.83–85). Hal has already indirectly answered this question, while playing at being his father in the tavern scene. When asked whether he would banish Falstaff, he says "I do, I will." We know Henry V would want his son disciplined.

The Chief Justice's capacity to impose the law impartially is exactly what Henry V needs. So Henry V, contrary to all expectations, including the Chief Justice's own, embraces him:

> You are right, Justice, and you weigh this well.
> Therefore still bear the balance and the sword;
> And I do wish your honors may increase
> Till you do live to see a son of mine
> Offend you and obey you, as I did.
> So shall I live to speak my father's words:
> "Happy am I, that have a man so bold
> That dares do justice on my proper son;
> And not less happy, having such a son
> That would deliver up his greatness so

Into the hands of justice." You did commit me:
For which I do commit into your hand
Th'unstained sword that you have us'd to bear,
With this remembrance—that you use the same
With the like bold, just, and impartial spirit
As you have done 'gainst me. There is my hand.
You shall be as a father to my youth,
My voice shall sound as you do prompt mine ear,
And I will stoop and humble my intents
To your well-practis'd wise directions.
(*Henry IV, Part 2*, 5.2.102–21)

Henry V seems finally to have chosen a father: "You shall be as a father to my youth."

The Chief Justice is an ideal father for Henry V at this moment of transition because he can defend the new king from both the lawlessness of Henry IV from above and the lawlessness of Falstaff from below. Henry V recognizes that he has a superior claim to legitimacy than did his own father, because he has acquired the crown through lineal inheritance. The new king can stand for the law as his father could not, and the Chief Justice can help him do so. The Chief Justice is enough like Henry IV to represent him, but also enough unlike Henry IV that he can outlive him to represent Hal.

As Ernst Kantorowicz demonstrates in his book *The King's Two Bodies,* medieval political theory split the atom of sovereignty into two "bodies." One body was the king's natural body, which was a mortal body susceptible to decay like that of any other human being. The other was the king's political body, which was immutable and eternal, representing the unity of the nation. Shakespeare knew of this theory. He invokes it in *Hamlet,* where the prince, after killing the king's advisor Polonius, observes that "[t]he body is with the King, but the King is not with the body" (*Hamlet*, 4.2.25–26). Here, the Chief Justice observes that when Hal struck the Chief Justice, he struck the king in his "second body." The Chief Justice is the king's "second body" because as the nation's highest judicial officer, he represents the immutable and eternal law that constitutes the nation. The Chief Justice offers Hal nothing less than the immortal political body of the king, now that the mortal natural body of Henry IV no longer contains it.

The Chief Justice can also defend Henry V against the threat Falstaff poses from below. When Falstaff approaches Henry V, he addresses him in the old familiar way: "God save thy Grace, King Hal, my royal Hal!" (*Henry IV, Part 2*, 5.5.41). Falstaff puts it sharply enough—it is still "Hal" rather than "Henry," which he then amends to a possessive: "*my* royal Hal." Henry V ignores him, but Falstaff will not be so easily put off: "God save thee, my sweet boy!" (5.5.43). So the new king turns to his new legal representative to avoid a direct confrontation: "My Lord Chief Justice, speak to that vain man" (5.5.44). The Chief Justice swiftly provides the needed assistance: "Have you your wits? Know you what 'tis you speak?" (5.5.45). There may be some retaliation here—recall that Falstaff falsely accused the Hostess of madness in the Chief Justice's presence, when the Chief Justice was able to do little about it.

Falstaff disregards the Chief Justice. He has already bested his adversary while Hal was a mere prince. Now that Hal is king, Falstaff must believe he will outrank any officer of the law. He does mend his speech a little, switching from "my sweet boy" to "My King! My Jove! I speak to thee, my heart!" (5.5.46). Yet he never surrenders his familiarity—"I speak to thee (the more familiar form of "you," just as Hal is the more familiar form of Henry). Falstaff forces Henry V to address him directly. Finally and terribly, the king does:

> I know thee not, old man. Fall to thy prayers.
> How ill white hairs becomes a fool and jester!

I have long dreamt of such a kind of man,
So surfeit-swell'd, so old, and so profane;
But being awak'd I do despise my dream.
Make less thy body hence, and more thy grace;
Leave gormandizing; know the grave doth gape
For thee thrice wider than for other men.
Reply not to me with a fool-born jest;
Presume not that I am the thing I was;
For God doth know, so shall the world perceive,
That I have turn'd away my former self;
So will I those that kept me company.
When thou dost hear I am as I have been,
Approach me, and thou shalt be as thou wast,
The tutor and the feeder of my riots.
Till then I banish thee, on pain of death,
As I have done the rest of my misleaders,
Not to come near our person by ten mile.
For competence of life I will allow you,
That lack of means enforce you not to evils;
And as we hear you do reform yourselves,
We will, according to your strengths and qualities,
Give you advancement.
[To the Lord Chief Justice]
Be it your charge, my lord,
To see perform'd the tenor of my word.
Set on.
(5.5.47–72)

Henry's resolve is not as strong as it sounds. He slides into the joshing mode of the tavern when he refers to Falstaff's obesity: "know the grave doth gape / For thee thrice wider than for other men." This is the new king's most vulnerable moment in this speech, for it opens him to the old daffy banter. We reflexively anticipate Falstaff's response, which we wish we were clever enough to formulate. Henry V foresees the danger, and hastily preempts Falstaff's return: "Reply not to me with a fool-born jest." He distances himself first not from Falstaff, but from his former self—"Presume not that I am the thing I was." Only after he has accomplished this self-estrangement can he banish the friend of his youth: "That I have turn'd away my former self; / So will I those that kept me company." Tellingly, Henry V does not banish Falstaff from England, but from coming within ten miles of his person. The most direct threat Falstaff poses is not to the nation, but to Henry, wherever Henry is.

The rejection is necessary: Falstaff's anarchic charisma would destroy the state. As A. D. Nuttall says, Henry V "is doing this for us." But the repudiation is no more bearable for being indispensable. Again, the Chief Justice shoulders what no ordinary mortal could— Hal turns to him, in stoic misery, to carry out his orders: "Be it your charge, my lord, / To see perform'd the tenor of my word." Then, banishing plump Jack and all the world, Hal sets on.

Critics divide sharply on Falstaff. Yet Falstaff is *both* inexhaustibly seductive and threatening. The relationship Hal has to Falstaff is similar to the relationship Plato's Socrates had to the poet in *The Republic*. Aristotle did not love the poet, but let him stay. Plato, in contrast, loved the poet and banished him because of, rather than in spite of, that love. It was because Plato loved the poet that he understood the poet's anarchic charisma. Similarly, Hal comes to recognize Falstaff as the most sublime of scofflaws. Falstaff is the fattest lamb literature ever sacrificed on the altar of the law.

Yet once Henry V makes the transition to kingship, he also relinquishes the Chief Justice. In *Henry V,* the next and final play in the *Henriad,* the Chief Justice has disappeared without explanation.

Henry V takes legal advice at the inception of the play from the Arch-bishop of Canterbury. The young king wishes to know whether he has the legal right to invade France. In contrast to the Chief Justice, the Archbishop is deeply partial in this case. The Parliament is about to pass a bill that would decimate the church's coffers. The Arch-bishop believes that if Henry V invades France, Parliament will not pass the bill. So Canterbury's conclusion is that Henry has a dynastic right to France. Henry does caution the Archbishop not to bend the law to suit his convenience: "And God forbid, my dear and faithful lord, / That you should fashion, wrest or bow your reading" (*Henry V*, 1.2.13–14). Nonetheless, Henry's appeal to such a biased judge raises the suspicion that he, like many an executive, is making an authority out of the individual who will serve up the opinion he wants.

BY THE BEGINNING of *Henry V*, then, Henry V has rejected all three of his father figures. These rejections, however, testify only to the extent that Henry V has *absorbed* the forms of legitimacy each fa-ther represents. In *Henry V*, we see him use a strategic combination of feudal, charismatic, and legal authority to consolidate his power.

With respect to feudal authority, Henry V attacks France in part because he has a dynastic claim to it that he cannot assert over his own country. The useful Archbishop of Canterbury explains that under Salic Law, which is thought to obtain in France, the throne cannot be inherited through the female line. England, however, allows matri-lineal inheritance. Because Henry V's great-great-grandmother was a daughter of the King of France, Henry V would be the rightful heir to the French throne.

France would presumably deem Salic Law, rather than English law, to control the dispute. However, Canterbury has an answer to this as well. On its own terms, the bar on female succession applies only to "Salic land" (*Henry V*, 1.2.39). Canterbury opines that those lands are entirely encompassed by Germany, because the law was enacted to punish German women "[f]or some dishonest manners of their life" (1.2.49). For this reason, Salic Law is not relevant to the dispute over France.

Before his death, Henry IV tells his son "to busy giddy minds / With foreign quarrels" (*Henry IV, Part 2*, 4.5.213–14). Henry V recognizes this advice to be sound—a foreign war will quiet civil unrest. But unlike his father, who wished to go on a crusade to the Holy Land, Henry V picks France as his target. This decision shows him to be the shrewder statesman. At least under Canterbury's interpretation, Henry *does* have title to France. His feudal claim over those lands is arguably more secure than his claim on England. This is the hidden irony in Henry's claim before setting sail for battle: "No king of England, if not king of France!" (*Henry V*, 2.2.194).

Henry draws as well on the charismatic authority of Falstaff, though of course he channels it to favor regal authority rather than to undermine it. In *Henry IV, Part 1*, Henry IV berates his son for being too familiar with the masses, observing that he would never have been able to acquire the crown if he had pursued that course. Henry IV attributes his success to his *distance* from the masses: "By being seldom seen, I could not stir / But, like a comet, I was wondered at" (*Henry IV, Part 1*, 3.2.46–47). Hal adopts a different strategy, both as a prince and as a king. His time in the tavern has given him a populist touch. The night before the battle, the chorus observes how Harry moves among his troops so that everyone feels "[a] little touch of Harry in the night" (*Henry V*, 4.0.47). That night, he also mingles in disguise with three common soldiers to hear their perspectives on the battle.

Moreover, like Falstaff, Henry V uses his redoubtable rhetorical skills to recast reality. On the day of battle, Westmorland bemoans that the English are woefully outnumbered (Exeter puts it at "five to one" [4.3.4]), and wishes they had more soldiers. Henry rebuffs him with his famous Saint Crispin's Day speech. He begins by telling Westmorland that he would not wish for a single additional soldier because "[t]he fewer men, the greater share of honour" (4.3.22). Noting that the day is known as Saint Crispin's Day, he proclaims that their exploits on this day will never be forgotten:

> This story shall the good man teach his son,
> And Crispin Crispian shall ne'er go by
> From this day to the ending of the world
> But we in it shall be remembered,
> We few, we happy few, we band of brothers.
> For he today that sheds his blood with me
> Shall be my brother; be he ne'er so vile,
> This day shall gentle his condition.
> And gentlemen in England now abed
> Shall think themselves accursed they were not here,
> And hold their manhoods cheap whiles any speaks
> That fought with us upon Saint Crispin's day.
> (4.3.56–67)

By the end of this speech, Henry V has completely turned Westmorland. When asked if he still wants more help from England, Westmorland responds: "God's will, my liege, would you and I alone, / Without more help, could fight this royal battle!" (4.3.74–75).

Finally, Henry V makes a great show of his legal authority when he enforces the law against one of his old tavern cronies. In France, one of the Gad's Hill robbers, Bardolph, is caught stealing a pax (a sacred tablet made of precious metal) from a church. His friend Pistol appeals to Captain Fluellen to ask Henry to pardon Bardolph. Fluellen refuses to do so, observing that the penalty is the proper punishment for looting. Henry V agrees. Kenneth Branagh's steely 1989 film version renders the scene well: Henry V allows his friend to be executed, but watches the execution through tears. As Branagh's rendition underscores, Bardolph stands for Falstaff, who has already died offstage.

It is easy, then, to celebrate Henry as the perfect convergence of the three sources of authority—feudal, charismatic, and legal. At Agincourt, Henry wins a victory against seemingly impossible odds. In Shakespeare, the final death toll for the French is ten thousand (4.8.88). The English dead number twenty-nine (4.8.104–107). Henry ends the play as the King of England and the inheritor of France. Nonetheless, the veneer of Henry V's self-presentation is thin. His feudal claim to France is a highly contestable one made by a biased source. This is a war of choice, not necessity, and it is motivated to an uncomfortable extent by a desire to distract England from its own civil strife. Henry's charismatic Saint Crispin's speech is also disingenuous. He obviously would prefer to have more men, but must do the best with those he has. It is also not the case that the commoners who fight for him will have their conditions "gentled" once they return to England. Finally, while Henry makes a great show of being bound by legal authority in having Bardolph hanged, he also violates the laws of war. When he hears the French are rallying, Henry V orders his men to kill all their prisoners. Law professor Theodor Meron carefully explores whether this order could have been justified either on grounds of reprisal (the French had done the same to the English pages) or necessity (the French POWs still represented a threat, as they could be rescued). Meron rejects both rationales under the law of war as it stood in Henry's time. Even Winston Churchill, a staunch fan of Henry, recoiled from this moment in the play.

Henry V, then, is less a completely virtuous ruler than one who has mastered the stagecraft of appearing to be one. Shakespeare shows that Henry has this instinct from the start. Even as he riots in the tavern world in act 1, Prince Hal pauses in soliloquy to describe the company he keeps:

> I know you all, and will awhile uphold
> The unyoked humour of your idleness.
> Yet herein will I imitate the sun,
> Who doth permit the base contagious clouds
> To smother up his beauty from the world,
> That, when he please again to be himself,
> Being wanted, he may be more wondered at
> By breaking through the foul and ugly mists
> Of vapours that did seem to strangle him.
> If all the year were playing holidays,
> To sport would be as tedious as to work;
> But when they seldom come, they wished-for come,
> And nothing pleaseth but rare accidents.
> So when this loose behaviour I throw off
> And pay the debt I never promised,
> By how much better than my word I am,
> By so much shall I falsify men's hopes;
> And, like bright metal on a sullen ground,
> My reformation, glittering o'er my fault,
> Shall show more goodly and attract more eyes
> Than that which hath no foil to set it off.
> I'll so offend to make offence a skill,
> Redeeming time when men think least I will.
> (*Henry IV, Part 1*, 1.2.185–207)

This justly celebrated passage shows that Hal, like his father, understands that sovereignty subsumes stagecraft. As literature professor

David Scott Kastan points out, father and son simply make different directorial decisions about how to achieve the same end of being "wondered at" (a phrase they both use). While Henry IV removes himself to make his emergence more dramatic, Hal covers himself in "the base contagious clouds." If Henry IV is the "comet," Hal is the "sun."

Shakespeare had cause to insert this speech soon after introducing Hal. The historical Henry V was a semidivine figure to the Elizabethans. The audience may have been concerned to see their national hero introduced in a tavern surrounded by rakehells. They could have asked, as Claudius asks of the play-within-the-play in *Hamlet*: "Have you heard the argument? Is there no offense in't?" (*Hamlet*, 3.2.226–27). This soliloquy would have reassured them.

It should *not* reassure us. Prince Hal is shown here to be a calculating figure from the outset. Shakespeare does not allow us to bask in a celebration of just rule. To the contrary, he shows us how the impression of great leadership is achieved without giving us any reassurance that any substance lies beneath the immaculate veneer.

IN CONTRAST TO other characters I have explored, Henry V has already been firmly assigned a modern-day analog: our forty-third president, George W. Bush. The comparison dates back at least to 1998, before Bush was even elected, when the London *Guardian* saw Bush as "a sort of Texan prince Hal putting aside his debauched youth in preparation for the ascent to power." The analogy perhaps reached its climax in the immediate aftermath of 9/11. At that moment, Bush, like Henry V, seemed to possess the perfect confluence of the three forms of Weberian authority—feudal, charismatic, and legal.

It may seem odd to speak of Bush's feudal authority when the United States has so formally and self-consciously moved away from

Shakespeare's monarchical society. Yet the United States has long had political dynasties, as represented by the Adamses, the Harrisons, the Roosevelts, the Kennedys, and the Bushes. (It is simply what Falstaff would call "the effect of gravy" to point out that the Bushes can supposedly trace their lineage back to British royalty.) As historian Richard Brookhiser puts it, political dynasty in the United States is the "tribute democracy pays to aristocracy."

The instance of George W. Bush may help us understand why we are so enamored of dynastic rule. Dynasties permit us to tell rich intergenerational stories, like that of the prodigal son who makes good. As Marjorie Garber observes: "George W. Bush's hard-drinking, hard-partying youth and his 'conversion' seem directly to parallel the wild youth and reformation of Prince Hal; the tension with a strong paternal predecessor and namesake marks 'George II' as a version of Henry V." Ken Adelman, who runs leadership seminars based on *Henry V* as part of his series Movers and Shakespeares, agrees that the intergenerational dynamic is key: "[a] son who wishes to redeem his father's reign, Hal puts the indiscretions of his youth behind him to get serious and go straight."

This brings us to Bush's charismatic authority. As we have come to perceive him, Bush may strike us as the opposite of charismatic. While, like Shakespeare, Bush invented a lot of words, most of his creations were unintentional. However, I believe this portrayal "misunderestimates" Bush's populist appeal. In his autobiography, Bush frankly admits to being an alcoholic, and rumors of his serious drug use have never been rebutted. He is also widely known to be the disfavored son, as his father President George H. W. Bush vested his political hopes in his son Jeb, much as Henry IV favored Hotspur over Hal. (Incidentally, the analogy could also be made to how Joseph P. Kennedy Sr. initially pinned his dynastic aspirations on Joseph P. Kennedy Jr., rather than on John F. Kennedy.) Bush's rise as an underdog from the tavern world is part of his populist charisma. As English professor Scott Newstok points out, what Hal and Bush both represent is a "blend of vertical authority with horizontal camaraderie in a way that evokes the best of both worlds, or at least effaces the worst of each."

By the time 9/11 occurred, President Bush's charisma was on full display. As conservative editor Rich Lowry observed: "I thought that last Friday, as Bush stood atop part of the rubble of the World Trade Center, he came as close as he ever will to delivering a St. Crispin's Day speech. That spirit and resolve carried over into the House chamber last night, and it was something to behold." Journalist Balint Vazsonyi agreed: "'He to-day that sheds his blood with me shall be my brother, be he ne'er so vile,' exclaims King Henry as dawn breaks over the fields of Agincourt. I do not know whether the President's speech writers study Shakespeare. . . . Yet the world fell silent when he extended the call, even to the ever-so vile, to join him." Political commentator David Gergen, who appears to have established himself as the expert on the V/W link, observed, "when trouble hit, how rapidly we left behind the pages of Henry the 4th [for] the pages of Henry the 5th. . . . Now, to be sure, [Bush] has not won his Agincourt, but he has set sail, and for that the country can be grateful."

Bush swiftly received the legal mandate to fight his Agincourt. One week after the attacks, Congress enacted the Authorization for Use of Military Force. This law gave Bush the mandate to use all "necessary and appropriate force" to bring the terrorists responsible for 9/11 to justice. While his tendency to distort the law later proved to be a major stumbling block for his administration, Bush heavily relied on the "AUMF" for much of his subsequent international military activity.

The infinitely arguable nature of Henry V's own authority, however, can be seen in how easily critics were able to deploy the play against Bush. The sinister advice Henry IV gives to his son to "busy giddy minds / with foreign quarrels" was raised by the *New York Daily News* in 2003: "This year's Shakespeare in Central Park production is about the leader of a country who diverts the people's attention away from the dubious way he came to power by invading another country. President George W. Bush? No, Henry V." Taking a shot at Bush's populism, London's *Observer* said of a 2003 National Theatre production: "if there is any topical resonance in Shakespeare's play, it comes from the story of a national leader going to war on highly dubious grounds and who, in the play's best scene on the night before the battle, is put on the spot by one of his common soldiers: 'the king hath a heavy reckoning to make if his cause be not good.'" Describing attacks on Bush's legal authority, Jack Lynch observes, "Henry V's justification of his war with France—based on a very tenuous reading of the old Salic Law, backed up by legal scholars paid to tell the king what he wanted to hear—reminded some critics of the arguments in favor of invading Iraq." (Columnist David Brooks wittily compared the neoconservative advocates of Bush's war to the Archbishop of Canterbury by calling them "theocons.") On a more sober note, Henry's decision to kill the prisoners of war and his threatened ill-treatment of those who refused to surrender has been compared to acts of U.S. cruelty reported from Fallujah and Abu Ghraib.

As Bush's presidency became more unpopular, the comparisons between Bush and Henry V declined. It seems that we still wish to keep Henry V's reputation untarnished. I believe this is a mistake. The major difference between Bush and Henry V is that Bush did not win his Agincourt. After all, in the immediate aftermath of 9/11, Bush was just as celebrated as Henry V. Moreover, many of Bush's faults can be attributed to Henry. We should not use Bush's unpopularity to distinguish him from Henry V. We should use it to call Henry V's popularity into question.

The stakes of this debate extend beyond the fictional Henry V. In Shakespeare's ten history plays, Henry V is the ruler we are meant to admire most. To run through the others, Shakespeare presents King John as illegitimate and murderous, Richard II as a tyrant, Henry IV as a chilly usurper, Henry VI as young and inexperienced, Richard III as a thorough villain, and Henry VIII as a gull of the church. To assail Henry V, then, is tantamount to assailing the possibility of just sovereignty itself.

I wish to posit that Shakespeare endorsed this assault. There are characters in Shakespeare who stand purely for justice, but they are often the minor, interstitial ones—Escalus in *Measure,* the Venetian nobles in *Othello,* or the anonymous servant who rises up against Cornwall in *Lear.* In the *Henriad,* this character is the Chief Justice. Shakespeare ushers him quickly off the stage for a reason—he is too pure for the political world unfolding around him. Shakespeare showed us how a savvy leader gains power, and part of this strategy is not to bind oneself to one source of authority, even—or perhaps especially—to a pillar of rectitude. In doing so, the Bard left us in the troubled knowledge that the just ruler may be more unique than rare, and perhaps more unreal than unique. Then as now, ultimate power is ultimately unclean.

SIX

THE NATURAL WORLD

Macbeth

MACBETH **HAS A DISTINCTIVE REPUTATION NOT JUST AMONG** Shakespeare's plays, but among *all* plays. As stage historian Richard Huggett notes: "There is one superstition so old, so all-consuming, so intimidating, that just about everyone in theater believes it, no matter how cynical, how materialistic, or hard boiled he is." This is the superstition that *Macbeth* is cursed. A long stage history of deaths, injuries, technical malfunctions, and acting fiascoes has been adduced to support the curse's existence. Actors avoid saying "Macbeth" or quoting lines from the play outside rehearsal or performance, referring to it as the "Scottish play" and its protagonists as "Mr. and Mrs. M."

They often refuse to wear a cloak or helmet if they learn it was used in a production of *that* play. In the days of traveling repertory companies, when props and scenery for productions were intermingled, the furniture, costumes, and settings for *Macbeth* were scrupulously quarantined.

Special purification rituals exist for those who slip. If an actor speaks the word "Macbeth," or a line from the play, he or she must "go out of the dressing room, turn around three times, spit, knock on the door three times, and beg humbly for readmission." Alternatively, the actor can quote one of two Shakespearean lines. The first is "Angels and ministers of grace defend us!" (*Hamlet,* 1.4.39), which Hamlet utters to protect himself from his father's ghost. The other is Lorenzo's line from *Merchant:* "Fair thoughts and happy hours attend on you!" (*Merchant,* 3.4.41). While less on point, it draws on *Merchant's* general reputation as a lucky play.

Given this history, I was struck on rereading *Macbeth* by how oddly comforting the play is about the justice of the universe. The Macbeths' undeniable evil, which trails like squid ink behind them, dissipates by the play's end. The Macbeths die miserably, Duncan's virginally pure son Malcolm takes the throne, and the bright side of the witches' prophecy—that the virtuous Banquo's issue will claim the crown—is imaginatively fulfilled in the watching King James I, for whom the play was written.

Most important, the evil in the play often seems to call "naturally" for its own correction. In act 1, Macbeth almost decides to spare Duncan because he fears "[b]loody instructions, which, being taught, return / To plague th'inventor" (1.7.9–10). He continues: "this evenhanded Justice / Commends th'ingredience of our poison'd chalice / To our own lips" (1.7.10–12). Lady Macbeth talks him out of this belief, but stages its truth at the other end of the play. When the doctor watches the tormented, sleepwalking Lady Macbeth, he diagnoses:

"Unnatural deeds / Do breed unnatural troubles" (5.1.68–69). If the play has a moral, this is it.

Merchant and Macbeth pair well not only because Merchant is deemed lucky and Macbeth is deemed unlucky, but also because Merchant is not as lucky, and Macbeth is not as unlucky, as each seems. Merchant is often designated a "problem comedy" because its happy ending is stained with troubling implications. Macbeth is the opposite—a "solution tragedy," if you will. The deaths of the "butcher, and his fiend-like Queen" (5.9.35) are characterized not only as just, but also as the inevitable consequence of their crimes. I shall call this belief in the self-correcting universe "natural justice." Under natural justice, moral laws are as unbreakable as physical ones—human law is as inescapable as the law of gravity. This quality lends a sanguine aspect to one of Shakespeare's most sanguinary plays.

Yet we should not accept the comfort Macbeth offers, because natural justice does not exist in the real world. While art and nature are often seen as contrasting terms, poetic justice is more like natural justice than either is like actual justice. The perfect punishments of Dante's Inferno, where the fortune tellers have their heads twisted backward, or the wrathful battle against each other, for instance, could never be achieved in the world in which we live.

This gap between natural and actual justice can be seen in how aggressively Shakespeare had to revise his historical sources to create Macbeth's self-correcting universe. Shakespeare's main source for the play was Raphael Holinshed's Chronicles. But in the Chronicles, the line between the "good" and "evil" characters is much less distinct. Moreover, punishments are not so tightly tailored to crimes. Closer examination of Macbeth shows that our wish to believe in natural justice in the actual world is just that—a wish.

In our enlightened times, it may seem unnecessary to caution that natural justice is a fallacy. Yet the belief in the self-correcting world has remained surprisingly stubborn. The fallacy led Susan Sontag to publish *Illness as Metaphor* in 1978 while battling cancer, out of her outrage that her illness was treated as a punishment for some bad act. Harold Kushner's 1981 book, *When Bad Things Happen to Good People* would not have been a bestseller if it had not so successfully challenged the underlying assumption that bad things happen only to bad people. In 2001, Jerry Falwell attributed responsibility for the 9/11 attacks to "the pagans, and the abortionists, and the feminists." Many of us are still in the thrall of such magical thinking: anything that looks like a punishment must have been caused by a crime.

Indeed, I read the ostensible curse attending *Macbeth* as an enduring example of the fallacy. As conventionally told, the play is cursed because it contains actual witches' spells. To invoke it is an "unnatural deed" that breeds "unnatural troubles." The curse is the continuing life of the play's moral. If you play by the rules of the curse, then you will not be punished. If you disrespect those rules, then you will be punished outside the play according to the same principles of natural justice imposed on the characters within it.

The alleged curse is harmless Halloween entertainment. But the belief it represents—the "natural justice fallacy"—is not. Justice is not a natural phenomenon but a fragile human achievement. We seem to need constant reminders of this simple truth. I seek to provide such a reminder in positing that the play is much brighter, and the world much darker, than we seem to think.

HUMAN LAW AND divine law do little work in *Macbeth*. No one seeks to prosecute the Macbeths for their crime, even when their guilt becomes manifest. There is a historical reason for this—King James I disapproved of all regicides, even when the king had killed a king to become king. Lady Macbeth can make the "sovereign immunity" argument literally in her sleep: "What need we fear who knows it, when none can call our power to accompt?" (5.1.35–37). Once Lady Macbeth gains sovereignty, she is confident that she has simultaneously acquired sovereign immunity, traveling beyond anyone's capacity to hold her accountable. Similarly, while God and angels are both mentioned in this play, they remain distant abstractions. In contrast, the "supernatural" (1.3.130) witches—those androgynous antitheses of nature—are vividly present. Starting the play amidst thunder and lightning, they summon their own atmosphere—literally and figuratively.

Human justice and divine justice retreat from the play to give central stage to natural justice. Every act riffs on the word "nature," which occurs with insistent regularity over Shakespeare's shortest tragedy. In act 1, Macbeth gets an early warning that the witches are evil because they make his heart beat "against the use of nature" (1.3.137); Lady Macbeth fears Macbeth will not murder Duncan because his "nature . . . is too full o'th'milk of human kindness" (1.5.16–17); she asks to be "unsex[ed]" (1.5.41) so "no compunctious visitings of Nature" (1.5.45) will stand between her murderous intention and its fulfillment. Duly persuaded, Macbeth takes comfort that "Nature seems dead" (2.1.50) and successfully kills Duncan, in part because Lady Macbeth has drugged Duncan's guards so "Death and Nature do contend about them" (2.2.7). Yet Nature is far from dead. Each of the gashes in Duncan's head is "like a breach in nature" (2.3.111), and the sovereign's death produces prodigies in "nature" (2.4.16). Because the witches have prophesied that Banquo's issue will assume the throne, Macbeth begins to fear Banquo's "royalty of nature" (3.1.49). He enlists two murderers, who leave Banquo in a ditch "[w]ith twenty trenched gashes on his head; / The least a death to nature" (3.4.26–27). But Banquo's ghost returns to haunt Macbeth. When her husband grows increasingly paranoid, Lady Macbeth says he "lack[s] the season of all natures, sleep" (3.4.140). By act 4, Macbeth reveals to the witches that his only wish is to "live the lease of Nature" (4.1.99). This too is not to be. Lady Macbeth herself sleeps only after a fashion: her sleepwalking is described as "[a] great perturbation in nature" (5.1.9). She dies, allegedly by her own hand. Macbeth is defeated by external forces (here human justice plays its part), but those human agents carry the boughs of Birnam wood before them, as if nature were marching on the castle.

The definition of "nature" shifts across the play to mean physiology, temperament, conscience, life, inanimate physical forces, fauna and flora, order, character, or normalcy. But while the word's meanings mutate, its sense remains stable. In the absence of angels, nature stands on their side.

Natural justice operates most obviously in the prodigies accompanying King Duncan's death. Nature blazons its condemnation to a terrified populace. Macbeth's murder of the good King Duncan produces daylight darkness:

ROSSE
Thou seest the heavens, as troubled with man's act,
Threatens his bloody stage: by th'clock 'tis day,
And yet dark night strangles the travelling lamp.
Is't night's predominance, or the day's shame,
That darkness does the face of earth entomb,
When living light should kiss it?

OLD MAN
'Tis unnatural,
Even like the deed that's done. On Tuesday last,

A falcon, towering in her pride of place,
Was by a mousing owl hawk'd at, and kill'd.
(2.4.5–13)

The exchange produces two images of inferior bodies supplanting superior ones—the moon blotting out the sun, and the mousing owl killing the regal falcon. Inanimate nature speaks not just through the eclipse, but also through storms (2.3.53–55) and earthquakes (2.3.59–60). The animal kingdom speaks not just through the falcon's death but also through another "obscure bird" that "clamour[s] the livelong night" (2.3.58–59) and—the image everyone remembers—through Duncan's horses, which turn "wild in nature" (2.4.16) and "eat each other" (2.4.18).

Natural justice also works on the two human culprits. Lady Macbeth's case is clearer. Worrying that Macbeth's "nature" is too kind, she deliberately sets herself against it:

Come, you Spirits
That tend on mortal thoughts, unsex me here,
And fill me, from the crown to the toe, top-full
Of direst cruelty! make thick my blood,
Stop up th'access and passage to remorse;
That no compunctious visitings of Nature
Shake my fell purpose, nor keep peace between
Th'effect and it! Come to my woman's breasts,
And take my milk for gall, you murth'ring ministers,
Wherever in your sightless substances
You wait on Nature's mischief! Come, thick Night,
And pall thee in the dunnest smoke of Hell,
That my keen knife see not the wound it makes,

Nor Heaven peep through the blanket of the dark,
To cry, "Hold, hold!"
(1.5.40–54)

In this incantatory passage, Lady Macbeth uses the imperative "Come . . . Come . . . Come" three times to invite evil into her body. With each repetition, her unthinkable thought of regicide gains force and specificity. After the first "Come," her references are "equivocal" (to use a word famously associated with this play). The "spirits that tend on *mortal* thoughts" could be "spirits that tend on *murderous* thoughts," or "spirits that tend on *human* thoughts." She asks these spirits to prevent any "natural" interruption between intent and act, but leaves the deed without a name. After the second "Come," the spirits are now "murth'ring ministers," an appellation that identifies the contemplated act. With the final "Come," she imagines the act itself—the keen knife in the dark that "see[s] not the wound it makes." Across these lines, an inchoate wish congeals into a specific intent to kill.

Modern feminism protects us to some extent from the horror an early modern audience would have felt in hearing this speech. The request for androgyny would have been seen as blasphemy against God and nature. When Banquo first meets the witches on the heath, he observes their "unsexed" quality: "you should be women, / And yet your beards forbid me to interpret / That you are so" (1.3.45–47). In asking to be unsexed, Lady Macbeth is asking to be made into the fourth witch, as Macbeth may make himself into the mysterious "third murderer."

Initially, Lady Macbeth's strategy appears successful. She convinces her husband to overcome his compunctions by showing how she has overcome her feminine nature:

I have given suck, and know
How tender 'tis to love the babe that milks me:
I would, while it was smiling in my face,
Have pluck'd my nipple from his boneless gums,
And dash'd the brains out, had I so sworn
As you have done to this.

(1.7.54–59)

Lady Macbeth inspires horror not because she lacks feelings "proper" to her sex—she knows "[h]ow tender 'tis to love the babe that milks me"—but because she can fully experience those feelings and cast them aside.

Lady Macbeth's "unnatural" repudiation of her femininity gradually destroys her. This couple's morale is on a pulley system—as Macbeth's confidence rises, Lady Macbeth's falls. One crisp instance relates to Duncan's blood. Horrified by his bloodstained hands after the murder, Macbeth asks: "Will all great Neptune's ocean wash this blood / Clean from my hand? No, this my hand will rather / The multitudinous seas incarnadine / Making the green one red" (2.2.59–62). The ocean will not cleanse the hand; rather, the hand will pollute the ocean. Lady Macbeth scoffs that "[a] little water clears us of this deed" (2.2.66). But in act 5, while Macbeth girds for war, Lady Macbeth echoes her husband, lamenting that "all the perfumes of Arabia will not sweeten this little hand" (5.1.47–48).

When Macbeth hears of his wife's madness, he asks the doctor: "Canst thou not minister to a mind diseas'd?" (5.3.40). His plea for psychoanalysis or psychiatry comes centuries too soon: the doctor remonstrates that "the patient / Must minister to himself" (5.3.45–46). Yet even the father of psychoanalysis would later confess to being stymied by Lady Macbeth's case. In an essay on "those wrecked by success," Freud begins by observing that the thesis of psychoanalytic work is "that people fall ill of a neurosis as a result of *frustration*." Freud then takes up the "more surprising" idea "that people fall ill precisely when a deeply-rooted and long-cherished wish has come to fulfillment." Taking Lady Macbeth to be such a character, he purports to be confounded by her case. Yet he offers a diagnosis in keeping with Jacobean conceptions of women's nature:

> It would be a perfect example of poetic justice in the manner of the talion if the childlessness of Macbeth and the barrenness of his Lady were the punishment for their crimes against the sanctity of generation. . . . I believe Lady Macbeth's illness, the transformation of her callousness into penitence, could be explained directly as a reaction to her childlessness, by which she is convinced of her impotence against the decrees of nature, and at the same time reminded that it is through her own fault if her crime has been robbed of the better part of its fruits.

In the world of the play, Lady Macbeth's sterility must be an imagined by-product of the murder, as only a week passes between her crime and her contrition. (In the source materials, the timing is less compressed.) The logic still holds. No sooner does Lady Macbeth acquire the crown than she wishes to pass it to her posterity. Because she has, imaginatively, made herself incapable of procreation by unsexing herself, this wish is frustrated. I am surprised that Freud seems to think her case an exceptional one, because under his own hypothesis, Lady Macbeth represents the *ordinary* case undone by frustration. She is eventually overwhelmed by arguments she has temporarily overcome.

Nature also overtakes Macbeth. Unlike his wife, Macbeth is

apparently undone by external forces: Duncan's son Malcolm and his English supporters. Yet Macbeth's foes have an ally in Macbeth himself. Long before forces muster against him, Macbeth finds himself so unable to sleep, so racked by his conscience, that he begins to envy his victim. He can be said to be undone in much the way Lady Macbeth is.

Macbeth gets his "natural" comeuppance through his imagination. As Harold Bloom has pointed out, Macbeth's character note is the power of his imagination. It is not just that he can imagine himself king (a trivial extension for anyone remotely in line for the throne), but that he has concrete visions. Directly before he murders Duncan, Macbeth is led to the act not by Lady Macbeth, but by an imagined dagger:

> Is this a dagger, which I see before me,
> The handle toward my hand? Come, let me clutch
>   thee:—
> I have thee not, and yet I see thee still.
> Art thou not, fatal vision, sensible
> To feeling, as to sight? or art thou but
> A dagger of the mind, a false creation,
> Proceeding from the heat-oppressed brain?
> I see thee yet, in form as palpable
> As this which now I draw.
> Thou marshall'st me the way that I was going;
> And such an instrument I was to use.—
> Mine eyes are made the fools o'th'other senses,
> Or else worth all the rest: I see thee still;
> And on thy blade, and dudgeon, gouts of blood,
> Which was not so before.—There's no such thing.
> It is the bloody business which informs

Thus to mine eyes.—Now o'er the one half-world
Nature seems dead. . . .
(2.1.33–50)

We are privy to an internal transformation here, played out again over a triple repetition: "I see . . . I see . . . I see." After the first "I see," the phantom dagger is merely described; after the second, Macbeth confesses that it leads him where he wishes to go; after the third, he imagines that wish fulfilled by the "gouts of blood" staining its blade and hilt.

In a world governed by natural justice, those who live by the dagger of the imagination die by it. Macbeth murders Duncan out of ambition, but the subsequent murders he commits (or commands others to commit) are motivated by a wish for security. The new King Macbeth cannot stop imagining threats to his crown. This again is an ordinary exercise of the imagination, to which the "reasonable regicide" would be susceptible. But after he has Banquo killed, Macbeth has a vision as idiosyncratic as the dagger—Banquo's ghost. Unlike the witches, this ghost appears only to Macbeth. Macbeth's response would be comically querulous were it not desperate with distress:

Blood hath been shed ere now, i'th'olden time,
Ere humane statute purg'd the gentle weal;
Ay, and since too, murthers have been perform'd
Too terrible for the ear: the time has been,
That, when the brains were out, the man would die,
And there an end; but now, they rise again,
With twenty mortal murthers on their crowns,
And push us from our stools. This is more strange
Than such a murther is.
(3.4.74–82)

Macbeth's complaint is that people have committed murders since time immemorial without being visited by ghosts. Human law—the "humane statute" against murder—makes a cameo here only to be characterized as irrelevant. Macbeth is saying that both before and after this law, murders were committed without the victims coming back to haunt their murderers. His plaint resonates with present-day bars on "cruel and unusual" punishment, for it maintains that this form of punishment—by ghost—is more unusual than the murder itself: "This is more strange / Than such a murther is." What he misses is that punishment by ghost is the punishment tailored to his own "nature."

Shakespeare's contemporaries would have been intimately familiar with the concept of a self-correcting universe. As literary scholar Jeff Dolven has demonstrated, the "emblem books" of the Elizabethan era showed crimes breeding punishments without human intervention. One scene shows a burglar being strangled by the sack of loot he has tied around his neck; another depicts a murderer assailed by his shadow as he raises his sword. *Macbeth* is in essence an extended dramatic version of the emblem of the murderer accosted by his shadow. Like the emblem books, the play conveys a profoundly comforting message.

UNFORTUNATELY, BECAUSE THE message is false, so is its comfort. Real life does not work like this, as can be seen in the case of *Macbeth* itself. Like the *Henriad*, *Macbeth* draws on the 1587 edition of Holinshed's *Chronicles*. But Duncan, Macbeth, and Banquo are more complex characters in Holinshed than in Shakespeare. Shakespeare had to alter his sources significantly to have his play convey its message of natural justice.

In Holinshed, Duncan is a much less sympathetic king, described as younger and, like Duke Vincentio in *Measure for Measure,* overly lenient. Some vestiges of this can be seen in Shakespeare's play—Macbeth is originally responsible, after all, for putting down a *civil* rebellion by Macdonwald. But any such traces are effaced by Macbeth's encomium to Duncan:

> this Duncan
> Hath borne his faculties so meek, hath been
> So clear in his great office, that his virtues
> Will plead like angels, trumpet-tongu'd, against
> The deep damnation of his taking-off. . . .
> (1.7.16–20)

Shakespeare reverses the spin of Duncan's "meekness." By making the soft young king into a holy older one, Shakespeare heightens Macbeth's guilt.

If Duncan is less sympathetic in Holinshed, Macbeth is more so. In the *Chronicles,* Macbeth has a legitimate grievance against Duncan. Under the applicable rules of succession, Macbeth has a viable claim to succeed Duncan until one of Duncan's sons reaches majority. By prematurely naming his minor son Malcolm the heir apparent, Duncan flouts those rules. For this reason, Holinshed describes Macbeth's bid for the throne as a war between two clans, rather than a naked usurpation. Moreover, after gaining the throne, Holinshed's Macbeth is a good ruler for ten years. Only after that decade produces no heir does he begin to fear the prophecy regarding Banquo's progeny.

As for Banquo, Holinshed describes the thane as an *accomplice* of Macbeth. As the *Chronicles* note: "At length therefore, communicating his purposed intent with his trustie friends, amongst whome Banquo was the chiefest, upon confidence of their promised aid, he slue the

King." In Shakespeare's version, Banquo staunchly refuses Macbeth's louche conspiratorial offer to participate in the crime.

Some of Shakespeare's changes are more immediately understandable than others. Because Banquo was (according to legend) the ancestor of King James I, Shakespeare had to absolve him of complicity. It is generally bad form to depict the ancestor of your patron as the accomplice to murder. But the alterations to Holinshed's nuanced portrayals of Duncan and Macbeth still require explanation. E. M. Forster draws a distinction between "flat" and "round" characters. In other plays, Shakespeare generally takes "flat" characters in his source materials and makes them "rounder." Here he seems to have done the opposite, making Duncan and Macbeth embodiments of good and evil. But why?

Stephen Greenblatt's wonderful answer reads the play as a response to the Gunpowder Plot. As early as 1603, the English Catholic nobleman Robert Catesby had hatched a plot to assassinate King James I. Catesby belonged to a radical Catholic conspiracy, which believed that James had broken his promise to extend more religious toleration to Catholics. Beginning in 1604, the conspirators set a plan into motion to destroy not just James, but his entire Parliament. They rented a house that abutted the Parliament building to gain access to its cellar. As historian Alan Stewart observes, this was their own attempt at "poetic justice." King James would later recount that Parliament was where "the cruel laws (as they say) were made against their religion" so they deemed it appropriate that "both place and person should all be destroyed and blown up at once." The plot was discovered at the last moment—on the evening before the opening of Parliament, officials found the Catholic plotter Guy Fawkes in the basement of Parliament with thirty-six barrels of gunpowder. The rescue was seen as providential, but the magnitude of the threat still beggared the imagination. Had it been successful, the entire country could have been plunged into anarchy.

Greenblatt understands *Macbeth* as an attempt to quiet the anxieties created by the Plot:

> In *Macbeth*, Shakespeare seems to have set out to write a play that would function as a collective ritual of reassurance. Everyone had been deeply shaken: the whole of the ruling elite, along with the king and his family, could have been blown to bits, the kingdom ripped apart and plunged into the chaos of internecine religious warfare. The staging of the events of eleventh-century Scotland— the treacherous murder of the king, the collapse of order and decency, the long struggle to wrest the realm from the bloody hands of traitors—allowed its seventeenth-century audience to face a symbolic version of this disaster and to witness the triumphant restoration of order.

While oblique, the link between *Macbeth* and the Gunpowder Plot is unmistakable. In act 2, the Porter pretends to be the gatekeeper of hell. In this capacity, he welcomes the "equivocator, that could swear in both the scales against either scale; who committed treason enough for God's sake, yet could not equivocate to heaven" (2.3.9– 11). Jacobean audiences would have understood "the equivocator" to be an allusion to Father Henry Garnet, a Jesuit who was privy to the Gunpowder Plot as a confessor. Although he did not participate in the plot, he was charged for his failure to reveal it. Garnet defended his decision according to the doctrine of mental reservation, which allowed the clergy to refrain from revealing matters learned during confession. The doctrine was also known as the doctrine of equivocation. The defense was rejected and Garnet was executed—he could not "equivocate his way to heaven."

Macbeth, then, is propaganda. It flatters James in several ways—by comforting the king about his ancestry, by indulging his interest in witchcraft, and, most of all, by reassuring him and his court that regicides would come to no good end. As Huggett writes, "There is evidence that Shakespeare went out of his way to please his royal patron to an extent he had never done before or was to do again."

The play's transcendence of its context makes it dangerous. I know of no other work of propaganda that has so successfully kicked over the traces of the political events that called it into being. Few read *Uncle Tom's Cabin* without thinking of the Civil War. But many read *Macbeth* without thinking of the Gunpowder Plot. If all readers knew that *Macbeth* was written against the background of the Gunpowder Plot, it would be more clear that Shakespeare was not trying to assert that good was always rewarded and evil was always punished. Shorn of its context, however, *Macbeth* can be read as a morality tale.

One might think that in our enlightened age, *Macbeth's* message of natural justice would not reach a broad audience. Yet if anything, the reverse seems true. Of all Shakespeare's plays, only *Macbeth* is believed to be cursed. The curse serves as a bridge across which the idea of natural justice travels from the play world to the real one.

ACCORDING TO COMMON account, the curse arises from the play's use of actual incantations. As Huggett (rather fancifully) puts it:

> Shakespeare grew up in a countryside where the people
> lived and practiced, where they believed in witches and
> their powers, where they were ducked in ponds, tortured,
> humiliated, and killed in dreadful, unspeakable ways. . . .
> He would have heard of their spells and incantations,

these being the living tradition of country life in which he grew up. In his natural and praiseworthy desire for authenticity, he went a little too far. . . . [The "Double, double toil and trouble" spell of act 3] is taken from an actual black-magic incantation which he would certainly have known about during those years in which he lived in Stratford.

Under this theory, whenever one invokes the play, one invokes an actual witches' spell. In the play, Banquo's ghost appears only when Macbeth mentions his name in the banquet scene (along the disingenuous lines of "I wish Banquo were here"). In the real world, the same logic also allegedly obtains—when one mentions "Macbeth," Macbeth comes.

Closer scrutiny of the curse reveals a cauldron of cognitive biases. The biggest problem with many curse stories is that they ignore alternative explanations. My favorite instance involves Charlton Heston. While performing the play in Bermuda in an open-air theater in 1953, Heston rode in on a horse for the first scene with Banquo, dismounted, and then ran off the stage groaning. Someone had dipped Heston's tights in kerosene, which had severely burned his thighs and groin when he rubbed against the horse. I suppose it is possible this "someone" was a demonic spirit. It seems more plausible that a mere mortal may have had it in for Heston.

I also have no need of the supernatural to explain why Diana Wynyard fell fifteen feet off a stage while playing Lady Macbeth's sleepwalking scene in a 1948 Stratford production. During dress rehearsals, she had rehearsed the scene with her eyes open. She decided on opening night that sleepwalkers do *not* walk with their eyes open. (Incidentally, many do.) She thought she knew the layout of the stage well enough to perform the scene with her eyes closed. She was wrong.

Other gossamer evidence for the curse dates back to 1744. In that year, David Garrick tried to improve on the play by adding a death scene for Lady Macbeth. According to Huggett, Garrick added "some of the most ludicrously inept blank verse in the history of the theater":

> Tis done! The scene of my life will quickly close!
> Ambitions, vain delusive dreams are fled
> And now I wake in darkness and guilt.
> I cannot bear it, let me shake it off.
> It will not be, my soul is clogged with blood.
> I cannot rise! I dare not ask for mercy.
> It is too late; hell drags me down. I sink.
> I sink. I sink, my soul is fled for ever. Oh! Oh!

This is, admittedly, bad. But is it bad enough to suggest a curse? If I were a minion of hell, I hope I could do more damage than this.

A separate problem with the "curse" stories is that they focus only on negative outcomes. As Marjorie Garber observes:

> One classic example of the "curse" at work involves the director Orson Welles. Welles actually staged two famous productions of *Macbeth*. The first, in 1936, became known as the "Voodoo Macbeth." It was performed at the Lafayette Theater in Harlem, and set in Haiti. Welles's *Macbeth* production was part of the Depression's Federal Theater Project, had an all-black cast of more than one hundred, and was an enormous success. When at the end of the play Hecate says, "the charm's wound up," everybody cheered. Welles was barely twenty-one—and the performance made him famous. In 1948, though, Orson

Welles decided to make a film of *Macbeth*. His objective was to make the performance as "authentic" as possible— and so he insisted that his characters speak in a real Scots burr. The film was produced inexpensively and was shot in twenty-three days. The verbal sound track was prerecorded, Scots burr and all. The problem was, once the film had been made, audiences couldn't understand a word of it. So they reissued Welles's *Macbeth* in 1950, redubbing all the actors' lines in BBC accents. A classic "curse" story.

While Garber is not defending the validity of the "curse," which she puts in scare quotes, she suggests that this story could be interpreted to support the curse's existence. But the evidence is at best "equivocal." On the first go-round, *Macbeth* put Welles on the map; on the second, it presented a serious but surmountable inconvenience. On net, the play seems to have been a lucky one for him.

A similar point can be made about Laurence Olivier's experience with *Macbeth*. When he played the title role in 1937, Olivier narrowly escaped death when a heavy weight fell from the flies onto the chair where he had been sitting. Had this been a production of a "lucky" play like *Merchant,* commentators would probably have described the escape as providential.

Still another problem with the "curse" stories is a confusion about the direction of causation. Michael Knox Beran describes how Abraham Lincoln read from *Macbeth* while steaming down the Potomac toward Washington, D.C., in April 1865. His traveling companions observed that he dwelt on a particular passage:

> Duncan is in his grave;
> After life's fitful fever he sleeps well;
> Treason has done his worst: nor steel, nor poison,

Malice domestic, foreign levy, nothing
Can touch him further!
(3.2.22–26)

Days later, Lincoln was dead. Curse proponents believe his invoca-
tion of *Macbeth* somehow led to the assassination. But it seems much
more logical to suppose that the fear of assassination directed the
president's attention to this play. Beran notes that Lincoln had already reported a nightmare in which he followed a crowd of people to
the East Room of the White House, only to find his dead body laid
out in state. A president in this frame of mind might understandably
dwell on the peaceful sleep of the murdered sovereign described in
his favorite Shakespeare play.

Several rational explanations have been proposed to explain away
the "curse." Some hypothesize that failing playhouses favored *Macbeth* because it is such a popular play. The weakness of those houses
caused the staging of the play, rather than vice versa. Others have
flatly disagreed that the production history of *Macbeth* contains more
mishaps than other plays with the same amount of onstage action,
such as dueling and special effects. Still others argue that a few negative experiences led the play to be branded as cursed and then the
bandwagon effect did the rest. Once the curse was established, the
person contemplating whether to dip Heston's tights in kerosene
might decide to add another page to the story. As Macbeth puts it:
"Things bad begun make strong themselves by ill" (3.2.55).

I think an additional rational explanation for the "curse" lies in
our deep-seated desire to believe in natural justice. This may seem
counterintuitive, as a curse implies supernatural forces beyond
human agency. Yet the curse does afford us agency. One can avoid
punishment by saying "the Scottish play" instead of "*Macbeth,*" or by
saying "Mr. and Mrs. M." rather than "the Macbeths." In the play,

people who do bad things are inexorably punished. The curse extends that axiom into the real world.

I do not wish to play the spoilsport. Little harm is done by a belief in the *Macbeth* curse. But great harm is done by subscribing to the belief in the natural justice that undergirds both the play and the curse. Natural justice is a form of justice that occurs only in art. When we blur the line between art and life, the consequences for justice can be disastrous.

SOMETIMES HUMAN BEINGS easily distinguish fiction from fact. At other times, we do not. It is unclear what separates these circumstances. I wish to contrast the witches' prophecies with the curse in this regard. I think most audiences watching *Macbeth* would understand that the prophecies of the witches will be fulfilled, but that the inexorability of those prophecies is a special pleasure of the stage that cannot be carried home. Not so with the curse.

Prophecies in literature are almost always fulfilled, though usually in unexpected ways. If an oracle says Oedipus will kill his father and marry his mother, we know Laius's resistance is futile. I know of only one "literary" prophecy that is arguably not fulfilled: God's promise to Jonah that he will destroy Nineveh. The vehemence with which interpreters argue that the prophecy *was* fulfilled (because Nineveh was destroyed and re-created when its people repented) serves only to underscore that in literature, we need prophecies to come true.

Shakespeare's prophecies are no exception to this general rule. To the contrary, the oracle in *The Winter's Tale* supplies the most abrupt fulfillment of a prophecy with which I am familiar. In that play King Leontes irrationally decides that his wife has committed adultery with his best friend, Polixenes. The court sends to the oracle for an answer, who unambiguously exonerates Hermione and threatens that Leontes' only son will die if the king does not come to his senses. When Leontes scoffs, "There is no truth at all i' th' Oracle" (Winter's Tale, 3.2.140), news comes one line later that his son has died. The closest contender for this kind of immediate corroboration lies in *Macbeth*, where the witches hail Macbeth as the "Thane of Cawdor" (*Macbeth*, 1.3.49) directly before he is greeted as such by Duncan's messengers.

It is more usual for prophecies to be fulfilled gradually, with the person who is trying to evade the inevitable slowly realizing the futility of his or her efforts. Macbeth contains this pattern as well. The witches guarantee that Macbeth will not be deposed unless two seemingly impossible conditions are met. First, "none of woman born / Shall harm Macbeth" (4.1.80–81); second, he will not be defeated "until Great Birnam wood to high Dunsinane hill / Shall come against him" (4.1.93–94). Macbeth finds deep solace in the witches' promises. Part of that comfort must be that the conditions of his downfall are so unnatural that they return him to the side of nature.

But audiences know those conditions will, somehow, be met. Macbeth understands the prophecy to say "none of *woman* born" shall harm Macbeth. To emphasize the last word—"none of woman *born*"—is to get a sharper picture of the threat, which is that "Macduff was from his mother's womb / Untimely ripp'd" (5.8.15–16). In other words, Macduff was not born "naturally," but through a cesarean section. Once we put the emphasis on "born," we can return some of the stress to "woman." In Shakespeare's time, midwives could oversee natural births. But only surgeons, who were at that time all men, could perform cesarean sections. Because Macduff was not of "woman *born*" he was also (with respect to the person superintending the birth) not of "*woman* born."

A similar point can be made about the final prophecy, which

states that Macbeth is safe until "Birnam wood" comes to Dunsinane hill. Macbeth interprets "wood" to mean "forest." But the apparition says "wood," meaning a stick from the forest will do. The apparition who speaks these lines is a "child crowned, with a tree in his hand" and the closest thing we have seen to a child crowned in this play is Malcolm, named Prince of Cumberland in act 1. When he masses troops outside the castle, Malcolm tells the soldiers marching from Birnam wood to Dunsinane to carry branches before them to hide their numbers. In the end, nature, in the form of a marching forest, moves against Macbeth.

The literary interest in prophecies is that they are always fulfilled, though in unexpected ways. One of the great things about literary works is that prophecies can come true in them. Prophecies in literature are *promises* to the audience. Prophecies in life are not.

IN AN IMPORTANT 1996 essay, criminal defense lawyer and law professor Alan Dershowitz reminds us that "life is not a dramatic narrative." He begins by observing how Anton Chekhov once told a writer that "If in the first chapter you say that a gun hung on the wall, in the second or third chapter it must without fail be discharged." Literary narratives, Dershowitz argues, are governed by the premise that we live in a purposive universe. In that universe, "chest pains are followed by heart attacks, coughs by consumption, life insurance policies by murders, telephone rings by dramatic messages." But in our actual lives, "most chest pains are indigestion, coughs are colds, insurance policies are followed by years of premium payments, and telephone calls are from marketing services."

Dershowitz argues that the gap "between teleological rules of drama and interpretation, on the one hand, and the mostly random rules of real life, on the other, has profoundly important implications for our legal system." As a criminal defense lawyer, Dershowitz is particularly concerned with how juries reflexively assume that if a gun was on the wall, it must have been discharged. But his more general point is that we need to free ourselves from the assumption that we live in a universe where everything has a meaning. If we do not, we become agents of injustice rather than justice.

This is the danger of the natural justice fallacy. In works of art like *Macbeth,* justice is an expression of the natural order of the universe. But to import that assumption into our daily lives is to invite complacency. If we are sure that justice will be done, we are much less likely to take action.

My favorite warning, as a civil rights lawyer, against the "natural justice" fallacy comes from our sitting president. In honoring the anniversary of Martin Luther King Jr.'s death, President Obama quoted one of Dr. King's most famous lines:

> When our days become dreary with low hovering clouds of despair, and when our nights become darker than a thousand midnights, let us remember that there is a creative force in this universe, working to pull down the gigantic mountains of evil, a power that is able to make a way out of no way and transform dark yesterdays into bright tomorrows. Let us realize the arc of the moral universe is long but it bends toward justice.

This quotation accords with Malcolm's claim in *Macbeth* that "The night is long that never finds the day" (4.3.240). The imagery is natural—the "mountains of evil" are ground down by erosion, as the "dark yesterdays" are transformed into "bright tomorrows." No direct claim about natural justice is made, but the imagery suggests that it obtains.

President Obama's gloss was that the moral arc of the universe should not be understood to be governed by the iron laws of physics. As he put it:

> Dr. King once said that the arc of the moral universe is long but it bends towards justice. It bends towards justice, but here is the thing: it does not bend on its own. It bends because each of us in our own ways put our hand on that arc and we bend it in the direction of justice.

President Obama was warning the polity against the fallacy of natural justice, urging us that the universe would not correct itself.

In *Macbeth,* the character of Hecate is seen as an "unfortunate" and possibly inauthentic addition to the play. But in a play rife with fallacy, she sounds a true note. She instructs her witches to draw on human quiescence, our lazy tendency to believe that the universe will bend toward justice without our help. We need to be galvanized by her gloat: "And you all know, security / Is mortals' chiefest enemy" (3.5.32–33).

CHAPTER SEVEN

THE INTELLECTUAL

Hamlet

INTELLECTUALS MAY REJOICE THAT THE MOST CANONICAL text of Western imaginative literature figures one of our tribe as its protagonist. Prince Hamlet is undeniably an intellectual, a student at the University of Wittenberg whose "inky cloak" (1.2.77) swaddles him not just in melancholy but in "[w]ords, words, words" (2.2.189). At the same time, we may be justifiably concerned that many believe Hamlet's intellectualism hobbles him from doing justice.

The central question of *Hamlet* is why the prince takes so long to avenge his father's murder. Psychoanalysts, literary critics, and philosophers have all offered their answers, many of which reflect their general explanations for procrastination. Following suit as a legal scholar, I contend that Hamlet's delay arises from an intellectual commitment to perfect justice. Faced with a terrible injustice, he is forced to correct it himself because, as in *Titus Andronicus*, his adversary controls the state. Hamlet certainly has the ingenuity to correct that injustice immediately. However, he bides his time because he wishes to secure not only justice but poetic justice. With respect to Claudius, he arguably attains that perfect justice. But he inflicts so much collateral damage in the process that his actions are ultimately unjustifiable.

Hamlet shows why those committed to social justice often feel ambivalence toward intellectuals. On the one hand, the critical distance that intellectuals have from the world allows us to imagine idealized forms of justice. On the other hand, when we cling too tightly to those ideals, we dissociate from reality. Hamlet adds another layer to the lesson of *Macbeth*. It is not just that poetic justice does not naturally come into being. It is also that, when human beings are perfectionists about justice, we risk doing immense harm.

HAMLET **BUILDS ON** a revenge tragedy composed by the Dane Saxo Grammaticus in the thirteenth century, reworked by the French author François de Belleforest in 1570, and reproduced yet again for the English stage by an unknown author (possibly Shakespeare) in the lost *Ur-Hamlet* of the 1590s. Shakespeare's rendition begins with Prince Hamlet of Denmark mourning the loss of his illustrious father, also named Hamlet. King Hamlet allegedly died after being stung by a serpent while sleeping in his garden. To make matters worse, Prince Hamlet's uncle, Claudius, married Queen Gertrude less than two months after Hamlet Sr.'s death. In doing so, Claudius took the crown that should have descended to Hamlet. Early in the play, a ghost resembling Hamlet's father appears to Hamlet and his friend Horatio. Declaring that Claudius has murdered him, the ghost enjoins Prince Hamlet to avenge his death.

While Hamlet initially agrees to do so, he comes to doubt whether the ghost is truly his father's spirit, or a devil sent to tempt him. He decides to stage a play reenacting the murder (the famous play-within-the-play titled *The Mousetrap*) to gauge Claudius's response. When Claudius reacts with consternation, Hamlet is satisfied of his guilt. Hamlet's next opportunity for revenge, however, occurs when Claudius is praying alone in his chapel. Hamlet does not kill Claudius because he believes that if Claudius is killed while praying for forgiveness, his soul will mount directly to heaven. During a later conversation with his mother, Hamlet becomes aware that someone is eavesdropping on them behind an arras, or tapestry. The prince draws his sword and kills the counselor Polonius in the belief he is the king.

Realizing the threat Hamlet poses to him, Claudius sends him to England in the custody of two of the prince's childhood companions, Rosencrantz and Guildenstern, with a letter secretly ordering his death. Hamlet rewrites the letter to require the execution of his two erstwhile friends. He then returns to Denmark, where Ophelia, who is Polonius's daughter and Hamlet's former lover, has gone mad with grief and committed suicide. Ophelia's brother Laertes begins an uprising against Claudius, but Claudius successfully redirects Laertes' fury toward Hamlet. The youth challenges Hamlet to a fencing match. Though purportedly just an athletic contest, the duel has been arranged by Claudius and Laertes with murderous intent. Claudius has poisoned Hamlet's drink, and Laertes has envenomed the tip of his foil.

During the fencing match, Gertrude dies after she drinks from the cup meant for her son. Laertes and Hamlet mortally wound each other with the poisoned rapier, which changes hands during the match. On the brink of death, Hamlet finally kills Claudius. Word arrives from England that Rosencrantz and Guildenstern have been executed according to Hamlet's plan. Horatio wishes to follow the dying Hamlet by committing suicide, but Hamlet asks him instead to live and tell his story. Fortinbras, the prince of Norway, takes over the kingdom, restoring order at the cost of Denmark's independence.

The core question of the play is why Hamlet delays his revenge. As literary critic A. C. Bradley states, "But why in the world did not Hamlet obey the ghost at once, and so save seven of those eight lives?" (The seven lives, in order of demise, belong to Polonius, Ophelia, Rosencrantz, Guildenstern, Gertrude, Laertes, and Hamlet.) The psychoanalyst Ernest Jones called the mystery of Hamlet's delay "the Sphinx of modern Literature."

Many have tried to solve the riddle. Freud believes Hamlet's delay derives from an Oedipus complex: "Hamlet is able to do anything—except take vengeance on the man who did away with his father and took that father's place with his mother, the man who shows him the repressed wishes of his own childhood realized." Goethe deems Hamlet too delicate: "a lovely, pure and most moral nature, without the strength of nerve which forms a hero, sinks beneath a burden which it cannot bear and must not cast away." Nietzsche takes him for a nihilist: "In this sense the Dionysian man may be said to resemble Hamlet: both have for once seen into the true nature of things,—they have *perceived,* but they are loath to act; for their action cannot change the eternal nature of things."

As Marjorie Garber observes, critics have a powerful identification with Hamlet. (I assume this is because critics are themselves intellectuals.) Because we see ourselves in him, we see his reasons for delay as our own: Freud sees Oedipus, Goethe sees his own sorrowful

Werther, and Nietzsche sees his Dionysian man. I see no reason to depart from these great predecessors in proposing an explanation inflected by my own professional background. So I contend that Hamlet's delay can best be explained by his pursuit of perfect justice. I do not think Hamlet delays because he is sexually conflicted, weak, or nihilistic. I think he defers his revenge because he wants it to be perfect. This explanation justifies his delays without justifying the ends they serve.

MY INITIAL POINT is that there is not one delay, but two. They occur during what a modern trial lawyer might call the "guilt" and "sentencing" phases of the play's action. First, Hamlet delays because he is uncertain of Claudius's guilt. This is a period of approximately two months between the ghost's appearance and the performance of the play-within-the-play. Only after *The Mousetrap* does Hamlet become convinced of Claudius's guilt. The second delay is more brief and more consequential. It is the delay in which Hamlet forgoes the chance to kill Claudius while Claudius is praying in the chapel. Both delays can be explained by Hamlet's desire for perfect justice.

Everything begins with the ghost. Stephen Greenblatt notes, "[t]he ghost in *Hamlet* is like none other—not only in Shakespeare but in any literary or historical text. . . . It does not have very many lines— it appears in three scenes and speaks only in two—but it is amazingly disturbing and vivid." These qualities are in sharp evidence during the ghost's first speech to Hamlet:

> I am thy father's spirit,
> Doomed for a certain term to walk the night
> And for the day confined to fast in fires
> Till the foul crimes done in my days of nature

Are burnt and purged away. But that I am forbid
To tell the secrets of my prison-house
I could a tale unfold whose lightest word
Would harrow up thy soul, freeze thy young blood,
Make thy two eyes like stars start from their spheres,
Thy knotted and combined locks to part
And each particular hair to stand on end
Like quills upon the fearful porpentine—
But this eternal blazon must not be
To ears of flesh and blood.
(1.5.9–22)

The ghost is in purgatory, the place where his "foul crimes" are "purged away" so he can enter heaven. The spirit says his torments are horrible, and we believe him in part because he describes them as indescribable.

The ghost is not just the object of punishment, but its agent. The ghost's imperative is often summarized as follows: "If thou didst ever thy dear father love . . . Revenge his foul and most unnatural murder!" (1.5.23, 25). Yet the ghost's commandment is a good deal more specific. The ghost gives a meticulous description of both the crime and the proposed punishment:

Sleeping within my orchard—
My custom always of the afternoon—
Upon my secure hour thy uncle stole
With juice of cursed hebona in a vial
And in the porches of my ears did pour
The leperous distilment whose effect
Holds such an enmity with blood of man
That swift as quicksilver it courses through

The natural gates and alleys of the body
And with a sudden vigour it doth possess
And curd like eager droppings into milk
The thin and wholesome blood. So did it mine
And a most instant tetter barked about
Most lazar-like with vile and loathsome crust
All my smooth body.
Thus was I sleeping by a brother's hand
Of life, of crown, of queen at once dispatched,
Cut off even in the blossoms of my sin,
Unhouseled, disappointed, unaneled,
No reckoning made but sent to my account
With all my imperfections on my head.
O horrible, O horrible, most horrible!
If thou hast nature in thee bear it not,
Let not the royal bed of Denmark be
A couch for luxury and damned incest.
But howsomever thou pursues this act
Taint not thy mind nor let thy soul contrive
Against thy mother aught; leave her to heaven
And to those thorns that in her bosom lodge
To prick and sting her. Fare thee well at once:
The glow-worm shows the matin to be near
And 'gins to pale his uneffectual fire.
Adieu, adieu, adieu, remember me.
(1.5.59–91)

On this account, Claudius poured poison into Hamlet Sr.'s ears, curdling his blood. The ghost's tale, poured into our ears, is likewise bloodcurdling. The horror begins with the description of the poison's physical effect: how "swift as quicksilver" the "leperous distilment" moved through "[t]he natural gates and alleys of the body." The conflation of the sovereign body and the body politic, made frequently in Shakespeare, arises here in the comparison of valves and veins with "gates and alleys." The sovereign has been poisoned—we now know why "[s]omething is rotten in the state of Denmark" (1.4.90). Yet the physiological effects of the murder are as nothing compared to the religious ones. The ghost decries how he was "[c]ut off even in the blossoms of my sin, / Unhouseled, disappointed, unaneled." Deprived of last rites, he is sent to final judgment "[w]ith all [his] imperfections on [his] head." The descriptions of physical and religious corruption merge. The body morphs into a disgusting object, as if the king's sins were surfacing—"a most instant tetter barked about / Most lazar-like with vile and loathsome crust / All my smooth body."

Three instructions follow. First, "Let not the royal bed of Denmark be / A couch for luxury and damned incest." Prince Hamlet must kill Claudius. Second, "howsomever [he] pursues this act," Hamlet must not "contrive / Against [his] mother." Finally, he must remember his father: "Adieu, adieu, adieu, remember me." Hamlet immediately agrees to the ghost's commands—he asks to be emptied out and made into a pure instrument of revenge.

Upon cooler consideration, however, Hamlet's shock cedes to skepticism, resulting in the first delay. This skepticism is justified, especially in historical context. Ghosts were widely seen as instruments used by the devil to lure the virtuous to perdition. Sir Thomas Browne wrote in *Religio Medici* (1643) that those "apparitions and ghosts of departed persons are not the wandering souls of men, but the unquiet walks of Devils, prompting and suggesting us unto mischief, blood and villainy." More specifically, as students from Wittenberg, known in Shakespeare's time as Martin Luther's bastion of Protestantism, both Horatio and Hamlet would presumably have doubts about a ghost returning from Catholic purgatory. Horatio warns Hamlet that the ghost may intend to "draw [him] into madness" (1.4.74). Even in his preliminary agreement to the ghost's commands, Hamlet ponders where to place him: "O all you host of heaven . . . And shall I couple hell?" (1.5.92–93). On reflection, he begins to take the latter possibility seriously: "The spirit that I have seen / May be a de'il, and the de'il hath power / T'assume a pleasing shape" (2.2.533–35).

Hamlet's doubts about the ghost may be heightened by Claudius's outward respectability. At this point, we, like Hamlet, are not certain that Claudius has murdered Hamlet Sr. The consummate politician, Claudius has allied himself solidly with the law on as many counts as possible. Before we even meet Claudius, Horatio observes that Hamlet Sr. and Fortinbras Sr. fought over some land. When Hamlet Sr. won that duel, land belonging to Fortinbras Sr. passed to Hamlet Sr. through "a sealed compact / Well ratified by law and heraldry" (1.1.85–86). However, Fortinbras's son now seeks to reclaim that land, having "[s]harked up a list of lawless resolutes" (1.1.97) to help him. Part of the fault lies with the new Norwegian king, who has exercised inadequate supervision over Prince Fortinbras. In Norway as in Denmark, the crown has moved from the original king to his brother, rather than to the king's son. The unnamed King of Norway is thus Claudius's foil in this play.

Claudius outshines his counterpart, making a plausible case that he is a savvy and competent monarch. He observes that Fortinbras is seeking to reclaim "lands / Lost by his father with all bands of law / To our most valiant brother. So much for him" (1.2.23–25). He dismisses the legitimacy of Fortinbras's claim with the abruptness that a lawless claim deserves. He also intuits that the bedridden King of Norway does not know of Fortinbras's plan, and sends messengers to the invalid king, telling the messengers that they have no more scope than certain "delated articles allow" (1.2.38). The sense that gradually rises from this scene is that Claudius is an effective king. Confronted with Fortinbras's attempts to challenge the law, he does not overreact. He sends messengers to alert the King of Norway that his nephew is acting outside the law, and informs the messengers that they must not do so themselves.

Of course, Hamlet has plenty to criticize about Claudius, including his "overhasty" and "incestuous" marriage to Gertrude. Yet the speed of the marriage may also be explicable in legal terms. As legal scholar J. Anthony Burton has pointed out, Gertrude had legal reasons for her "wicked speed." Under the prevailing law, a widow was given a dower, a one-third interest in the real property of her deceased husband. She would hold this share until her death, at which point it would descend to her male heir. To give her time to settle on her third, she was given a "quarantine," a forty-day period in which she could remain on her husband's estate. Applying early modern English law, Hamlet should have inherited two-thirds of his father's land when Hamlet Sr. died. But if Gertrude married during this forty-day period, she could have made a more plausible claim to keep all her lands jointly with her new husband.

The question is whether Gertrude married during the crucial forty-day period. According to Hamlet, she did. Hamlet first complains that Gertrude married when his father was "[b]ut two months dead" (1.2.138). Yet he immediately corrects himself: "nay not so much, not two" (1.2.138). He later insists three times on how less than one month has elapsed between Hamlet Sr.'s death and Gertrude's remarriage, observing that it occurred "within a month" (1.2.145), "[a] little month" (1.2.147), and, again, "[w]ithin a month" (1.2.153). If Gertrude remarried within a month, she did so within her period of quarantine.

Of course, Claudius may have used the law for the nefarious purpose of disinheriting Hamlet. But Claudius seems genuinely to love Gertrude, saying to Laertes that she is "conjunct to my life and soul" (4.7.15). Mischievous scholars like to point out that Claudius and Gertrude represent one of the few happy marriages in Shakespeare. Given that Claudius and Gertrude are in love, it is plausible they would marry. Once they decided to marry, it also made sense for them to marry speedily to quiet any uncertainty about Claudius's title to Denmark's throne and lands. The elimination of this uncertainty was not just in Claudius's interest, but in Denmark's. As is repeatedly emphasized in the play, the sovereign cannot act like a private individual. As Rosencrantz observes: "Never alone / Did the king sigh but with a general groan" (3.3.22–23).

A decent king in Claudius's position would recognize the effects of his hasty marriage on Hamlet. Claudius repeatedly does so. His first address to Hamlet is "my cousin Hamlet, and my son" (1.2.64). Soon thereafter, he makes an unambiguous public declaration of Hamlet's status as heir apparent: "let the world take note / You are the most immediate to our throne" (1.2.108–109). When Hamlet says to Rosencrantz: "Sir, I lack advancement" (3.2.331), Rosencrantz asks incredulously: "How can that be, when you have the voice of the King himself for your succession in Denmark?" (3.2.332–34).

Hamlet's other charge—that a brother who marries his dead brother's widow commits incest—is harder for Claudius to evade. In Shakespeare's time, this charge was topical. King Henry VIII had married his older brother Arthur's widow, Catherine of Aragon. Under prevailing ecclesiastical law, such marriages were broadly prohibited as incestuous. As it states in Leviticus, "Thou shalt not uncover the nakedness of thy brother's wife: it is thy brother's nakedness." And further: "if a man shall take his brother's wife, it is an unclean thing: he hath uncovered his brother's nakedness; they shall be childless." However, Deuteronomy states an exception to this rule: "If brethren dwell together, and one of them die, and have no child, the wife of the dead shall not marry without unto a stranger: her husband's brother shall go in unto her, and take her to him to wife." Because Arthur and Catherine had no children, Henry easily acquired permission from Pope Julius II to employ the Deuteronomy exception to the Leviticus rule. Henry could argue that he was not only permitted but obligated to marry his brother's widow under what the Mosaic law termed "levirate marriage."

To be sure, Claudius's case is easily distinguishable from Henry VIII's. Claudius's brother has left a son, namely Hamlet. Claudius cannot avail himself of the exception in Deuteronomy. Indeed, legal scholar Jason Rosenblatt has argued that Claudius's attempt to fob off his marriage as legitimate contributes to Hamlet's depression because it negates Hamlet's existence.

It does not follow, however, that Claudius has gone beyond the pale of legality. Hamlet insists four times in the play that the relationship between Claudius and Gertrude is "incestuous." Even in the biblical prohibitions, however, incest between individuals related directly by blood was distinguished from incest between individuals who were related only through marriage. Claudius may simply have been willing to violate this prohibition and suffer its consequences. Those consequences were either literal childlessness (if one took Deuteronomy at its word) or figurative childlessness (because the normal punishment for incest included the bastardization and disinheritance of children who were a product of it). Claudius certainly seems reconciled to childlessness, because Gertrude is probably beyond childbearing years. He also readily embraces Hamlet as his son and heir. So the charges of "incest," while technically true, may be overblown in the play.

Given Claudius's seeming adherence to the law and the ghost's dubious provenance, Hamlet has something less than perfect proof of Claudius's guilt. Hamlet is self-aware enough to know this. He worries that the devil is taking advantage of him through the ghost: "Yea, and perhaps / Out of my weakness and my melancholy, / As he is very potent with such spirits, / Abuses me to damn me!" (2.2.535–38). This skepticism is indeed characteristic of Hamlet, and of intellectuals. It is an old saw in Shakespearean criticism that if Othello and Hamlet had switched plays, neither would have been a tragedy. Hamlet, the man of thought, would have seen through Iago. Othello, the man of action, would have killed Claudius in act 1. Literary critic Maynard Mack contends, "Othello in Hamlet's position, we sometimes say, would have [had] no problem." Yet this insight is hardly an indictment of Hamlet. In his own play, Othello's temperament leads him to trust a human devil and kill an innocent.

Rather than relying on the ghost, Hamlet looks for an alternative means to determine Claudius's guilt. This takes time, but only because the means have not materialized. When traveling actors arrive at the palace, Hamlet swiftly realizes that they offer the solution:

> Hum, I have heard
> That guilty creatures sitting at a play
> Have by the very cunning of the scene
> Been struck so to the soul that presently
> They have proclaimed their malefactions.
> For murder, though it have no tongue, will speak
> With most miraculous organ. I'll have these players
> Play something like the murder of my father
> Before mine uncle. I'll observe his looks,
> I'll tent him to the quick. If 'a do blench
> I know my course.
>
> (2.2.523–33)

Hamlet's uncertainty about the ghost is reflected in his claim that murder has "no tongue." (What is the ghost if not the tongue of murder?) In constructing his alternative test of Claudius's guilt, Hamlet cures the deficiencies of the ghost's testimony. Instead of trafficking in the supernatural, the play will appeal to natural human psychology. In lieu of relying on a private exchange, the play will be staged. Hamlet seeks a de facto public confession from Claudius: "The play's the thing / Wherein I'll catch the conscience of the King" (2.2.539–40).

In Hamlet's view, *The Mousetrap* is a resounding success. Hamlet scrutinizes Claudius to see if he will "blench" (or flinch). The king does far more than cringe. After a few lines, "[t]he King rises" (3.2.258) and, in agitation, leaves the play: "Give me some light, away" (3.2.261). Hamlet is jubilant. Horatio is less certain of *The Mousetrap*'s success, perhaps because, as Judge Richard Posner observes, Hamlet has publicly announced the murderer in the play to be the nephew of the king. Claudius could therefore have been innocent, but still terrified that his "mad" nephew was going to kill him. Yet for all his alleged indecisiveness, from this point on, Hamlet never wavers with respect to Claudius's guilt. He has shifted from the guilt phase to the sentencing phase of his self-created trial. He waits now only for the right moment to execute Claudius.

THAT MOMENT SEEMS to present itself immediately. After *The Mousetrap*, Claudius goes to the chapel to pray, where Hamlet finds him alone and unarmed. Before Hamlet enters, Claudius confesses his guilt: "O, my offence is rank: it smells to heaven; / It hath the primal eldest curse upon't— / A brother's murder" (3.3.36–38). This is a crucial moment, because it is the first time that we, the audience and readers of the play, are given the "full proof" of Claudius's uncoerced confession to the murder. Hamlet has come to the right conclusion after all.

The allusion is to God's curse on Cain for murdering his brother Abel. (This reference to Genesis resonates with the Edenic image of Hamlet Sr. sleeping contentedly in his garden until stung by the "serpent.") The train of thought leads Claudius to contrast worldly and divine justice. Claudius first acknowledges that "[i]n the corrupted currents of this world / Offence's gilded hand may shove by justice, / And oft 'tis seen the wicked prize itself / Buys out the law" (3.3.57–60). He speaks from experience. By murdering Hamlet's father, Claudius took the crown. That "prize itself" immunized him from legal accountability. Later in the play, when threatened by Laertes, Claudius will brazenly assert sovereign immunity, observing that "[t]here's such divinity doth hedge a king / That treason can but peep to what it would" (4.5.123–24). However it is acquired, the crown retains its prerogatives.

Yet Claudius recognizes that in the afterlife, "[t]here is no shuffling, there the action lies / In his true nature, and we ourselves compelled / Even to the teeth and forehead of our faults / To give in evidence" (3.3.61–64). The idea that there might be a right against self-incrimination had already been introduced in Shakespeare's time, though it had not yet been fully embraced by the courts. But Claudius knows he will not be able to assert any right against "compelled" evidence when called to account by his god.

While seemingly describing only the omniscient justice of heaven, Claudius is also describing what has just happened to him. Through *The Mousetrap,* Hamlet has "compelled" him to "give in evidence" of his crime. And this, more broadly, is the kind of justice Hamlet seeks to mete out on Claudius—celestial rather than earthly justice. Hamlet makes this patent when he happens on Claudius at prayer. He draws his sword, but then declines to take his revenge:

Now might I do it. But now 'a is a-praying.
And now I'll do it
[Draws sword.]
—and so 'a goes to heaven,
And so am I revenged! That would be scanned:
A villain kills my father, and for that
I, his sole son, do this same villain send
To heaven.
Why, this is base and silly, not revenge.
'A took my father grossly full of bread
With all his crimes broad blown, as flush as May,
And how his audit stands who knows, save heaven,
But in our circumstance and course of thought
'Tis heavy with him. And am I then revenged
To take him in the purging of his soul
When he is fit and seasoned for his passage?
No.
[Sheathes sword.]
Up sword, and know thou a more horrid hent
When he is drunk, asleep or in a rage,
Or in th'incestuous pleasure of his bed,
At game a-swearing, or about some act
That has no relish of salvation in't.
Then trip him that his heels may kick at heaven
And that his soul may be as damned and black
As hell whereto it goes.
(3.3.73–95)

Hamlet sheathes his sword because if a person is killed praying for forgiveness, he or she will go directly to heaven. Again, Othello is Hamlet's foil here. Before he kills Desdemona, he not only permits but also exhorts her to say her final prayers: "I would not kill thy unprepared spirit, / No, heaven forfend, I would not kill thy soul" (*Othello*, 5.2.31–32). Hamlet, in contrast, wishes not only to execute Claudius but to consign his soul to hell.

Critics have deemed Hamlet's sentiment barbaric. Samuel Johnson thought the speech was "too horrible to be read or uttered"; others who agreed often cut it in performance. Yet we should expect nothing less of Hamlet's sense of poetic justice. Throughout the play, Hamlet draws a sharp distinction between his life and his soul, showing a remarkable disregard for the former. When warned not to pursue the ghost, Hamlet says: "Why, what should be the fear? / I do not set my life at a pin's fee, / And for my soul—what can it do to that, / Being a thing immortal as itself?" (1.4.64–67). Hamlet's celebrated "To be or not to be" speech is also a meditation on how suicide would be rational if the soul did not outlive the body. It seems natural, then, that Hamlet would consider taking Claudius's life to be insufficient vengeance. Perfect justice requires not just a life for a life, but a soul for a soul. This requirement has accrued more force because Hamlet, in the wake of *The Mousetrap*, seems fully to credit the ghost. The ghost has cried out that he is in greater torment because Claudius took him "unhouseled, disappointed, unaneled." Hamlet thinks back to that plaint here: "'A took my father grossly full of bread." Claudius must be taken the same way.

We also cannot take Hamlet's refusal to kill Claudius in the chapel as a simple excuse for inaction. When Hamlet thinks he can dispatch Claudius properly, he acts promptly. After the chapel scene, Hamlet goes to Gertrude's bedchamber. Polonius is concealed behind the arras to eavesdrop on their conversation. Remembering his father's injunction not to harm Gertrude, Hamlet decides he "will speak daggers to her but use none" (3.2.386) against her. But as their conversation grows heated, Gertrude thinks Hamlet intends to murder her. When she cries for help, Polonius stirs behind the arras, and Hamlet stabs him to death.

Hamlet's murder of Polonius is often characterized as rash. Here is Bradley: "When he acts, his action does not proceed from this deliberation and analysis, but is sudden and impulsive, evoked by an energy in which he has no time to think." This criticism of how Hamlet acts is also a criticism of how he thinks. It suggests that because Hamlet is so intellectual, he can act only when not given a chance to think, making him less a man of action than a man of reaction. Yet while Hamlet does not deliberate in that moment, he is acting on a *prior* deliberation. In the chapel scene, Hamlet says he will kill Claudius when he is engaged in an "act / That has no relish of salvation in't." Eavesdropping would qualify as such an act. Given that we are in the queen's bedchamber, Hamlet reasonably assumes Claudius is behind the arras. (As he regretfully says when he discovers Polonius: "I took thee for thy better" [3.4.30]). So Hamlet makes good on the pledge he makes in the chapel—although, unluckily, against the wrong target.

If the punishment neatly fits the crime, Hamlet not only acts but also takes affirmative pleasure in acting. After he kills Polonius, he tells Gertrude that he knows Claudius has some sinister purpose in sending him to England with Rosencrantz and Guildenstern. He relishes the opportunity to turn Claudius's treachery on him:

> For 'tis the sport to have the enginer
> Hoist with his own petard, and't shall go hard
> But I will delve one yard below their mines
> And blow them at the moon. O, 'tis most sweet
> When in one line two crafts directly meet.
>
> (3.4.204–208)

The metaphor concerns landmines—the "enginer / Hoist with his own petard" is the engineer blown up by his own bomb. Hamlet enjoys his plan for poetic justice, which he then smoothly implements. Rosencrantz and Guildenstern bear a commission telling the English king to kill Hamlet. Hamlet swaps their names for his, and they are duly executed.

In the last act of the play, Hamlet achieves his perfect revenge, though at great cost. As the play concludes, bodies fall like leaves. Gertrude drinks from the poisoned cup intended for Hamlet. Laertes and Hamlet each wound the other with the poisoned rapier. After he realizes they are both fatally wounded, Laertes confesses that he has outsmarted himself: "I am justly killed with mine own treachery" (5.2.292). He tells Hamlet that "[i]n thee there is not half an hour's life" (5.2.300) and that "the King, the King's to blame" (5.2.305).

Hamlet undoes Claudius in a similar fashion. He "hurts" the king with his rapier, thereby assuring that the king will die in the same way he will. The lords cry "Treason!" (5.2.307), but there is little they can do, as Hamlet himself is not long for the world. Claudius is ignominious to the end: "O, yet defend me, friends, I am but hurt" (5.2.308). Hamlet ensures that these are his last words by forcing the king to drink from the poisoned chalice: "Here, thou incestuous, damned Dane! / Drink of this potion. Is the union here? / Follow my mother. [King dies.]" (5.2.309–11).

Compelling the king to drink perfects Hamlet's revenge in several ways. For starters, Hamlet ensures that the king will die. The king has planned the poisoned "union," or pearl, as a fail-safe in case Laertes' poisoned foil does not do its work. Hamlet also uses it as insurance after the king claims he is only hurt. In making the king "follow" Gertrude according to his "union" with her, Hamlet also does symbolic justice to his mother, forcing the king to die as she did. Moreover, by making Claudius drink, he forestalls the king from speaking. He takes Claudius as Claudius took his father, barring him from saying his prayers. Hamlet merges with his father here, as both are now phantoms tarrying on the threshold between life and death. In this moment, Hamlet manages both to be and not to be.

Viewed from any of these perspectives, Hamlet's punishment of Claudius constitutes poetic justice. So Hazlitt is wrong to say that because Hamlet "cannot have his revenge perfect, according to the most refined idea his wish can form, he declines it altogether." As Laertes says directly before Claudius's death, "He is justly served. / It is a poison tempered by himself" (5.2.311–12). Early in his play, Macbeth muses: "this even-handed justice / Commends th'ingredience of our poison'd chalice / To our own lips" (Macbeth, 1.7.10–12). Here that figure becomes literal.

IT IS DANGEROUS to disagree with Freud, Goethe, and Nietzsche all at once. But their explanations of Hamlet's delays all seem less plausible than the one offered here. Contrary to Freud, I see little evidence that Hamlet has a particularly pronounced Oedipus complex. Claudius is deemed "incestuous" because he has married his dead brother's wife. So while the play refers repeatedly to incest, it always means fraternal incest rather than the parent-child incest associated with the Oedipus complex.

I see even less evidence that Hamlet is weak or nihilistic. A weak man would not have been able to take action against Polonius, Laertes, or Claudius. En route to England, Hamlet boards a pirate ship in a manner that seems downright swashbuckling. Similarly, a nihilistic man would have welcomed his impending execution in England. In a dark moment early in the play, Hamlet says that he wishes he could die without violating the "canon 'gainst self-slaughter" (1.2.132). His rejection of the opportunity to be killed without committing suicide shows that sentiment to be temporary.

Hamlet's delays make more sense if seen as part of his active pursuit of poetic justice. Hamlet first delays to confirm Claudius's guilt. He then delays to ensure that he is perfectly revenged. In fact, Hamlet shows an unswerving commitment to his ideal form of justice that reflects the strength, not the weakness, of his will.

Nonetheless, I do not come to praise Hamlet. Like many intellectuals in the grip of an idea, he is largely oblivious to its consequences on others. Totting up the seven avoidable deaths does not begin to capture the magnitude of the harm Hamlet inflicts. His cruelty to Ophelia is the prime example. Here, at least, he shows remorse at her graveside. In contrast, he manifests enduring indifference toward Rosencrantz and Guildenstern, telling Horatio that "[t]hey are not near [his] conscience" (5.2.57). After he kills Polonius, he similarly lets the counselor bleed out on the floor of the bedchamber while he has an extended conversation with Gertrude. When later asked where he has stashed the corpse, he jokes about how Polonius is at supper: "Not where he eats but where 'a is eaten" by a "convocation of politic worms" (4.3.19–20). This indifference extends to the fate of Denmark. Hamlet's actions lead to the collapse of the state, leaving it in the hands of the invading Norwegians. What we see in Hamlet is not just a commitment to moral perfectionism, but also the bottomless cost of that commitment.

IN A 1931 essay titled "Law and Literature," soon-to-be Supreme Court Justice Benjamin Cardozo explores both the importance of idealism and the importance of containing it. Cardozo observes that dissents tend to be more idealistic than majority opinions:

The voice of the majority may be that of force triumphant, content with the plaudits of the hour, and recking little of the morrow. The dissenter speaks to the future, and his voice is pitched to a key that will carry through the years. Read some of the great dissents, the opinion, for example of Judge Curtis in Dred Scott vs. Sandford, and feel after the cooling time of the better part of [a] century the glow and fire of a faith that was content to bide its hour. The prophet and the martyr do not see the hooting throng. Their eyes are fixed on the eternities.

Cardozo observes that dissents can afford to be more idealistic because they have no immediate force in the world. The dissenter, who has already lost, can express an ideal justice for "the eternities."

Conversely, one of the costs of power is that it must be more careful: "The spokesman of the court is cautious, timid, fearful of the vivid word, the heightened phrase. He dreams of an unworthy brood of scions." The coercive effect of his words disciplines his rhetoric: "The result is to cramp and paralyze. One fears to say anything when the peril of misunderstanding puts a warning finger to the lips."

Cardozo correctly intuits an inverse relationship here between force and fancy. The coercive force of a majority opinion places constraints on the way its authors can exercise their imaginations. In contrast, the dissenter has no such constraints, and so can engage in more aggressive acts of imagination. Cardozo celebrates the value of both genres. The dissenting opinion is valuable because it permits a legal actor to articulate ideals of justice at a crystalline level of purity for future majority opinions to take up, or not. The majority opinion is valuable because it adjusts those ideals for the world we inhabit.

Cardozo's example clarifies this dynamic. In the 1857 case of *Dred Scott v. Sandford,* Justice Benjamin Curtis vigorously dissented from a majority opinion arguing that the descendants of slaves were not citizens under the federal Constitution. That dissent later became a basis for enacting the Fourteenth Amendment (1868), the home of the equality principle in our Constitution. Yet while the Fourteenth Amendment overrode the *Dred Scott* majority, its language is much more restrained than the soaring rhetoric of Curtis's dissent.

Cardozo is not speaking about intellectuals in this essay. Nonetheless, he captures something important about us. The general run of intellectuals—academics, journalists, writers, and the like—generally are in the position of the dissenter. We are not the decision makers, and this gives us the freedom to engage in flights of fancy. In the realm of social justice, we can imagine utopias.

The danger arises when we lack the self-consciousness to understand that our ideals are just that—ideals. For them to be rendered functional, an additional act of translation is necessary. When we or our acolytes seek to impose them in their pure form on society, the results are usually disastrous. Consider the tradition of literary utopias, extending from Sir Thomas More's *Utopia* through Étienne Cabet's *Travels in Icaria* to B. F. Skinner's *Walden Two*. French socialist readers of Cabet founded a real Icaria in the United States; disciples of Skinner created communal societies modeled on his book in Mexico, Virginia, and Missouri. As literary critic Northrop Frye acidly observes, "There have been one or two attempts to take utopian constructions literally by trying to set them up as actual communities, but the history of these communities makes melancholy reading."

This is Hamlet's mistake. He clings to his intellectual conception of poetic justice with extraordinary tenacity and seeks to impose it on the world. Such is the force of his will that he is able to do so with respect to Claudius, but only at immeasurable cost to the world around him. A more pragmatic person would either have assassinated

Claudius in private in the chapel or, alternatively, like Laertes, have considered leading an insurgency to take over the state. But Hamlet wishes to have all the imaginative freedom of a dissent with none of the caution of a majority opinion. In the end, while his delays are justifiable, the purpose they serve is not. Hamlet's failed justice stands as a cautionary tale to intellectuals in the play-outside-the-play.

CHAPTER EIGHT

THE MADMAN

King Lear

IT MAY SEEM THAT WE HAVE COME TO A PRETTY PASS WHEN
we turn to the madman for insights into justice. But Shakespeare's
Lear moves beyond Hamlet in showing us how madness permits a
more profound apprehension not only of justice, but of its limits. *Lear*
is about a king who, after abdicating his sovereignty, suffers so intensely that he goes insane. Ironically, while this madness is inimical
to law, it may be necessary to justice. Only by surrendering his relationship to reality is Lear able to see a perfectly distilled form of
justice. Once he finds this, he never returns to mortal law. Yet as law
professor Paul Kahn points out, even this movement from mortal law
to immortal justice is not enough. At the end of the play, he turns
from justice to love. It is said that at the beginning of the play we

know more than Lear does, but at the end of the play, he knows more than we do. He passes us somewhere on the heath. I seek to know what he knows at his death.

THE TRAGIC ACTION of the play flows from the "love trial" of the daughters in the first scene. Critics charge Lear with several errors: surrendering and dividing his kingdom before his death, dividing it according to the "love test," and misperceiving which daughter loves him most. I read the scene in a way that is more sympathetic to Lear. Lear is trying to extricate himself from a difficult legal predicament while preserving the rule of law. Traditional readings, which tend to see this scene solely through a psychological lens, fail to apprehend his dilemma fully.

The case against Lear begins with his belief that he can surrender his kingdom during his lifetime and "[u]nburdened crawl toward death" (1.1.40). Lear understands that he is—or will soon become— unfit to rule his country. He is over eighty years old and wishes to leave the country to "younger strengths" (1.1.39). When and how transfers of power should occur is a profound question. I cannot say Lear answers it incorrectly.

We might still fault Lear for dividing his kingdom. In *Basilicon Doron,* King James I urged his son to keep the three kingdoms of Britain (England, Ireland, and Scotland) together, were he fortunate enough to inherit them all:

> And in case it please God to provide you to all these three
> Kingdoms, make your eldest son Isaac, leaving him all your
> kingdoms; and provide the rest with private possessions:
> Otherwise by dividing your kingdoms, ye shall leave the
> seed of division and discord among your posterity; as befell

to this Isle, by the division and assignment thereof, to the
three sons of Brutus: Locrine, Albanact, and Camber.

The allusion to the mythical King Brutus, who partitioned the island among his three sons, harks back to a legendary unified Britain
akin to Lear's. The historical Lear reigned in about the ninth century
B.C., long before the Norman Conquest brought primogeniture (the
law under which the eldest son would inherit the entire estate) to
England. Yet the logic of primogeniture—that dividing the kingdom
would lead to civil strife (at least in the short run)—is transhistorical.
Read against that logic, Lear's statement that he wishes "to publish /
Our daughters' several dowers, that future strife / May be prevented
now" (1.1.42–44) seems naïve. As early as act 2, we hear rumors of
"likely wars toward 'twixt / the two dukes of Cornwall and Albany"
(2.1.11–12). By act 3, Gloucester bluntly describes "division between
the dukes" (3.3.8–9).

Yet Lear may be choosing the lesser evil. Even in the absence of
a formal rule, birth order carries privileges in the play. In the love
trial, the daughters speak in that order: Lear says "Goneril, / Our
eldest born, speak first" (1.1.53–54), while leaving Cordelia to the end
because she is "last and least" (1.1.83). Kent also initially believes the
king favored Goneril's consort over Regan's. If Lear did not divide
the kingdom among his daughters, Goneril would take it all. Surely
this is not the correct solution.

Lear sensibly appears to be trying to give as much land to Cordelia as possible while placating her older sisters. His original intent
(as he laments after his scheme goes awry) was "to set [his] rest / On
her kind nursery" (1.1.123–24). Luckily for Lear, unlike money, land
is unique, and so can never be divided evenly. Lear says he will divide the country into thirds, but while two of these thirds are roughly
equal, the last is more "opulent" (1.1.86). Even this is an understate-

ment. Albany is the ancient name of the lands that became Scotland, while Cornwall represents the southwest of England and Wales. The remainder of Britain that Lear wishes to reserve for Cordelia is the lion's share of England.

Critics still fault Lear for imposing the so-called love trial, through which he ostensibly proportions his largesse to their expressions of love:

> Since now we will divest us both of rule,
> Interest of territory, cares of state—
> Which of you shall we say doth love us most,
> That we our largest bounty may extend
> Where nature doth with merit challenge.
> (1.1.49–53)

Lear is accused of making the category mistake of confusing love and statecraft. Yet if Lear refuses to divide the kingdom according to birth order ("nature"), he must permit that default to be challenged on some other ground, such as "merit." Filial piety was one of the few ways daughters could show merit in that time.

Perhaps most important, Lear only meant the "love test" to play a minimal role in his original scheme. What leaps out to a lawyer's eye is that the lands have already been divided and assigned before any daughter speaks a word. In the first lines of the play, we learn that Gloucester has seen Lear's grants to the Dukes of Albany and Cornwall. Kent and Gloucester do not know Lear's "darker purpose" (1.1.35), announced directly before the love trial, of abdicating and surrendering the remaining land to Cordelia. But even the bounds of that territory have been determined. As the king states before the ceremony begins: "Know that we have divided / In three our kingdom" (1.1.36–37).

This scene, then, contains less a love test than the most high-stakes real estate closing in English history. All the preparatory work has been done—the territories have been mapped and allocated. This is merely the event in which title publicly changes hands. Each daughter need only show up and make a ceremonial speech to show her gratitude and—in Cordelia's case—provide a justification for why she, "the last and least," nonetheless merits the most "opulent" third. Only when the ceremony goes disastrously wrong does it swerve from its carefully choreographed course.

The strongest criticism of Lear is his failure to distinguish the specious statements made by Goneril and Regan from the sincere one made by Cordelia. Even this criticism must be tempered. *All* these speeches are meant to be ceremonial. The genre demands puffery—like toasts children make at a parent's retirement party. To disrespect the conventions of the ceremony is to disrespect the parent. Only a child with a particular family history or temperament would do so.

Cordelia has that history and temperament. One common way to defend Lear is to demonize Cordelia—recent productions have made her a prig or a cipher. This, too, is a mistake. Unlike Lear, Cordelia sees her sisters clearly: "I know you what you are, / And like a sister am most loath to call / Your faults as they are named" (1.1.271–73). She understandably wishes to distinguish herself as much as possible from her sisters. Her sisters adhere only to the forms of love. So Cordelia avoids those forms.

Goneril's and Regan's set pieces to Lear are worth repeating to show how closely they box in Cordelia rhetorically.

GONERIL
Sir, I do love you more than word can wield the matter,
Dearer than eyesight, space and liberty,

Beyond what can be valued, rich or rare,

No less than life, with grace, health, beauty, honour.

As much as child e'er loved, or father found,

A love that makes breath poor and speech unable,

Beyond all manner of so much I love you.

(1.1.55–61)

These lines are exquisitely tuned to the occasion. Cordelia immediately recognizes her own love will now be harder to express—"What shall Cordelia speak? Love, and be silent" (1.1.62).

Cordelia could have spoken Goneril's words sincerely. She would not stoop to say so. Regan, though as insincere as Goneril, has no such compunctions:

REGAN

Sir I am made of that self mettle as my sister,

And prize me at her worth. In my true heart

I find she names my very deed of love:

Only she comes too short, that I profess

Myself an enemy to all other joys

Which the most precious square of sense possesses,

And find I am alone felicitate

In your dear highness' love.

(1.1.69–76)

Regan has found something new to say here. She accuses Goneril of not going "far enough," and of being insincere even in going as far as she does. Regan's phrase "my true heart" implicitly contrasts with "her false heart." Cordelia feels her predicament intensify: "Then poor Cordelia, / And yet not so, since I am sure my love's / More ponderous than my tongue" (1.1.77–79).

When Cordelia is charged to speak, her most natural response is to say "Nothing" (1.1.89). If her sisters will "speak and purpose not" (1.1.227), she will purpose and speak not. In making that choice, she reveals the contradiction they articulate. Goneril's statement that her love is indescribable is a description of her love. A truly ineffable love should not be accompanied by words.

Would Cordelia have "played the game" if she had known its stakes? I think not. Her comments after her sisters' speeches have the tremor of incapacity about them. Many characters in Shakespeare state that they are inarticulate before bursting into lyricism, as we have seen with Othello. Cordelia may be the only character in Shakespeare who states she is inarticulate, and is. She favors action over words, "since what I well intend, / I'll do't before I speak" (1.1.227–28). As A. C. Bradley reminds us, Cordelia makes her indelible impression upon us while speaking little more than a hundred lines in the play.

I do not wish to minimize how Lear misreads Cordelia's love, a failure of perception for which I do fault him. But psychological readings of this play have blocked equally illuminating political readings. When we look at the love trial not as a *metaphorical* legal event (a love trial) but as an *actual* legal event (a transfer of sovereignty), Lear's actions are more understandable.

I find Lear's original scheme defensible, even sensible. He sees himself as unfit to rule and wishes to transfer as much power as possible to his favorite daughter. His favorite daughter is also his youngest, so he must find a way to give her the lion's share of the kingdom without appearing unfair to her elder sisters. So he devises the "love test," because he knows she loves him best.

Given Cordelia's response in the public ceremony, Lear cannot bequeath her portion on the basis of her "merit." He scrambles to devise an alternate scheme. He divides the land meant for Cordelia

between Goneril's and Regan's husbands, vowing to move his residence back and forth between his elder daughters. He develops this
plan in a white rage. His rage is that of a heart-stricken parent. But it
is also the rage of a sovereign. Cordelia's response has profound consequences not just for him, but for all of Britain, which now descends
to Goneril and Regan.

In accepting the love trial's outcome, Lear shows himself bound
by law. The constraint he feels can be seen in his exchange with Kent,
who urges him to recant.

> KENT
> Royal Lear,
> Whom I have ever honoured as my king,
> Loved as my father, as my master followed,
> As my great patron thought on in my prayers—
>
> LEAR
> The bow is bent and drawn; make from the shaft.
>
> KENT
> Let it fall rather, though the fork invade
> The region of my heart: be Kent unmannerly
> When Lear is mad. What wouldst thou do, old man?
> Think'st thou that duty shall have dread to speak,
> When power to flattery bows? To plainness honour's
>   bound
> When majesty falls to folly. Reserve thy state,
> And in thy best consideration check
> This hideous rashness. Answer my life my judgement,
> Thy youngest daughter does not love thee least,

Nor are those empty-hearted, whose low sounds
Reverb no hollowness.
(1.1.140–54)

Kent is, of course, right that Cordelia "does not love [Lear] least" simply because her "low sounds reverb no hollowness." In act 5, Lear will
pick up on the "low" quality of her voice—the quietness of Cordelia—
when he says "[h]er voice was ever soft, / Gentle and low, an excellent
thing in woman" (5.3.270–71).

Again, though, I understand why Lear resists. Kent wants Lear
to change his mind. "See better, Lear" (1.1.159), Kent admonishes, introducing the metaphor of sight that pervades the play. But the point
is not whether Lear has judged correctly or incorrectly. The point is
that Lear has *judged*. Kent is treating this dispute as if Lear were not
bound by the legal proceeding. He wants Lear to "reserve his state"
even though he has publicly given it away. He challenges not just
Lear's authority, but the authority of the rule of law. The vehemence
of Lear's response shows the affront he feels this to be:

Hear me, recreant, on thine allegiance, hear me:
That thou hast sought to make us break our vows,
Which we durst never yet, and with strained pride
To come betwixt our sentences and our power,
Which nor our nature, nor our place can bear,
Our potency made good, take thy reward.
Five days we do allot thee for provision,
To shield thee from disasters of the world,
And on the sixth to turn thy hated back
Upon our kingdom. If on the next day following
Thy banished trunk be found in our dominions,

The moment is thy death. Away! By Jupiter,
This shall not be revoked.
(1.1.168–80)

If Kent urges Lear to "see" better, Lear urges Kent to "hear" better—"Hear me, recreant, on thine allegiance, hear me." Lear is furious because Kent has not heard the king speak as a king. Kent has sought to make the king "break our vows, / Which we durst never yet." The key word is "durst," meaning "have dared." Lear does not just say he has never broken his word, but also that he has never *dared* do so. Lear feels himself bound by a higher authority, the authority of law. He has committed himself to give lands according to a public showing of merit by his daughters. Now that Cordelia has declined to show her "merit," he must abide by his earlier commitment.

To break the link between law and its effects—"our sentences and our power"—is to attack the idea of legal authority itself. If a speaker says "Let there be light" and no light materializes, the speaker is not God. In the same way, if a speaker makes a legal utterance—"I banish Cordelia"—and no banishment follows, the speaker is not a sovereign. Lear is the supreme legal authority in the state. His warning to Kent not to come between his "sentences and their power" echoes his earlier warning to Kent to "[c]ome not between the dragon and his wrath" (1.1.123). Since pre-Christian times, the dragon has symbolized the British state. Lear charges Kent not to confuse the "old man" Kent sees with the larger, mythical state Lear embodies. Kent's punishment for attempting to challenge a legal judgment, which includes the legal banishment of Cordelia, is that he himself is legally banished. Those who resist the law are pushed from its jurisdiction, made literally into "outlaws." And lest Kent repeat the error of challenging *that* judgment, Lear concludes: "This shall not be revoked."

We see an enraged and capricious ruler in this scene who in many ways cannot command our admiration. But we also see a king who respects the rule of law. Even when he abhors the outcome, Lear abides by the legal procedure to which he has committed himself. Lear believes law should constrain power. Unhappily for him, his elder daughters do not share that view.

LEAR BEGINS TO see Goneril and Regan for what they are when he spars with them over the hundred knights he reserves to follow him. Shakespeare increases the number of knights from a king's ordinary retinue, which might have numbered a dozen or so, to a number tantamount to a personal army. For this reason, Goneril and Regan's anxiety about housing them may seem plausible. Yet again, viewed through a legal lens, these knights represent more than their numbers. The hundred knights represent a legal entitlement.

When Lear grants his powers to Albany and Cornwall, he withholds two things: the title of king and the right to a retinue:

> I do invest you jointly with my power,
> Pre-eminence and all the large effects
> That troop with majesty. Ourself, by monthly course,
> With reservation of an hundred knights
> By you to be sustained, shall our abode
> Make with you by due turn; only we shall retain
> The name, and all th'addition to a king; the sway,
> Revenue, execution of the rest
> Beloved sons, be yours. . . .
> (I.I.131–37)

Lear makes both his grant and his reservations clear. (Ian McKellen's version of the play has a scribe furiously memorializing both as Lear intones them.) These knights are the legal remnant of Lear's force.

After Lear exits the love trial in a rage, he goes to Goneril's palace. Goneril complains that Lear's followers "grow riotous" (1.3.7). She instructs her trusty servant Oswald to neglect them, saying that she would "have it come to question" (1.3.14)—that is, that she would like to provoke a dispute with Lear. She quickly gets her wish. When Lear asks why she appears unhappy, she replies that his hundred knights are "so disordered, so debauched and bold" (1.4.233) that they have made her home "more like a tavern or a brothel / Than a graced palace" (1.4.236–37). Lear retorts: "Detested kite, thou liest / My train are men of choice and rarest parts / That all particulars of duty know" (1.4.254–56). The text—here and elsewhere—is wonderfully ambiguous. We do not know whether the knights are "debauched and bold" or "choice and rare." Directors must take sides. In Peter Brook's production, the knights leave Goneril's banquet hall in a shambles. Other productions have made the knights close to invisible, or at most prankish.

Again, however, the point is not whether the knights are riotous. The point is that Lear has an absolute legal right to them. Goneril and Regan's failure to respect this right shows how little they respect law. Goneril dismisses fifty of Lear's knights "at a clap" (1.4.286). Lear appeals to Regan. Yet to his chagrin, he finds her equally hostile. Lear then reminds them of his legal rights:

LEAR
I gave you all—

REGAN
And in good time you gave it.

LEAR
—Made you my guardians, my depositaries
But kept a reservation to be followed
With such a number. What, must I come to you
With five and twenty? Regan, said you so?

REGAN
And speak't again, my Lord: no more with me.
(2.2.439–44)

Notice that Regan does not—because she cannot—refute Lear's legal claim. She merely reiterates her position. With brutal efficiency, the daughters then work in tandem to whittle down the number of knights in Lear's retinue. They pare Lear's one hundred men to fifty, then to twenty-five, then to ten, then to five, and then to nothing. In doing so, Goneril and Regan savagely invert the first scene. It is now Lear who is required to quantify the unquantifiable.

As in the first scene, the psychological and the political processes occur simultaneously. The loss of knights is not only a symbol of lost respect for Lear, but also of lost respect for the rule of law. Lear acts against his own interest to give Goneril and Regan power out of respect for the law. Yet once they have that power, they refuse to pay him—or the law—the same courtesy.

In the battle over the knights, Lear gradually realizes he can appeal neither to power nor to law. We see his appeals shift from law to justice, and from mortal authorities to immortal ones. When Goneril first seeks to strip him of his knights, Lear calls down his famous curse:

Hear, Nature, hear, dear goddess, hear:
Suspend thy purpose if thou didst intend
To make this creature fruitful.

Into her womb convey sterility,
Dry up in her the organs of increase,
And from her derogate body never spring
A babe to honour her. If she must teem,
Create her child of spleen, that it may live
And be a thwart disnatured torment to her.
Let it stamp wrinkles in her brow of youth,
With cadent tears fret channels in her cheeks,
Turn all her mother's pains and benefits
To laughter and contempt, that she may feel
How sharper than a serpent's tooth it is
To have a thankless child.
(1.4.267–81)

The "poetic justice" Lear demands here—that Goneril have an equally thankless child—could not be meted out by a human tribunal. Lear's appeal toward nature as his goddess may reflect a growing understanding of his increasingly tenuous legal position.

One other character invokes nature as his goddess in this play: Edmund. In his opening lines, Gloucester's villainous bastard son says, "Thou, Nature, art my goddess; to thy law / My services are bound" (1.2.1–2). Edmund makes nature his law because mortal law—"the plague of custom" (1.2.3)—works against him. Under the common law, a bastard was considered a *filius nullius,* "a child of no one." Because of his illegitimacy, Edmund is introduced to us as the quintessential anti-legal figure in the play. Lear's appeal to nature signals his impending marginalization by echoing the character who in the first act of the play occupies the position most opposed to his. For if Lear represents the center of the legal universe, Edmund represents its outermost margin.

When Lear curses Goneril, he has not yet surrendered faith in mortal authority. His curse predates his appeal to Regan, as well as the legal claim he makes on both sisters. Only when the sisters unite to reject this legal claim does he turn his back on human civilization, including law, and walk into the storm on the heath. His exit speech is one of the most brilliant in Shakespeare for its combination of speech and stage direction:

> No, you unnatural hags,
> I will have such revenges on you both
> That all the world shall—I will do such things—
> What they are yet I know not, but they shall be
> The terrors of the earth! You think I'll weep,
> No, I'll not weep.
> [Storm and tempest.]
> I have full cause of weeping, but this heart
> Shall break into a hundred thousand flaws
> Or e'er I'll weep. O fool, I shall go mad.
> [Exeunt Lear, Gloucester, Kent, Fool.]
> (2.2.467–75)

Lear is heartbreakingly childlike in his threat of revenge. His simultaneous impotence and grandiosity are reflected in the threat—he cannot name the punishment, but it will be terrible!—and also in the coincidence between the claim "No, I'll not weep," and the beginning of the "Storm and tempest." Lear will not weep, so nature will weep for him, recalling the sympathetic disturbances in nature that followed the murder of Duncan in Macbeth. But nature is a much more ambiguous force here than in Macbeth, because it threatens Lear himself. His enemies retreat from the storm into the house, into civilization, while Lear, stripped of his hundred knights, exits onto the heath. As he recognizes, his madness begins here.

* * *

THE GREAT IRONY of this play is that Lear finds his most fully realized conception of justice in madness. In the first scene, Kent calls Lear "mad," but Lear cannot fairly be called so in that scene, at least if we define madness as total dissociation from reality. We see true madness when Lear begins to rail on the heath about a vision of justice that could never be attained in a human society. It is a vision of Judgment Day, of Armageddon, of the Apocalypse, in which the gods can perfectly perceive and perfectly punish all wrongdoers.

> Let the great gods
> That keep this dreadful pudder o'er our heads
> Find out their enemies now. Tremble, thou wretch,
> That hast within thee undivulged crimes,
> Unwhipped of justice. Hide thee, thou bloody hand,
> Thou perjured, and thou simular of virtue
> That art incestuous. Caitiff, to pieces shake,
> That under covert and convenient seeming
> Has practised on man's life. Close pent-up guilts
> Rive your concealing continents and cry
> These dreadful summoners grace. I am a man
> More sinned against than sinning.
> (3.2.49–59)

Lear is a man "more sinned against than sinning" because Goneril and Regan have hidden their evil from him. He imagines a world in which all such dissimulation is exposed. This is a radically different world from the world of limited justice we have seen in other plays. Think of Angelo in *Measure for Measure* defending "the laws / That thieves do pass on thieves" (*Measure,* 2.1.22–23) on the ground that justice can seize only "[w]hat's open made to justice" (*Measure,* 2.1.21). In Lear's ideal world, all is made open to justice, and all is seized. To embrace this vision of justice, however, is to surrender the world. Even Lear, the man who has "ever but slenderly known himself" (*Lear,* 1.1.294–95), recognizes this—almost directly after he limns this vision of justice, he observes, "My wits begin to turn" (3.2.67).

The change that occurs inside Lear on the heath is permanent. He returns physically from the heath into Gloucester's house, but he never returns psychologically to ordinary society. Again, this can be seen in his relationship to law. When he enters Gloucester's house, some creature comforts are restored to him. Kent urges him to take that solace rather than standing "so amazed" (3.6.33)—that is, rapt in his own madness. Lear, however, associates civilization with the return of law and stages one of the most extraordinary legal scenes in literature—the "mad trial" of Goneril and Regan.

KENT

How do you sir? Stand you not so amazed.

Will you lie down and rest upon the cushions?

LEAR

I'll see their trial first. Bring in their evidence.

[to Edgar]

Thou robed man of justice, take thy place.

[to the Fool]

And thou, his yoke-fellow of equity,

Bench by his side.

[to Kent]

You are o'the commission;

Sit you too.

EDGAR

Let us deal justly.

(3.6.33–40).

LEAR

Arraign her first, 'tis Goneril—I here take my oath
before this honourable assembly—kicked the poor King
     her father.

FOOL

Come hither, mistress: is your name Goneril?

LEAR

She cannot deny it.

FOOL

Cry you mercy, I took you for a joint-stool.

LEAR

And here's another whose warped looks proclaim
What store her heart is made on. Stop her there!
Arms, arms, sword, fire, corruption in the place!
False justicer, why hast thou let her 'scape?

(3.6.46–55)

This "trial" seems initially to be a case of the inmates taking over the asylum, a direct ancestor of the Red Queen's "mad trial" in *Alice in Wonderland.*

Yet there is method to Lear's madness. In his 1913 *Commentaries on the Law in Shakespeare,* Edward J. White observes that legal procedures are being followed punctiliously in this ostensibly insane proceeding. White first observes that "[a]t common law, no one charged with a crime could be put upon trial without first being arraigned, and asked whether he or she was guilty or not guilty of the charge." (Notice that the joint stool that stands for Goneril can say "nothing" in a manner reminiscent of Cordelia in the love trial.) White continues that Lear correctly addresses Edgar as the "justice" and the Fool as his "yoke-fellow of equity," for "[a]t common law, the occupant of the judgment seat was called a 'justice' and he was said to occupy the Bench; the Chancellor, or judge who dispensed equity, on the equity side of the court, could be likened to a 'yoke-fellow' in the team of jurists, working to dispense justice." White further notes that "when two or more judges sat in judgment they were called a Commission," meaning that Kent could properly be said to be "of the Commission." Finally, he observes that "[a]fter the arraignment, it was always essential to establish the guilt of the accused, by competent evidence, as guilt was never presumed, but all persons were presumed innocent of crime, until proven guilty." So it is appropriate that "the mad king after the arraignment, calls for the evidence and deposes and gives evidence, under oath, of the offense he thinks his daughter guilty of."

The mad trial is the distilled expression of Lear's broken faith in law. In fantasy, he can create the perfect legal proceeding. But even in fantasy, law cannot produce justice. To Lear's dismay, Regan gets away, revealing the "justicer" to be "[f]alse." This imagined escape so disrupts the proceedings that Goneril is never convicted. The justice of the gods, invoked on the heath, is perfect; the law of mortals, invoked in Gloucester's house, is not. Lear can return from heath to house, but not from justice to law. Lear gives up on the trial because law is ultimately unsatisfying. We see this again when the king "recognizes" Edgar as "one of my hundred" (3.6.76), that is, as a fragment of his legal entitlement of one hundred knights. But again, this fragment is inadequate—"I do not like the fashion of your garments . . . let them be changed" (3.6.76–78).

Lear's repudiation of the law may be too categorical. After all, "[s]ome five- or six-and-thirty of his knights" (3.7.15) save his life by carrying him from Gloucester's house to Dover. Law also furthers the ends of the good characters in the play as they seek to restore justice in the state. Leading the troops of France, Cordelia hears Lear is in the fields of Dover and sends "[a] century" (4.4.6) to find him. A century is a hundred soldiers. Literary critic R. A. Foakes wonders if it is a symptom of her anxiety that she sends out so many. Yet I understand the hundred soldiers as Cordelia's conscious or unconscious restoration of the hundred knights of which Lear has been deprived, a symbolic restoration of the rule of law. Law also constrains the evil characters. In formulating his plan to avenge himself on Gloucester, Cornwall observes that law prevents him from taking Gloucester's life—"we may not pass upon his life / Without the form of justice" (3.7.24–25) ("justice" here meaning a legal trial rather than the divine justice of the gods).

For all this, however, I share Lear's skepticism. Directly after he recognizes the constraints of law, Cornwall states he will still get his way—"yet our power / Shall do a courtesy to our wrath, which men / May blame but not control" (3.7.25–27). Cornwall puts out both of Gloucester's eyes in a scene that for many years was thought to be unstageable.

As it happens, Cornwall's belief that he can torture with impunity is wrong. An unnamed servant rises up and kills Cornwall for his treatment of Gloucester. But this is an act of justice, not of law. The servant raising arms against the master was, in the early modern period, almost the paradigmatic illegal activity. When Albany hears of it, he praises heavenly justice for the act: "This shows you are above, / You justicers, that these our nether crimes / So speedily can venge" (4.2.79–81). Albany does not—because he cannot—praise the punishment as a legal act.

The capping instance in which law bends to power rather than constraining it can be seen in Goneril's actions in the final act of the play. After Edgar mortally wounds Edmund in a trial by battle, she cries out that the wager was unlawful: "By the law of war thou wast not bound to answer / An unknown opposite. Thou art not vanquished, / But cozened and beguiled" (5.3.150–52). Her insistence on the law is too much for her husband, Albany, who confronts her with her own adulterous and treasonous plan to incite Edmund to murder him. Goneril's response—"the laws are mine, not thine. / Who can arraign me for't?" (5.3.156–57)—echoes claims of sovereign immunity made by Lady Macbeth and Claudius. In a scant three lines, we see Goneril state that the law is a constraint on others, but not on her, because she is a sovereign, and Edgar is not. Yet her claim that the laws *belong* to her strikes Albany, and us, as "[m]ost monstrous" (5.3.157). It is enough to make one lose one's faith in the law altogether.

While Lear recovers enough of a sense of reality to recognize Cordelia, he never returns to the "real world." After the French forces have been defeated, Cordelia wishes to confront her sisters. Lear wants nothing of this—he wants to go with her to prison. The sense here is one of dissociated joy:

> No, no, no, no. Come, let's away to prison;
> We two alone will sing like birds i'the cage.
> When thou dost ask me blessing I'll kneel down
> And ask of thee forgiveness. So we'll live
> And pray, and sing, and tell old tales, and laugh
> At gilded butterflies, and hear poor rogues
> Talk of court news; and we'll talk with them too—

Who loses and who wins, who's in, who's out—
And take upon's the mystery of things
As if we were God's spies. And we'll wear out
In a walled prison packs and sects of great ones
That ebb and flow by the moon.
(5.3.8–19)

Cordelia is all the world Lear wishes to know now, and this passage is one of the most moving descriptions of what it means to live in a universe composed of two people—lover and beloved. It is a madness and a bliss.

IF THE PLAY ended with the passage above, we might be able to say with more equanimity that justice had been served, even if it came at the cost of Lear's relationship to reality. But the play continues on to the death of Cordelia—the only injustice that can invade Lear's reality to destroy him. This death is all the more shocking for being gratuitous—at least in the narrow sense of departing from the source. In Holinshed, Cordelia saves Lear and restores him to the throne. Lear reigns for two years until his death, after which Cordelia succeeds him. Regan's and Goneril's sons then lead a successful revolt against her, after which Cordelia hangs herself in prison. Yet in the source materials, there is at least a period of time in which Lear and Cordelia live together. The death of Cordelia was deemed such an affront to justice that Nahum Tate rewrote the ending to permit Cordelia to live and to marry Edgar. Tate's version reigned on the stage from the Restoration well into the nineteenth century.

Lear himself experiences Cordelia's death as the cardinal injustice: "O thou'lt come no more, / Never, never, never, never, never"

(5.3.306–307). But then he believes she is reviving: "Do you see this? Look on her: look, her lips, / Look there, look there! *He dies*" (5.3.308–309). Bradley argues we should believe that Lear dies in joy, and that this is the redemptive value of Cordelia's death. I think this is sentimental. I incline more to Dr. Johnson's sense that the death of Cordelia is a seemingly senseless act of cruelty on Shakespeare's part. But I do not think the answer is to rewrite the play. I think the answer is to ask why Shakespeare inflicts this ending on us.

I BELIEVE CORDELIA must die in this play to help us understand the unavoidable injustice of death. It is a short step from being forced to confront the fact that even the most pure, most virtuous character must die, to being forced to confront the idea that all of us must die. It is difficult not to experience the inevitability of death as the inevitability of injustice. We seek to avoid this truth by leading virtuous lives that will be rewarded on whatever form of Judgment Day we believe in—that is, that death will be succeeded by ultimate justice, not ultimate injustice. Yet in this play, the virtuous die in a pagan universe that holds out little hope for redemption. Lear holding Cordelia is often figured as a reverse pietà, but the figure only reminds us that Christ is eight centuries away. No wonder Tate took out his blue pen.

For me, *Lear* unflinchingly delivers the adamantine truth. *Lear* is the most sublime of Shakespeare's plays because it helps us get as close to contemplating death as possible. Freud famously stated that our deaths were impossible to imagine, for whenever we sought to do so, there we would be, caught alive in the act of imagination. I agree with Freud's point, but it is when I read *Lear* that I find my death easiest to imagine. What I see is that in that moment, I will not wish to be thinking of justice.

Lear surrenders law for justice. The final trick of the play, though, is that he surrenders justice for love. As we slip life's jurisdiction, we slip not only the empire of law, but the empire of justice. Justice is the paramount virtue of the living. But only the unlucky think of justice on their deathbeds. The lucky think of love.

Chapter Nine

The Magician

The Tempest

The Tempest features a ruler who, because he is a magician, possesses greater power over a society than any actual ruler could ever have. That magician, Prospero, systematically imposes his own conception of justice on the island he controls. The play tests Lord Acton's famous 1887 observation that "[p]ower tends to corrupt, and absolute power corrupts absolutely." Prospero presents an important exception to the Acton rule.

The Tempest is rightly read as a colonialist allegory. The play was almost certainly inspired by the flurry of contemporary accounts of colonial activity, particularly William Strachey's 1609 account of a hurricane that drove the ship *Sea Venture* onto the rocky coast of the Bermudas. Many critics read Prospero as the colonizer of the island, which generally means he is cast in a negative light. Without a doubt, Prospero is guilty of gross injustices. Yet his final act is to relinquish his power voluntarily, in what I will argue is a profoundly ethical act. *The Tempest* shows that justice can often reside in the renunciation of power rather than in its exercise.

Our system of government is based on the conception that individuals will always seek to expand their power. This theory is perhaps best expressed in the Madisonian system of checks and balances, under which individual self-interest controls the self-interest of others. While this approach is generally wise, it should not obscure the exceptional case. Sometimes human beings will exhibit genuine self-restraint, relinquishing power for the greater good. George Washington, the first president under Madison's Constitution, repeatedly restrained himself in a way that Madison correctly did not expect the run of our nation's leaders to do. *The Tempest* teaches us to remember and celebrate the possibility that sometimes power does not corrupt, and to ask who our Prosperos are today.

THE PLAY OPENS with the tempest of the title, which shipwrecks a crew of Italian nobles on the island on which Prospero and his daughter, Miranda, live. Yet the events that stranded Prospero and Miranda on the island predate the shipwreck by twelve years. Prospero has often begun, but never finished, telling Miranda how they came to the island. As the tempest subsides, he finally does.

Prospero recounts that he was the Duke of Milan, who was displaced by his brother Antonio. He repeatedly attributes the loss of his dukedom to his commitment to scholarly life. After boasting that he was considered "for the liberal arts / Without a parallel" (1.2.73–74), he ruefully admits: "those being all my study, / The government I cast upon my brother / And to my state grew stranger, being transported / And rapt in secret studies" (1.2.74–77). Later, he observes he was guilty of "neglecting worldly ends, all dedicated / To closeness and the bettering of my mind" (1.2.89–90). He had no political ambition—his "library / Was dukedom large enough" (1.2.109–10).

Unlike his brother, Antonio *was* interested in political power. Viewing Prospero as "incapable" (1.2.111) of "temporal royalties" (1.2.110), Antonio decided to take over the state. He was so "dry . . . for sway" (1.2.112), or thirsty for power, that he joined with King Alonso of Naples to topple Prospero, even though Milan lost its independence to Naples in the bargain. As a result of this alliance, Prospero and Miranda were cast to sea on "[a] rotten carcass of a butt" (1.2.146), so unseaworthy that "the very rats / Instinctively ha[d] quit it" (1.2.147–48). They ultimately landed on the island.

Luckily for Prospero, the kind noble Gonzalo had placed some books from his library on the raft: "Knowing I loved my books, he furnished me / From mine own library with volumes that / I prize above my dukedom" (1.2.166–68). These books enabled Prospero to continue his studies. Prospero put these studies to practical use. Continuing the "secret studies" he had begun in Milan, Prospero became a magician.

Early modern audiences would have immediately recognized the character type. Magicians were commonly figured with certain symbols, including a robe, staff, and book. The title page to a 1620 printing of Christopher Marlowe's *Doctor Faustus* (first published in 1607) pictures the enrobed Faustus tracing a cabalistic circle with a staff held in his right hand, while consulting a book held open with his left. Prospero has all three accoutrements. When he relinquishes power, he removes his "magic garment" (1.2.24), breaks his "staff" (5.1.54), and drowns his "book" (5.1.57).

Prospero employs his magic to survive on the island. The island has two natives—Caliban, the son of the deceased witch Sycorax, and

Ariel, a spirit Sycorax has trapped inside a pine. Prospero liberated Ariel in exchange for an unspecified period of service. He also claims to have treated Caliban "with humane care" (1.2.347) until Caliban sought to rape Miranda. Now he uses both Ariel and Caliban as servants or slaves, threatening them with magical punishments if they refuse his commands.

After twelve years, fortune has brought Prospero's enemies within his grasp. Alonso, the King of Naples, has married off his daughter to the Prince of Tunis. The royal party's return course from Tunis to Naples brings it by Prospero's island. Prospero sees his only chance at redemption: "I find my zenith doth depend upon / A most auspicious star, whose influence / If now I court not, but omit, my fortunes / Will ever after droop" (1.2.181–84). Prospero has two goals—to get Alonso's son Ferdinand to marry Miranda to secure her future, and to punish the nobles who displaced him. He conjures the tempest, and sends Ariel to create the illusion that it is destroying the ship. Ariel ensures that the royal party is divided into three groups—he isolates Prince Ferdinand, strands Alonso and some of his retinue in a separate cluster, and stows the sleeping crew safely in a cove with the intact ship.

Prospero easily gets Ferdinand and Miranda to fall in love. Although his magic cannot compel them to do so, it certainly facilitates it. Ariel's music leads Ferdinand to Miranda and Prospero. Miranda is immediately smitten: "This / is the third man that e'er I saw, the first / That e'er I sighed for" (1.2.445–47). Ferdinand responds with equal alacrity: "O, if a virgin, / And your affection not gone forth, I'll make you / The Queen of Naples" (1.2.448–50). Prospero's problem is that their affair moves a bit *too* quickly, which he fears will lead the lovers to undervalue each other. "[L]est too light winning / Make the prize light" (1.2.452–53), Prospero pretends to be the blocking agent fathers represent in many of the plays—Brabantio in *Othello,* Egeus in *A Midsummer Night's Dream,* or the Old Athenian in *Timon of Athens.* He accuses Ferdinand of being an impostor who seeks control over the island and threatens to impress him into service. Ferdinand draws his sword in self-defense: "I will resist such entertainment till / Mine enemy has more power" (1.2.466–67). But then, according to the stage direction, he is "*charmed from moving.*" Prospero presumably fits deed to word in saying: "I can here disarm thee with this stick / And make thy weapon drop" (1.2.473–74). The contest between Prospero's magical power and Ferdinand's physical power could not be starker. The staff subdues the sword.

Prospero's magic may lie in his robe as well as in his books. In pleading for Ferdinand, Miranda clings to Prospero, drawing a strong, perhaps even frantic, response from her father: "Hence; Hang not on my garments" (1.2.474). When Miranda persists, he shakes her off: "Silence! One word more / Shall make me chide thee, if not hate thee" (1.2.476–77). Prospero may be motivated solely by the wish to excite Miranda's sympathies for Ferdinand. But he may also fear that physical contact with his robe will disrupt its power.

Prospero's opposition to Ferdinand has its intended effect. He forces Ferdinand to "remove / Some thousands of these logs and pile them up" (3.1.9–10). This punishment further stimulates Miranda's sympathy, shifting her fealty from her father to Ferdinand. When he asks her name, she says: "Miranda.—O my father / I have broke your hest to say so!" (3.1.36–37). Prospero, who is eavesdropping on them, approves of the transfer of loyalty. Soon Miranda has proposed to Ferdinand and he has accepted.

Prospero's second project—bringing those who usurped him to justice—is more complex. Prospero was a political naïf in Milan—as he says to Miranda, Antonio was the person "whom next thyself / Of all the world I loved" (1.2.68–69). Like many an older sibling, he still blames himself for Antonio's faults, saying his negligence "[a]waked an evil nature" (1.2.93) in his brother. As if he still cannot believe Antonio is truly evil, Prospero gives him another chance on the island. He sequesters Antonio with King Alonso, Alonso's brother Sebastian, Gonzalo, and a few other nobles. Ariel then puts all the nobles except Antonio and Sebastian to sleep.

Antonio fails this test of character spectacularly. He immediately sees an opportunity for still more professional advancement, urging Sebastian to commit regicide while the courtiers drowse. Sebastian remembers how Antonio overthrew Prospero: "You did supplant your brother Prospero" (2.1.272). Antonio shows as little remorse as Aaron or Iago: "And look how well my garments sit upon me / Much feater than before. My brother's servants / Were then my fellows; now they are my men" (2.1.273–75). Sebastian asks if Antonio's conscience troubles him. Antonio cheerfully reports that "[t]wenty consciences" (2.1.279) would not stand between him and his ambition. Antonio is— and always has been—a thorough villain. When Sebastian agrees to kill Alonso, and Antonio makes ready to kill Gonzalo, history looks to repeat itself. This time, however, Prospero contains the threat. Observing that his "master through his art foresees the danger" (2.1.298), Ariel rouses Gonzalo with a song. Music, one of the few subjects to receive uniformly positive treatment in Shakespeare, interrupts the effects of their treasonous words with its sweeter cadences.

The contest between Prospero's staff and Ferdinand's sword is a dress rehearsal for a more serious confrontation in act 3. There Ariel in the guise of a harpy denounces the "three men of sin" (3.3.53)— Alonso, Sebastian, and Antonio—for having colluded to depose Prospero a dozen years before. When the three nobles draw their swords, Ariel laughs their show of force to scorn:

> You fools! I and my fellows
> Are ministers of fate. The elements
> Of whom your swords are tempered may as well

THE MAGICIAN - 239

Wound the loud winds, or with bemocked-at stabs
Kill the still-closing waters, as diminish
One dowl that's in my plume. My fellow ministers
Are like invulnerable. If you could hurt,
Your swords are now too massy for your strengths
And will not be uplifted.
(3.3.60–68)

The men's swords, like Ferdinand's, are magically disabled. Moreover, in mocking their display of force, Ariel refers back to the tempest that has already overwhelmed them. They may as well attempt to wound the wind or waters as attempt to wound Ariel.

After establishing his authority, Ariel sentences Alonso, Antonio, and Sebastian for their crimes:

But remember
(For that's my business to you) that you three
From Milan did supplant good Prospero,
Exposed unto the sea, which hath requit it,
Him and his innocent child; for which foul deed,
The powers delaying, not forgetting, have
Incensed the seas and shores—yea, all the creatures—
Against your peace. Thee of thy son, Alonso,
They have bereft, and do pronounce by me
Ling'ring perdition, worse than any death
Can be at once, shall step by step attend
You and your ways, whose wraths to guard you from—
Which here, in this most desolate isle, else falls
Upon your heads—is nothing but heart's sorrow
And a clear life ensuing.
(3.3.68–82)

Ariel seemingly presents the notion of natural justice encountered in *Macbeth*—"[t]he powers delaying, not forgetting, have / Incensed the seas and shores." He states that nature itself is punishing the three miscreants for their unnatural crimes. But it is not nature that has raised the tempest, but Prospero's magic.

The three men reveal their characters in their reactions. King Alonso immediately repents and vows to sink himself in the mud with the son he thinks he has lost. In contrast, Sebastian contests the judgment: "But one fiend at a time, / I'll fight their legions o'er" (3.3.103–104)—that is, so long as the fiends come one at a time, he will fight them all. Antonio quickly follows: "I'll be thy second" (3.3.104). The men race off, and the elderly Gonzalo desperately calls to those of "suppler joints" (3.3.108) to stop them—he believes they have been driven mad by their former sins.

Ariel leads them to Prospero's cell, where the three men are magically transfixed. As Ariel reports to Prospero:

> They cannot budge till your release. The King,
> His brother and yours abide all three distracted,
> And the remainder mourning over them,
> Brimful of sorrow and dismay; but chiefly
> Him that you termed, sir, the good old Lord Gonzalo.
> His tears run down his beard like winter's drops
> From eaves of reeds. Your charm so strongly works 'em
> That, if you now beheld them, your affections
> Would become tender.
> (5.1.11–19)

Prospero asks: "Dost thou think so, spirit?" (5.1.19). Ariel responds, "Mine would, sir, were I human" (5.1.20).

Ariel's line is a favorite of mine, as it verges so tenderly on self-contradiction—he cannot feel empathy, but he can empathize enough with human beings to know that if he were human, he would feel empathy for these men. Prospero is moved:

> Hast thou, which art but air, a touch, a feeling
> Of their afflictions, and shall not myself
> (One of their kind, that relish all as sharply,
> Passion as they) be kindlier moved than thou art?
> Though with their high wrongs I am struck to th'quick,
> Yet with my nobler reason 'gainst my fury
> Do I take part. The rarer action is
> In virtue than in vengeance. They being penitent
> The sole drift of my purpose doth extend
> Not a frown further. Go, release them, Ariel.
> My charms I'll break; their senses I'll restore;
> And they shall be themselves.
>
> (5.1.21–32)

At a moment when he has complete control over his enemies, Prospero chooses the path of forgiveness. Prospero's forgiveness of Alonso is understandable—the king has repented and will soon be Miranda's father-in-law. But Antonio and Sebastian never express penitence in this play. Unlike Titus, Prospero stops the cycle of vengeance with an act of grace.

Magic also foils another unexpected political plot, in which the low characters mime the action of the high ones. Stephano, the butler of the royal party, and Trinculo, the jester, fall in with Caliban's plot to kill Prospero and to take over the island. Stephano escaped the wreck "upon a butt of sack" (2.2.119), or cask of wine. Caliban immediately recognizes Stephano for the Bacchic figure he is: "[t]hat's a brave god and bears celestial liquor" (2.2.115).

Realizing the source of his power, Stephano tells Trinculo and Caliban when they swear oaths to "kiss the book" (2.2.127, 139) as one would kiss the Bible in swearing fealty to a sovereign. Each "kiss" is a swig from the bottle. Like Prospero, Stephano has a "book" of "spirits," which he uses to control others. While Stephano assumes he will "inherit" (2.2.172) the island, Caliban informs him that Prospero already controls it. He suggests that Stephano murder Prospero while he lies asleep, but cautions him to seize his books first:

> Why, as I told thee, 'tis a custom with him
> I'th' afternoon to sleep. There thou mayst brain him,
> Having first seized his books, or with a log
> Batter his skull, or paunch him with a stake,
> Or cut his wezand with thy knife. Remember
> First to possess his books, for without them
> He's but a sot, as I am, nor hath not
> One spirit to command. They all do hate him
> As rootedly as I. Burn but his books.
> (3.2.87–95)

In this incantatory passage, Caliban thrice mentions Prospero's "books" as the source of his magic. The link between books and magic also surfaces in *Henry VI, Part 2*, where a weaver states that the "clerk of Chartham" (*Henry VI, Part 2*, 4.2.78) has "a book in his pocket with red letters in't" (4.2.83). The illiterate rebel leader Jack Cade takes this book to be evidence that "he is a conjuror" (4.2.84). (The book is probably an almanac with red-letter days in it.) This confusion has real-life analogs. Stephen Greenblatt refers to a Frenchman, Father Chaumonot, who maintained in 1640 that the Hurons "were convinced that we were sorcerers," whose killing spells "were shut up in our inkstands, in our books, etc." According to Chaumonot, this meant that "we dared not, without hiding ourselves, open a book or write anything."

Again, the magical counter to this political intrigue is music. Ariel leads the three plotters with his tabor through "[t]oothed briars, sharp furzes, pricking gorse and thorns" (4.1.180), leaving them at last in a "filthy-mantled pool" (4.1.182) behind Prospero's cell. The injury the rogues feel the most is the loss of their bottle along the way. Far from being deprived of his books, Prospero has divested Stephano of his "book" of sack.

By act 5 of the play, magic has secured almost all of Prospero's ends. He has brought Ferdinand and Miranda together, thwarted Antonio and Sebastian's attempted regicide, gotten Alonso to repent his earlier treachery, and foiled Caliban, Stephano, and Trinculo's plot on his life. To be sure, Prospero's magic has limits. Just as Prospero cannot force Miranda and Ferdinand to fall in love, he cannot force Antonio and Sebastian to feel remorse. Nonetheless, he can still contain Antonio and Sebastian with knowledge acquired through his magic. At the play's conclusion, he quietly warns them that he knows of their treason against Alonso and threatens to expose them if they attempt it again.

Prospero's reconciliation with Alonso reaches its climax when Prospero lifts a curtain to reveal Ferdinand and Miranda "discovered playing chess." On seeing the Neapolitan nobles, Miranda exclaims: "O wonder! / How many goodly creatures are there here! / How beauteous mankind is! O brave new world / That has such people in't" (5.1.181–84). Prospero dryly finishes the line: "'Tis new to thee" (5.1.184).

The tableau of the chess-playing lovers charms and troubles. It charms because rather than using their time alone to make love, the youngsters are decorously playing a game. But there is sadness here too. A game of chess begins with two equal kingdoms and ends with one conquering the other. Miranda accuses Ferdinand of cheating, but says she would surrender twenty kingdoms for him. In act 1, Prospero mourned to Miranda about how Antonio engaged in "most ignoble stooping" (1.2.116) to subject Prospero's Milan to Alonso's Naples. Milan and Naples were independent duchies until Antonio submitted "his coronet to [Alonso's] crown" (1.2.114). We might mourn anew on Prospero's behalf that they have returned to that political game, here figurative, soon through Miranda's marriage to be literalized. Miranda's naïveté, while understandable, is also worrisome. Some of the "goodly creatures" she admires sought to kill her.

Miranda's continuing vulnerability raises the question of why Prospero renounces his magic before returning to Milan. Magic has been the means through which Prospero has protected and advanced Miranda's interests throughout the play. Threats to those interests, such as Antonio and Sebastian, endure. The most obvious explanation is that absorption in his studies caused Prospero to be deposed in the first place. But this rationale is unpersuasive. Prospero's magic has advanced significantly since he was last in Milan. On the island, he can predict danger, as he does when Antonio and Sebastian plot to kill the king. To understand why he sacrifices his art, we must look more closely at its other effects.

THE DANGER OF the unnamed, unlocatable island is that its seemingly blank political canvas tempts new arrivals to project narcissistic visions onto it. It is predictable that the villainous characters, like Antonio and Sebastian, or the ignorant ones, like Stephano and Trinculo, will have imperial fantasies. But even the kind old counselor Gonzalo has one:

> I'th' commonwealth I would by contraries
> Execute all things, for no kind of traffic

Would I admit; no name of magistrate;
Letters should not be known; riches, poverty
And use of service, none; contract, succession,
Bourn, bound of land, tilth, vineyard—none;
No use of metal, corn, or wine or oil;
No occupation, all men idle, all;
And women, too, but innocent and pure;
No sovereignty—
(2.1.148–57)

Gonzalo's utopian vision comes directly from Montaigne's essay "Of the Cannibals" (available to Shakespeare through John Florio's 1603 translation), which describes how the much-maligned "cannibals" in Brazil are more civilized than their European peers. Superficially attractive, the vision conjures a commonwealth in which no law or need for law exists.

Yet as in many utopias, this state comes under the sole rule of the person who imagined it. When Gonzalo claims that his commonwealth would know "[n]o sovereignty," Sebastian responds, "Yet he would be king on't" (2.1.157). Antonio concurs that "[t]he latter end of his commonwealth forgets the beginning" (2.1.158–59). They are right: Gonzalo is the self-appointed king of his kingless country.

Like Gonzalo, Prospero wishes to impose a utopian order on his commonwealth. Unlike Gonzalo, Prospero has the means to do so. It may initially be hard to see Prospero as an imperialist, because he comes to the island as a castaway rather than as a conquistador, as a Crusoe rather than as a Cortés. Yet once he arrives on the island, he is so aggrieved by his own displacement that he seems insensible to the displacement of others. His behavior bears the darkest marks of the colonialist enterprise. I believe Prospero relinquishes his magic because he comes to see its corrupting effects.

Ariel is Prospero's main magical agent throughout the play. Trapped inside a pine for twelve years by Caliban's mother, Sycorax, Ariel is freed from his confinement by Prospero in return for a period of indenture. In act 1, Ariel refers to a modification of that contract: "Thou did promise / To bate me a full year" (1.2.249–50). Prospero does not deny the agreement to shorten Ariel's term, under which Ariel should already be free. Instead, he angrily reminds Ariel of the torments from which he saved him. Worse, he threatens him with more: "If thou more murmur'st, I will rend an oak / And peg thee in his knotty entrails till / Thou hast howled away twelve winters" (1.2.294–96). Prospero's answer to a claim of right is a claim of power.

Prospero's abuse of Caliban is worse still. Caliban also makes a legal claim—a property claim—asserting that "[t]his island's mine by Sycorax, my mother" (1.2.332). Prospero, in contrast, treats the island as if it were *terra nullius,* or legally unoccupied land. Commentary debates whether Caliban's ostensible illegitimacy would have made him unable to succeed. The debate is moot. Because Caliban was the only human inhabitant of the island when Prospero arrived, he would have had ownership regardless of parentage. Just as Antonio has dispossessed Prospero, Prospero has dispossessed Caliban. As Caliban mourns: "I am all the subjects that you have, / Which first was mine own king; and here you sty me / In this hard rock, whiles you do keep from me / The rest o'th' island" (1.2.342–45).

Prospero's retort is that he used Caliban "with humane care" (1.2.347) until Caliban sought "to violate / The honour of my child" (1.2.348–49). But this answer is unresponsive to Caliban's claim. Nothing suggests that Prospero recognized Caliban's possession of the island before the attempted rape. Moreover, while Caliban's crime deserves severe punishment, this punishment would not necessarily extend to divesting Caliban of title to the island, much less to enslaving him. This slavery is enforced through physical pain, which is not just threatened (as in Ariel's case) but inflicted. The gauzy atmospherics of the play may prevent us from seeing the "cramps," "side-stiches," and "pinch[es]" (1.2.326, 327, 330) Prospero inflicts on Caliban as torture. By the time Prospero looses dogs on Caliban, we must name it as such.

While Shakespeare does not idealize Caliban, he keeps his humanity steadily visible. Miranda at one point berates Caliban for ingratitude: "When thou didst not, savage, / Know thine own meaning, but wouldst gabble like / A thing most brutish, I endowed thy purposes / With words that made them known" (1.2.356–59). All Miranda establishes here is that she did not understand *his* language. Caliban retorts, "You taught me language, and my profit on't / Is I know how to curse" (1.2.364–65). Yet Caliban can do far more than curse. In comforting Stephano and Trinculo, he delivers one of the most lyrical speeches in Shakespeare.

> Be not afeard. The isle is full of noises,
> Sounds and sweet airs that give delight and hurt not.
> Sometimes a thousand twangling instruments
> Will hum about mine ears; and sometimes voices,
> That if I then had waked after long sleep,
> Will make me sleep again; and then in dreaming,
> The clouds, methought, would open and show riches
> Ready to drop upon me, that when I waked
> I cried to dream again.
> (3.2.135–143)

"Caliban" is a rough anagram of "cannibal," which leads us back again to Montaigne's essay. In this speech, the "savage" Caliban shows more refinement than Stephano or Trinculo, and more eloquence than Miranda.

Prospero's only conceivable defense for his treatment of Ariel and Caliban is necessity. Prospero and Miranda need Ariel to get off the island. As he reminds Miranda, they also both need Caliban: "We cannot miss him; he does make our fire, / Fetch in our wood, and serves in offices / That profit us" (1.2.312–14). I am not condoning Prospero's use of power for these ends. But at the point where Prospero's needs have been met, he lacks even a token excuse to continue to control them.

Prospero must relinquish his magic not just for the play's characters, but for its audience. *The Tempest* was performed for King James I in 1611. A self-styled expert on the occult, King James warned in his book *Daemonologie* (1597) that learned men too often step "upon the slipperie and uncertaine scale of curiositie; they are at last enticed, that where lawfull artes or sciences failes, to satisfie their restles mindes, even to seeke to that black and unlawfull science of *Magie*." Scholars who pursued the "black and unlawfull science" believed themselves to be gods, but "their knowledge, for all that they presume therof, is nothing increased, except in knowing evil, and the horrors of Hell for punishment thereof, as Adam's was by the eating of the forbidden tree."

Shakespeare's contemporaries would not have had to travel back to Adam to remember how the quest for knowledge could end in perdition. Other tales of this "unlawful" trajectory—some real, others fictional—lay close at hand. Queen Elizabeth's protégé John Dee is often said to be the basis for Prospero. (Dee allegedly commanded a spirit named Uriel, a close cognate of Ariel.) A man of immense learning, he became obsessed with the occult in the last decades of his life and died in 1608 in disgrace and poverty. The most famous contemporary fictional character who traveled this path was Christopher Marlowe's Doctor Faustus, who begins his play as a learned doctor, sells his soul to the devil in exchange for magical power, and ends up being carried off to hell. Prospero is the Italian for Faustus (both names mean "fortunate"), and it is Prospero's challenge in the play to redeem his name from his literary predecessor.

AT THE END of *Doctor Faustus,* Faustus offers to burn his books if the devils will spare his soul. It is too late for him because he has already availed himself of all of the advantages of his magical power. Prospero, on the other hand, renounces his book before giving his power full extension. Unlike Faustus, he can still redeem himself. Perhaps this is why he inverts the image, offering to drown his book, rather than to burn it:

> Ye elves of hills, brooks, standing lakes and groves,
> And ye that on the sands with printless foot
> Do chase the ebbing Neptune, and do fly him
> When he comes back; you demi-puppets that
> By moonshine do the green sour ringlets make,
> Whereof the ewe not bites; and you whose pastime
> Is to make midnight-mushrooms, that rejoice
> To hear the solemn curfew, by whose aid—
> Weak masters though ye be—I have bedimmed
> The noontide sun, called forth the mutinous winds,
> And 'twixt the green sea and the azured vault
> Set roaring war; to the dread-rattling thunder
> Have I given fire and rifted Jove's stout oak
> With his own bolt: the strong-based promontory
> Have I made shake, and by the spurs plucked up
> The pine and cedar; graves at my command
> Have waked their sleepers, ope'd and let 'em forth
> By my so potent art. But this rough magic

I here abjure; and when I have required
Some heavenly music (which even now I do)
To work mine end upon their senses that
This airy charm is for, I'll break my staff,
Bury it certain fathoms in the earth,
And deeper than did ever plummet sound
I'll drown my book.
(5.1.33–57)

This speech echoes a speech made by Medea (the paradigm black witch of antiquity) in Ovid's *Metamorphoses*. Some productions have Prospero pause after "graves at my command / Have waked their sleepers, ope'd and let 'em forth," before saying in hushed tones "By my so potent art," as if realizing anew the magnitude of his disruption of the laws of God and nature. But unlike Medea, Prospero is not just announcing his power, but renouncing it.

In abjuring his magical power, Prospero follows the more virtuous and likable characters in the play. We know Ferdinand is a decent fellow when he says he will be reconciled to his servitude to Prospero if he can see Miranda from his prison once a day: "All corners else o'th' earth / Let liberty make use of; space enough / Have I in such a prison" (1.2.492–94). Ferdinand values love over power. He reiterates this preference later in the play with respect to his father, noting that "I am, in my condition, / A prince, Miranda; I do think a king / (I would not so!)" (3.1.59–61). Ferdinand would rather be a prince with a father than a king without one.

Similarly, one of Ariel's many appealing traits is his desire for contraction rather than expansion. During his servitude to Prospero, he is forced to be larger than life. He "flame[s] amazement" (1.2.198) on the rigging of the ship to mimic St. Elmo's fire; he hands down judgment to the Italian miscreants in the terrifying figure of a harpy;

he directs the masque of the goddesses performed to celebrate Ferdinand and Miranda's impending nuptials. On the cusp of his manumission, however, he imagines himself smaller:

> Where the bee sucks, there suck I,
> In a cowslip's bell I lie;
> There I couch when owls do cry.
> On the bat's back I do fly
> After summer merrily.
> Merrily, merrily, shall I live now,
> Under the blossom that hangs on the bough.
> (5.1.88–94)

To suck where the bee sucks, to couch in a cowslip, to fly on a bat's back in pursuit of an endless summer—this is Ariel's vision of liberty. In this play of disabling freedoms and enabling constraints, Ariel's song is the most memorable formulation of freedom through constriction, as if the spirit were slipping through the eyes of a net rather than breaking its links. The vision is seductive enough to engender a cry of affection in Prospero: "Why that's my dainty Ariel! I shall miss thee, / But yet thou shalt have freedom" (5.1.95–96).

Prospero also releases Caliban. When he introduces Caliban to the Italian nobles, he says, "this thing of darkness I / Acknowledge mine" (5.1.275–76). The word "acknowledge" carries the sense of a father "acknowledging" an illegitimate child, as Gloucester has "blushed to acknowledge" Edmund (*Lear*, 1.1.9), but also the sense of a colonizer acknowledging a wrong. If Caliban has become a thing of darkness, Prospero has had agency in that transformation.

The magician's renunciation, understandably, is laden with regret. He expects that on his return to Milan, "[e]very third thought shall be my grave" (5.1.312), now that his powers have become "most faint" (Epilogue, 3). This elegy suggests why power is so difficult to renounce—it is a bulwark against the fear of decline and death. This recognition makes Prospero's surrender all the more admirable.

THE QUESTION RAISED by *The Tempest* is whether leaders in the real world will ever voluntarily relinquish their power. Our Founders thought it prudent to assume otherwise. As James Madison put it in *The Federalist Papers,* "[i]f men were angels, no government would be necessary." Men could be distinguished from angels in part because they constantly sought to aggrandize their power. To keep those imperial ambitions in check, it was not enough to rely on self-restraint. Instead, Madison argued that government needed to be structured to make self-interest cancel out self-interest: "Ambition must be made to counteract ambition." With this in mind, Madison proposed the system of checks and balances embodied in our federal Constitution.

While I endorse the brilliance of this solution, I hope it does not cause us to descend into cynicism. Sometimes men can be angels. The first president to be elected under the new Constitution seems to have had an entirely ethical stance toward power, repeatedly questioning his right to exercise it and repeatedly renouncing it. After winning the Revolutionary War, Washington resigned his position as general, sending his sword to Congress. As biographer Garry Wills observes, in this moment "the ancient legend of Cincinnatus—the Roman called from his plow to rescue Rome, and returning to the plow when danger had passed—was resurrected as a fact of modern political life." The painter John Trumbull similarly observed in a letter that the resignation "excites the astonishment and admiration of this part of the world. 'Tis a Conduct so novel, so inconceivable to People, who, far from giving up powers they possess, are willing to convulse the Empire to acquire more."

Of course, General Washington was called back to public life to become President Washington. But after serving two four-year terms in that capacity, he resigned again to return to Mount Vernon. As constitutional historian Akhil Reed Amar observes, "Washington set a striking example for his successors when in 1796 he declined to stand for the reelection at the end of his second term, even though he would have been a shoo-in." Washington was concerned that if he stayed in office too long, the fragile new republic would too much resemble a monarchy. Subsequent presidents took their cues from him. President Jefferson invoked "the sound precedent set by an illustrious predecessor" to decline to run for a third term. Madison and Monroe followed suit. In this way, Amar observes, "was a tradition born." It was only when Franklin Delano Roosevelt broke the eight-year limit that Congress had to propose the Twenty-second Amendment, ratified in 1951, which precludes a president from being elected more than twice for the office. It was a classic Madisonian moment—Roosevelt's self-interest had triumphed over his self-restraint, so the self-interest of others had to counteract it.

Who is our present-day Cincinnatus, our Prospero, our Washington? Sadly, no comparable figures come to my mind. Given *The Tempest*'s stature as a colonialist allegory, I have asked my colleagues in postcolonial studies if they can provide an instance where a colonizer has voluntarily ceded power over a colony, without pressure from a war of independence or the demands of a treaty. The answer was a resounding no. Turning to domestic affairs, constitutional limitations now constrain presidential ambition, so no self-restraint is needed. But where no such limitations exist, I am hard pressed to find truly altruistic renunciations. We live in an age where "I am resigning to spend more time with my family" is a euphemism for "I am getting ahead of the scandal that will force me from office."

Perhaps I am being too hard on humankind. It takes fortitude to descend from the pinnacle of one's profession. Prospero shows us the fears of impotence and death that attend such surrenders. This dynamic, of course, is not limited to politics, but extends to all of the professions. And so we turn, finally, to Shakespeare himself.

THE CONVENTIONAL WISDOM that Prospero is an avatar of his creator has, despite several backlashes, endured. The crux of the identification is that Prospero issues a series of famous valedictory utterances in what is widely viewed to be the playwright's last solo-authored play. Critics point out that Shakespeare definitely cowrote (and possibly solo-authored) plays after *The Tempest*. But one can say good-bye before one leaves. In fact, if one wishes to compose a farewell symphony, it is prudent to guard against dying before its completion.

Throughout the play, the word for magic is "art." The First Folio capitalized the word to emphasize its specialized meaning of "magical art." I endorse the decision of most subsequent editions to restore the lowercase "a" because the ambiguity it creates is generative, and arguably deliberate. At this time in history, the word "art" was acquiring its more spacious modern sense of the "liberal arts" and of "aesthetics."

In *The Tempest,* magical and aesthetic art are distinct and related. On the one hand, Prospero's magic is much more powerful than any aesthetic enterprise. Prospero's power allows him to raise the tempest and (according to him) the dead. On the other hand, much of Prospero's magic is the power to create illusions—as he tells Miranda, the tempest was not a "real" tempest but a persuasive facsimile. He elaborates on this point to Ferdinand:

> Our revels now are ended. These our actors
> As I foretold you, were all spirits and

Are melted into air, into thin air;
And—like the baseless fabric of this vision—
The cloud-capped towers, the gorgeous palaces,
The solemn temples, the great globe itself,
Yea, all which it inherit, shall dissolve,
And like this insubstantial pageant faded,
Leave not a rack behind. We are such stuff
As dreams are made on, and our little life
Is rounded with a sleep.
(4.1.148–58)

This quality of Prospero's magic is one of many grounds on which magic shifts into aesthetics, the magician shifts into the playwright, and Prospero shifts into Shakespeare.

The Tempest reads like Shakespeare's valediction in ways that extend beyond Prospero's famous speeches in act 5. An extraordinary number of Shakespeare's other plays clamor around this one. Just as Prospero must stave off threats to his happy ending, so too must Shakespeare prevent his earlier tragedies from intruding on his romance. The regicide of *Macbeth* must be averted; the fraternal betrayal of *Hamlet* must be contained; and the father-daughter death of *Lear* must be rewritten.

After having managed that feat, however, Shakespeare is ready to break his own staff. Shakespeare is an uncommon author in that he truly stopped writing before he died, retiring from London to Stratford. Stephen Greenblatt speculates from the prevalence of daughters in the Romances that Shakespeare stopped writing to be with his daughter Susanna. Yeats said, "[t]he intellect of man is forced to choose / Perfection of the life or of the work," and perhaps Shakespeare, like Prospero, knew a writing life would keep him from other forms of living.

While that is speculation, Shakespeare unquestionably demonstrated a striking insouciance toward the preservation of his work. He was willing, like Prospero, to drown his book. As Harold Bloom puts it: "It is as though an unpublished Freud threw what would have been the Standard Edition into the sea of space and time." Freud framed himself as a conquistador, but Shakespeare seems to have been reluctant to think of himself as even a literary imperialist. At the same time, the contrast between the drowned book and the burned book of *Doctor Faustus* should not elude us. We know from *The Tempest* that nothing goes into the sea that does not come out of it, transformed "into something rich and strange."

It was not until 1623, seven years after Shakespeare's death, that actors John Heminges and Henry Condell brought out the First Folio of Shakespeare's work. The first play in the First Folio is *The Tempest*. It is appropriate that the project of recovering Shakespeare's work—his book—began with this play about the creative process. The Folio, whose publication consolidated and confirmed Shakespeare's literary empire, made good on the promise that the drowned book would be recovered.

In his sonnets, which *were* published during his lifetime, Shakespeare shows imperial confidence in staking his claim to immortality on future generations of readers. "Not marble, nor the gilded monuments / Of princes," he says in Sonnet 55, "shall outlive this powerful rhyme." Still more famously, he ends Sonnet 18 with the couplet "So long as men can breathe or eyes can see, / So long lives this, and this gives life to thee." In the moment we read these lines, we realize we have been commandeered into keeping Shakespeare's work alive. We are the men and women who breathe, and our eyes are the eyes that see. Shakespeare coerces us to carry on his work and his name.

The epilogue to *The Tempest* is substantially more tentative, ac-

cording the audience or reader more agency to keep or break faith
with its author:

> Now my charms are all o'erthrown,
> And what strength I have's mine own,
> Which is most faint. Now, 'tis true
> I must be here confined by you,
> Or sent to Naples. Let me not,
> Since I have my dukedom got
> And pardoned the deceiver, dwell
> In this bare island by your spell;
> But release me from my bands
> With the help of your good hands.
> Gentle breath of yours my sails
> Must fill, or else my project fails,
> Which was to please. Now I want
> Spirits to enforce, art to enchant;
> And my ending is despair,
> Unless I be relieved by prayer,
> Which pierces so that it assaults
> Mercy itself, and frees all faults.
> As you from crimes would pardoned be,
> Let your indulgence set me free.
> (Epilogue, 1–20)

The poetry here is flatter, less imbued with the quality in the sonnets in which each line makes the next seem inexorable. The sim-
plicity of this verse can be seen as a gift of agency. In style as well
as substance, these lines frame a request, not a command. Prospero/
Shakespeare, who has controlled us for so long, allows us to make a
final judgment.

We know how we have ruled. The reach of *The Tempest,* like the reach of Shakespeare's work, is not only global but galactic. When assigning names to planetary bodies beginning in the mid-nineteenth century, astronomers decided to depart from the traditional practice of naming the moons after characters from Greco-Roman mythology. Because Uranus was unknown to the ancients, it seemed more appropriate to give its moons modern names. Twenty-five of Uranus's twenty-seven moons are named after characters from Shakespeare. Ten of those names come from *The Tempest,* as befits a play about the brave new worlds swimming into our ken.

Shakespeare's reluctance to rule may be the key to legitimate authority. If the book was meant to survive, others will pull it from the sea, others will read it and cherish it, others will sustain an empire of acquiescence rather than of force, of art rather than law. The plays are available for us to take up or discard, through a process that can only be described as democratic. We are not forced, but persuaded, one by one.

The final forgotten meaning of the "tempest" comes from the art of alchemy—it is the boiling in the alembic that transforms dross into gold. We know that this cannot happen; yet just thinking of that change will change us. That Shakespeare wrote this transformative, restorative play is his triumph; that he cast it on the waters is his trust. That we have kept it afloat is our contribution to the process through which we change and preserve art, and allow it to change and preserve us.

Épilogue

You see me Lord Bassanio where I stand,
Such as I am; though for myself alone
I would not be ambitious in my wish
To wish myself much better, yet for you,
I would be trebled twenty times myself,
A thousand times more fair. . . .
(*Merchant of Venice*, 3.2.149–54)

PORTIA SPEAKS THESE LINES IN *THE MERCHANT OF VENICE* directly after she is united with her lover, Bassanio. While I have taken a skeptical view of her role in that play, I think these lines capture something extraordinary about her, and us. This is our desire, particularly when we enter a community of love, to be better people than we are.

I wish to focus on Portia's desire to be "[a] thousand times more fair," because of the double meaning of the word "fair." I remember, when I was a young man, being asked the purpose of life, and responding, reflexively—"beauty and justice." This was before my career had taken shape; many of my life choices stood yet to be made. While I would go back and supplement that list—it is interesting to me, for instance, that "love" did not figure there—I stand by the original two terms.

The relationship between beauty and justice has been debated for millennia. Some believe in an innate relationship between them. Aristotle, for instance, characterized justice as a perfect cube. And as present-day literary critic Elaine Scarry reminds us, the word "fair" in its sense of justice derives from the word "fair" in the sense of beauty. Others, in contrast, believe beauty and justice are competing goods. Plato banished the poet from the city because the poet distracted us from justice. Modern-day skeptic Terry Eagleton points out that many of the guards in the Nazi concentration camps had a copy of Goethe in their back pockets. At that point, those who believed literature led inexorably to moral uplift "had some explaining to do."

I take a third view. I do not believe in any inherent link between beauty and justice, but I believe we can forge such a link. Shakespeare's contemporary Sir Philip Sidney got this right, in claiming that the task of the poet was to create "a speaking picture—with this end, to teach and delight." The poet, he said, should not come "with obscure definitions." Rather, he should come "with words set in delightful proportion . . . with a tale which holdeth children from play, and old men from the chimney corner." But Sidney did not believe in art for art's sake. At some point the poet, "pretending no more," had to reveal his true intention—the "winning of the mind from wickedness to virtue."

I still marvel at Shakespeare's capacity to hold children from play or to draw old men from the chimney corner. I am astonished that works this complex could nonetheless be so common. No other text but the Bible can make this claim. Our universal love of Shakespeare is a hopeful sign about how strong the drive toward beauty is within us.

What better use can we make of Shakespeare's allure than to let it draw us toward justice? While much of what passes for art these days is pabulum, the same could be said of what passes for justice. The aspiration of this book is to transcend the hurly-burly of our daily politics to find a deeper register. For I believe we yearn for that too.

Let us pause then to be grateful, not just to Shakespeare, but also to our own natures. It could easily have been otherwise. We could have had no higher ambitions in either direction. Instead, I think each of us has the desire to be a thousand times more beautiful and a thousand times more just. This is the call of fairness. We are human because we hear it.

Acknowledgments

To begin at the beginning, I wish to thank David Weber, English teacher at Phillips Exeter Academy. When my classmates and I were teenagers, David appended typewritten comments to handwritten papers. That confidence-inspiring service has extended into middle age: David sent detailed comments on every chapter of this book. I hope he has discerned some progress over the decades in which he has taught me.

As an English major at Harvard College, I had the glorious experience of taking Marjorie Garber's year-long introduction to Shakespeare. I also had the privilege of studying under Seamus Heaney and Helen Vendler. I cannot imagine better field guides to the slopes of Mount Parnassus. I look back on those four years of complete immersion in literature with reverence.

I enrolled in Yale Law School as a first-year student thinking I was leaving the humanities. I left fifteen years later as a chaired professor with the conviction that law was *one* of the humanities. I thank my sometime teachers, now my colleagues, for revealing this truth: Bruce Ackerman, Akhil Reed Amar, Ian Ayres, Jack Balkin, Peter Brooks, Bo Burt, Guido Calabresi, William Eskridge, Owen Fiss, Paul Gewirtz, Paul Kahn, Harold Hongju Koh, Anthony Kronman, Robert Post, Carol Rose, Jed Rubenfeld, Peter Schuck, and Reva Siegel.

I also thank those who taught me as colleagues: Anne Alstott, Richard Brooks, Amy Chua, Heather Gerken, Oona Hathaway, Christine Jolls, Daniel Markovits, Judith Resnik, Vicki Schultz, Scott Shapiro, and John Witt.

At NYU Law School, I have been given a better welcome than anyone could deserve. Dean Richard Revesz has supported me unstintingly in all my endeavors. Among my other colleagues here, Carol Gilligan gets marquee billing for letting me co-teach a freshman honors seminar with her titled Love and Law in Shakespeare's Plays, where this book first took shape. I also benefited from oral and written comments from Amy Adler, Rachel Barkow, Oren Bar-Gill, Barton Beebe, Cynthia Estlund, David Golove, Ryan Goodman, Stephen Holmes, Deborah Malamud, Troy McKenzie, Robert Rabin, David Richards, Catherine Sharkey, and Jeremy Waldron. For material support, I gratefully acknowledge the Filomen D'Agostino and Max E. Greenberg Research Fund.

In the fall of 2009, I tested many ideas in this book on a class of extraordinary students. At the end of our last session together, I promised to acknowledge them individually in the final product. I do so here, with enduring respect: Liran Avisar, Matthew Carhart, Avinoam Erdfarb, Adair Iacono, Joshua Kass, Kibum Kim, Summer Lacey, Matthew Lafargue, Christian Lang, Angela Libby, Silas Lum, Andrew Lutes, James Moody, Elizabeth Morris, Ranadeb Mukherjee, Dale Park, Michael Ray, Anne Redcross, Mark Rizik, Yoshinori Sasao, Tania Schrag, Matthias Swonger, Friedrich von Schoenfeld, Katrina Voorhees, and Jeffrey Wren. Six students also provided stellar research assistance: Graham Ballou, Noam Biale, Emma Dunlop, Ari Lazarus, Angela Libby, and Edward Lintz.

This project received unparalleled administrative support. My assistant, Rachel Jones, herself a great lover of Shakespeare, helped me forward in a myriad ways. Librarian Annmarie Zell showed such tireless efficiency that I pitied the poor sources that tried to elude her. I worked hard to keep up with them both.

Looking to the broader academic communities in which I work, I thank participants and colleagues in the following forums and institutions: the American Association of Law Schools annual meeting, the University of Chicago, the Cleveland-Marshall College of Law, Hong Kong University, the Shakespeare Association of America annual meetings of 2008 and 2009, Princeton University, and Waseda University. Through these and other channels, I received valuable comments from Anthony Appiah, Oliver Arnold, David Bevington, Harold Bloom, Anne Cheng, Bradin Cormack, Larry Danson, Elizabeth Emens, Henry Finder, George Fisher, Stephen Greenblatt, Elaine Ho, Martha Minow, Tetsu Motoyama, Martha Nussbaum, Richard Posner, Paul Raffield, Matthew Smith, Richard Strier, and Marco Wan. Special thanks go to Bernadette Meyler for her good cheer and wise counsel.

Many friends and family members were not professionally connected to the book, but did more than I can say to help me complete it: Bob Alsdorf, Matt Alsdorf, Sarah Alsdorf, Mary Ruth Bond, Ina Bort, Jessica Bulman-Pozen, Anne Calabresi, Bill Chinn, Sara Chinn, Kim Depole, Ariela Dubler, Christy Fisher, Adam Freed, Jesse Furman, Lee James, Aly Kassam-Remtulla, Michael Kavey, Emily Koh, Susan Lewis, Joseph Loy, Alison MacKeen, Jay Michaelson, Julie Nestingen, David Pozen, Tom Pulham, Paul Smith, Donna Stoneham, Chiyoko Yoshino, Kaye Yoshino, and Michael Yoshino.

At Ecco, I received tremendous support from the top down, starting with Dan Halpern. On the editorial side, Virginia Smith took the first leap of faith and Matt Weiland saw the project home with trenchant commentary. The entire team at Ecco—including Rachel Bressler, Suet Yee Chong, Rachel Elinsky, Michael McKenzie, Allison Salzman, Rebecca Urbelis, and Nancy Tan—is a credit to publishing. For her fathomless wisdom, I thank my longtime agent Betsy Lerner.

My greatest professional debt is to Robert Ferguson. The American dean of law and literature, he was the prime interlocutor for this book. More important, he models for me what a scholar, and human being, should be.

Anyone who has met our dogs will know that it is not overkill to thank them. Shakespeare has been accused of disliking dogs. Because he did not have the opportunity to meet Billy and Chloe, I need not qualify my bardolatry.

My deepest thanks go to my spouse, Ron Stoneham, to whom I have dedicated this book. To paraphrase an author he has come to know well, I do not know how I shall live and work to match his goodness.

Notes

Introduction

xi   *As the late law-and-literature scholar Robert Cover put it:* Robert M. Cover, "Nomos and Narrative," *Harvard Law Review* 97 (1983): 4.

xi   *Judge Richard Posner's memorable phrase:* Richard Posner, "The Ethical Significance of Free Choice: A Reply to Professor West," *Harvard Law Review* 99 (1986): 1433.

xii *as Mark Twain argued:* Mark Twain, *Is Shakespeare Dead?* (1909; Whitefish, Mont.: Kessinger Publishing, 2004), 27–35.

xii *I identify with James Joyce's:* James Joyce, *Ulysses* (1925; New York: Random House, 1986), 554.

Chapter One: The Avenger: *Titus Andronicus*

1   *Although it put Shakespeare on the map:* Jonathan Bate, introduction to *Titus Andronicus* by William Shakespeare, ed. Jonathan Bate (London: Arden Shakespeare, 2006), 1.

1   *T. S. Eliot:* T. S. Eliot, "Seneca in Elizabethan Translation," in *Selected Essays* (1932; New York: Harcourt Brace, 1964), 51, 67.

1   *Harold Bloom avers he:* Harold Bloom, *Shakespeare: The Invention of the Human* (New York: Riverhead Books, 1998), 86.

1   *Others have argued:* Philip C. Kolin, "*Titus Andronicus* and the Critical Legacy," in *Titus Andronicus: Critical Essays,* ed. Philip C. Kolin (New York: Garland, 1995), 3–4.

1   *While most critics now admit Shakespeare composed it:* Kolin, "*Titus Andronicus* and the Critical Legacy," 3; Bloom, *Shakespeare: The Invention of the Human,* 86.

2 *When Peter Brook:* Bate, introduction to *Titus Andronicus,* 5.

2 *Sir Laurence Olivier . . . said at least three audience members fainted every evening:* Ibid., 6.

2 *Jonathan Bate opines:* Ibid., 1.

2 *Coleridge writes that* Titus *was "obviously intended to excite vulgar audiences":* Samuel Taylor Coleridge, *Lectures and Notes on Shakespe[a]re and Other English Poets,* ed. T. Ashe (London: Bell, 1883), 9.

2 *That view of* Titus: Bate, introduction to *Titus Andronicus,* 58.

2 *Shakespeare lived in a time:* A. D. Nuttall, *Shakespeare the Thinker* (New Haven: Yale University Press, 2007), 44.

2 *As modern scholars:* William Ian Miller, *Bloodtaking and Peacemaking: Feud, Law, and Society in Saga Iceland* (Chicago: University of Chicago Press, 1990); Jon Elster, "Norms of Revenge," *Ethics* 100 (1990): 862–85.

3 *As Justice Oliver Wendell Holmes once said:* Oliver Wendell Holmes Jr., *The Common Law* (1938; New York: Dover Publications, 1991), 3.

3 As Bate observes: Bate, introduction to *Titus Andronicus,* 1.

3 *More recently, Julie Taymor's 1999 film:* Titus, DVD, directed by Julie Taymor (1999; Century City, Calif.: 20th Century Fox, 2006).

3 *has earned critical acclaim:* Stephen Holden, Film Review, "It's a Sort of Family Dinner, Your Majesty," *New York Times,* December 24, 1999; Mick LaSalle, "Taymor's *Titus* Twisted and Terrific," *San Francisco Chronicle,* January 28, 2000.

4 *"Wild justice," as Sir Francis Bacon:* Sir Francis Bacon, "Of Revenge," in *The Essays or Counsels Moral and Civil,* ed. Brian Vickers (1597; Oxford: Oxford University Press, 1999), 10.

4 *The Old Testament* lex talionis: Exod. 21:23–25 (King James Version).

4 *The literary scholar:* Fredson Thayer Bowers, *Elizabethan Revenge Tragedy 1587–1642* (Princeton: Princeton University Press, 1967), 23.

4 *James I described "factions and deadly feuds":* Ibid.

5 *One Shakespeare biographer:* William Holden, *William Shakespeare: The Man Behind the Genius* (Boston: Little, Brown, 2000), 139–40.

5 *The Long-Danvers feud:* Ibid.

5 *After Sir Walter rescued the servant:* Ibid., 140.

5 *Upon Sir Walter's release, a series of brawls:* Ibid.

5 *Sir Walter's brother Henry wrote abusive letters:* Lawrence Stone, *The Crisis of the Aristocracy 1558–1641* (Oxford: Clarendon Press, 1965), 224.

5 *Charles Danvers and his brother:* Holden, *William Shakespeare: The Man Behind the Genius,* 140.

5 *Charles attacked Henry:* Ibid.

5 *Southampton is the dedicatee:* William Shakespeare, *The Complete Works* (London: Arden Shakespeare, 2001), 49.

5 *widely believed to be the dedicatee:* John Kerrigan, "Shakespeare's Poems," in *The Cambridge Companion to Shakespeare,* eds. Margreta De Grazia and Stanley W. Wells (Cambridge: Cambridge University Press, 2001), 65, 73.

5 *Writing in 1609:* Bowers, *Elizabethan Revenge Tragedy,* 13.

5 *The passage in Exodus ceded to one in Romans:* Rom. 12:19–20 (King James Version).

6 *for Catholics and Protestants alike:* Bowers, *Elizabethan Revenge Tragedy,* 12.

6 *The Statute of Marlbridge: Statutes of the Realm,* 52 Hen. 3, c.6 (1257).

6 *The statute ordained:* Ibid., c.1.

6 *As Susan Jacoby writes:* Susan Jacoby, *Wild Justice: The Evolution of Revenge* (New York: Harper and Row, 1983), 35.

8 *Herodotus casts as:* Herodotus, *The Histories,* trans. G. C. Macaulay, rev. Donald Lateiner (New York: Barnes and Noble, 2004), 216.

9 *Though often invoked:* Morris J. Fish, "An Eye for an Eye: Proportionality as a Moral Principle of Punishment," *Oxford Journal of Legal Studies* 28 (2008): 57, 61.

11 *As critic Marjorie Garber points out, we need not be Freudians:* Marjorie Garber, *Shakespeare After All* (New York: Pantheon, 2004), 78.

13 *The controlling narrative is Ovid's Philomela:* Ovid, *The Metamorphoses,* ed. and trans. Allen Mandelbaum (New York: Harcourt, 1993), 194–204.

13 *Directors have struggled:* Alan Hughes, introduction to *Titus Andronicus* by William Shakespeare (New York: Cambridge University Press, 2006), 37.

13 *Brook used an overly:* Bate, introduction to *Titus Andronicus,* 60.

14 *Warner took a more literal tack:* Ibid., 61.

14 *Taymor found the middle ground:* Taymor, *Titus.*

14 *the Apollo and Daphne myth:* Ovid, *Metamorphoses* (Mandelbaum), 20.

15 *The actress Anna Calder-Marshall, who played Lavinia:* Bate, introduction to *Titus Andronicus,* 2.

17 *As Judge Richard Posner:* Richard A. Posner, *Law and Literature: A Misunderstood Relation* (Cambridge, Mass.: Harvard University Press, 1988), 29. Posner's book has gone through two subsequent editions, both of which

also make this point with phrasing that is slightly less on point for my purposes. Richard A. Posner, *Law and Literature*, 3rd ed. (Cambridge, Mass.: Harvard University Press, 2009), 78 (noting that vengeance breeds "intense loyalty within the extended family"); Richard A. Posner, *Law and Literature*, rev. ed. (Cambridge, Mass.: Harvard University Press, 2002), 52 (same).

18 *Prime among these:* Ovid, *Metamorphoses* (Mandelbaum), 1.1.150.

19 *As actor and legal scholar Paul Raffield:* Paul Raffield, "'Terras Astraea reliquit': *Titus Andronicus* and the Loss of Justice," in *Shakespeare and the Law,* ed. Paul Raffield and Gary Watt (Oxford: Hart Publishing, 2008), 204.

19 *The word "barbarous":* Edith Hall, *Inventing the Barbarian: Greek Self-Definition Through Tragedy* (Oxford: Oxford University Press, 1991), 4.

21 *Livy's* Roman History: Livy, *The Early History of Rome: Books I–V of the History of Rome from Its Foundations,* trans. Aubrey de Sélincourt (London: Penguin Books, 2002), 251–52.

21 *Ovid's* Metamorphoses: Ovid, *Metamorphoses* (Mandelbaum), 194–204.

21 *melds with Seneca's:* Seneca, *Thyestes,* ed. Joost Daalder, trans. Jasper Heywood (New York: W. W. Norton, 1982), act 5, sc. 3. The feast occurs throughout act 5, scene 3, with the revelation slowly unfolding and only made explicit at 5.3.66: "Atreus: 'Thou hast devour'd thy sons, and fill'd thyself with wicked meat.'"

21 *Garber says:* Garber, *Shakespeare After All,* 85.

21 *Posner describes this:* Posner, *Law and Literature: A Misunderstood Relation,* 39.

22 *We should remember:* John Milton, *Paradise Lost,* ed. David Scott Kastan (Indianapolis, Ind.: Hackett, 2005), bk. 9, ll. 171–72.

24 *But as for Polyneices:* Sophocles, *Antigone,* in *Antigone; Oedipus the King; Electra,* ed. Edith Hall, trans. Humphrey Davy Findley Kitto (Oxford: Oxford University Press, 1998), ll. 26–30.

24 *The statistics tell us:* "9/11 by the Numbers," *New York Magazine,* September 16, 2002, http://nymag.com/news/articles/wtc/1year/numbers.htm (accessed June 26, 2010).

24 *Stephen Holmes points out:* Stephen Holmes, *The Matador's Cape: America's Reckless Response to Terror* (Cambridge: Cambridge University Press, 2007), 2.

25 *"[o]ne theme that constantly":* Ibid.

25 *approval rating roared:* Richard Benedetto, "Support for Bush, Military Action Remains Firm," *USA Today,* September 24, 2001.

25 *As Bush said: "There's no need to discuss innocence":* "Bush rejects Taliban offer to hand Bin Laden over," *The Guardian* (U.K.), October 14, 2001, http://www.guardian.co.uk/world/2001/oct/14/afghanistan.terrorism5 (accessed June 26, 2010).

26 *Kissinger perhaps answered most honestly:* Bob Woodward, *State of Denial* (New York: Simon & Schuster, 2006), 408.

26 *As Richard Clarke:* Barry Bergman, "'Who's going to believe us?' Richard Clarke Faults Bush Team's Post–9/11 Policies," *U.C. Berkeley News,* September 8, 2004, http://berkeley.edu/news/media/releases/2004/09/08_clarke.shtml (accessed June 26, 2010).

27 *The photographs of Abu Ghraib prisoners:* Susan Sontag, "Regarding the Torture of Others," *New York Times Magazine,* May 23, 2004.

27 *quartet of opinions: Hamdi v. Rumsfeld,* 542 U.S. 507 (2004); *Rasul v. Bush,* 542 U.S. 466 (2004); *Hamdan v. Rumsfeld,* 548 U.S. 557 (2006); *Boumediene v. Bush,* 553 U.S. 723 (2008).

27 *"blank check": Hamdi,* 542 U.S. at 536.

27 *"bound to comply": Hamdan,* 548 U.S. at 635.

Chapter Two: The Lawyer: *The Merchant of Venice*

30 *"government of laws": Marbury v. Madison,* 5 U.S. (1 Cranch) 137, 163 (1803).

30 *Commentators generally see:* See, e.g., G. Midgley, "The Merchant of Venice: A Reconsideration," *Essays in Criticism* 10, no. 2 (1960): 119.

31 *Portrayals by Patrick Stewart:* Patrick Stewart, *Shylock: Shakespeare's Alien* (Leeds, England: 2001).

31 *Al Pacino in a 2004 film: The Merchant of Venice,* DVD, directed by Michael Radford (2004; Sony Pictures Classics, 2005).

32 *As Freud recognizes:* Sigmund Freud, *The Theme of the Three Caskets* (1913), reprinted in the *Standard Edition of the Complete Psychological Works of Sigmund Freud,* ed. and trans. James Strachey (London: Hogarth Press, 1955), 12: 292–93.

33 *Given that silver was used to make mirrors:* P. L. Jacob, *The Arts in the Middle Ages and the Renaissance* (New York: F. Ungar, 1964), 24.

34 *Critics dispute whether Portia helps him:* Compare Harry Berger Jr., "Marriage and Mercifixion in *The Merchant of Venice:* The Casket Scene Revisited," *Shakespeare Quarterly* 32, no. 2 (1981): 156 (arguing that Portia helps

Bassanio choose the correct casket) with Lawrence Danson, *The Harmonies of* The Merchant of Venice (New Haven: Yale University Press, 1978), 117–18 (rejecting this view).

35 *It is a critical commonplace:* Marjorie Garber, *Shakespeare After All* (New York: Pantheon, 2004), 290.

38 *This play is set:* Robert Bonfil, *Jewish Life in Renaissance Italy*, trans. Anthony Oldcorn (Los Angeles: University of California Press, 1994), 77; Max I. Dimont, *Jews, God, and History* (New York: Mentor, 1994), 231.

38 *forced to wear red hats:* Benjamin Ravid, "From Yellow to Red: On the Distinguishing Head-Covering of the Jews of Venice," *Jewish History* 6, no. 1 (1992): 179–210.

38 *Jews often turned to moneylending:* Bonfil, *Jewish Life in Renaissance Italy*, 79.

38 *Acte Against Usurie:* 13 Eliz. I, c. 8; see also R. H. Helmholz, *The Oxford History of the Laws of England* (Oxford: Oxford University Press, 2004), 1: 379.

38 *The 1571 Act only prohibited:* Helmholz, *The Oxford History of the Laws of England*, 1: 379.

40 *The only defenses:* Edith G. Henderson, "Relief from Bonds in the English Chancery: Mid-Sixteenth Century," *American Journal of Legal History* 18, no. 4 (1974): 298–306.

40 *Individuals bound by:* Mark Edwin Andrews, *Law Versus Equity in* The Merchant of Venice (Boulder: University of Colorado Press, 1965), xi.

40 *Chancery could not undo the bond:* Ibid.

40 *By the 1590s, Chancery's interventions:* Henderson, "Relief from Bonds," 298.

42 *Finally, when anthologized:* See, e.g., *The Complete Dictionary of Shakespeare Quotations*, ed. D. C. Browning (Poole, U.K., and New York: New Orchard Editions, 1986), 91–92.

44 *Portia's gambit is rightly seen as a "wretched quibble":* Rudolph von Ihering, *The Struggle for Law* (n.p., 1872), 411.

44 *As an 1858 legal treatise:* Freeman Oliver Haymes, *Outlines of Equity: A Series of Elementary Lectures* (Philadelphia: T. and J. W. Johnson and Co., 1858), 20.

49 *Shylock's ring is a relatively humble turquoise:* Jackson Campbell Boswell, "Shylock's Turquoise Ring," *Shakespeare Quarterly* 14, no. 4 (1963): 481–82.

50 *Portia Law School:* John F. O'Brian, "Opportunity for All," New England School of Law History Project, http://www.nesl.edu/historyProject/ (accessed June 26, 2010).

50 *"who now graces our Court":* John Paul Stevens, "The Shakespeare Canon of Statutory Construction," *University of Pennsylvania Law Review* 140 (1992): 1387.

50 *Ann Althouse has observed:* Ann Althouse, "When is it considered socially acceptable to joke to a stranger that people like you should all be dead?" Althouse blog, posted December 21, 2004, http://althouse.blogspot.com/2004/12/when-is-it-considered-socially.html (accessed June 26, 2010).

51 *Sophists of antiquity:* G. B. Kerferd, *The Sophistic Movement* (Cambridge: Cambridge University Press, 1981), 32.

51 *Law professor Marc Galanter:* Marc Galanter, *Lowering the Bar: Lawyer Jokes and Legal Culture* (Madison: University of Wisconsin Press, 2005), 17.

52 *Of all the hairsplitting: The Starr Report: The Findings of Independent Counsel Kenneth W. Starr on President Clinton and the Lewinsky Affair* (New York: Public Affairs, 1998), 325.

52 *In his Paula Jones deposition:* Ibid., 159.

52 *This statement dovetailed with an affidavit submitted by Lewinsky:* Ibid., 129.

52 *When questioned about the Lewinsky affidavit:* Ibid., 159.

52 *Clinton also remained silent:* Ibid., 36.

52 *At a White House press conference:* Ibid., 151.

52 *As it turned out:* Ibid., 32–36.

53 *In this appearance:* Ibid., 173.

53 *"If you said":* Office of the Independent Counsel, Transcript of Testimony of William Jefferson Clinton, President of the United States, Before the Grand Jury Empanelled for Independent Counsel Kenneth Starr, August 17, 1998, http://jurist.law.pitt.edu/transcr.htm (accessed June 26, 2010).

53 *Under that definition: Starr Report,* 37.

53 *The president had an answer:* Ibid., 38.

54 *Clinton's follow-up seemed:* Ibid.

54 *As The Starr Report:* Ibid.

54 *Asked whether the statement:* Ibid., 325.

54 *As he elaborated:* Ibid.

55 *conservative columnist George Will:* George F. Will, "In 'Forgiveness Mode,'" *Washington Post,* September 16, 1998.

55 *Thomas Reed Powell once said: AT & T Corporation v. Hulteen,* 129 S. Ct. 1962, 1980 (2009) (Ginsburg, J., dissenting).

55 *"I didn't inhale":* Gwen Ifill, "Clinton Admits Experiment with Marijuana in 1960's," *New York Times,* March 30, 1992.

55 *never "explicitly" told her to lie:* Starr Report, 207.

56 *However, she testified:* Ibid., 211–13.

56 *For instance, Clinton allegedly:* Ibid., 191.

56 *When Lewinsky tried:* Ibid., 76.

56 *Both parties used her:* Ibid., 75.

56 *"You were always there":* Ibid., 140.

56 *She admitted:* Ibid., 141.

Chapter Three: The Judge: *Measure for Measure*

60 *With the circumspection:* Charlie Savage, "A Nominee on Display, but Not Her Views," *New York Times,* July 16, 2009.

60 *President Barack Obama stated:* "Obama's Remarks on the Resignation of Justice Souter," *New York Times,* May 1, 2009.

60 *Senator Jeff Sessions:* Kathy Kiely and Joan Biskupic, "Sotomayor's Remarks Cap Emotional Day," *USA Today,* July 13, 2009.

60 *Empathy for some, he noted:* Ibid.

60 *The first sense:* Matt. 7:1–5 (King James Version).

61 *Old Testament ethic of commensurability:* However, in later Jewish tradition some sages claimed that the Temple was destroyed because when disputes arose, judges insisted on the strict letter of the Torah, and did not act with compassion in the interest of peace to reach a compromise, i.e., go beyond the letter of law. Menachem Elon, "Law, Truth, and Peace: The Three Pillars of the World," *New York University Journal of International Law and Politics* 29 (1996): 439, 444.

61 *As it says in:* Exod. 21:23–25 (King James Version).

65 *Albert Einstein opposed:* Albert Einstein, "My First Impressions of the U.S.A.," in *Berliner Tageblatt,* July 7, 1921, reprinted in Albert Einstein, *Ideas and Opinions,* ed. Carl Seelig, trans. Sonja Bargmann (1954; New York: Wing Books, 1988), 3, 6.

67 *Machiavelli points out:* Niccolò Machiavelli, *The Prince,* eds. Quentin Skinner and Russell Price (1515; Cambridge: Cambridge University Press, 1988), 58.

68 *the doctrine of "desuetude":* Daniel J. Kornstein, *Kill All the Lawyers?: Shake-*

speare's Legal Appeal (Lincoln: University of Nebraska Press, 2005), 46–69.

69 *Like Angelo, the Puritans:* Havelock Ellis, *The Psychology of Sex* (1910; Philadelphia: F. A. Davis, 1913), 356; Edmund Morgan, "The Puritans and Sex," *The New England Quarterly* 15, no. 4 (1942): 591, 594.

69 *Shakespeare had reason:* Stephen Greenblatt, *Will in the World: How Shakespeare Became Shakespeare* (New York: W. W. Norton, 2004), 120.

70 *The order of Saint Clare:* Natasha Korda, *Shakespeare's Domestic Economies: Gender and Property in Early Modern England* (Philadelphia: University of Pennsylvania Press, 2002), 159.

70 *New York City in the mid-1980s:* Malcolm Gladwell, *The Tipping Point* (Boston: Little, Brown, 2000), 133–68.

70 *I like Northrop Frye's:* Northrop Frye, *Northrop Frye on Shakespeare,* ed. Robert Sandler (New Haven: Yale University Press, 1986), 146.

73 *Indeed, Supreme Court Justice:* Michael Lipkin, "Justice Breyer Speaks on Shakespeare and Law," *Chicago Maroon,* May 19, 2009, http://www .chicagomaroon.com/2009/5/19/justice-breyer-speaks-on-shakespeare-and-law.

75 *is as old as Plato:* Plato, *The Republic of Plato,* ed. and trans. Allan Bloom (New York: Basic Books, 1991), 369b.

75 *As Harold Bloom says, "Had the Marquis de Sade":* Harold Bloom, *Shakespeare: The Invention of the Human* (New York: Riverhead Books, 1998), 365.

76 *two examples:* Paul Kane and Chris Cillizza, "Sen. Ensign Acknowledges an Extramarital Affair," *Washington Post,* June 17, 2009; Danny Hakim and William K. Rashbaum, "Spitzer Is Linked to Prostitution Ring," *New York Times,* March 10, 2008.

82 *"I neede not to trouble":* James I, *The Political Works of James I,* ed. Charles Howard McIlwain (Cambridge, Mass.: Harvard University Press, 1918), 37.

83 *In opposing the confirmation:* Statement of Senator Obama, *Congressional Record* 151 (September 22, 2005): S10365.

83 *But he continued:* Ibid.

84 *When asked during:* See, e.g., Chris Weigant, "Is the Media Misinterpreting Obama's 'Empathy' Dog Whistle?," *Huffington Post,* May 7, 2009, http:// www.huffingtonpost.com/chris-weigant/is-the-media-misinterpret _b_198389.html (discussing Obama's 2007 speech to Planned Parent-

hood); Barack Obama, interviewed by Wolf Blitzer, *The Situation Room*, CNN, May 8, 2008.

84 *Karl Rove called:* Karl Rove, "'Empathy' Is Code for Judicial Activism," *Wall Street Journal*, May 28, 2009.

84 *"Judges are like umpires":* Bruce Weber, "Umpires v. Judges," *New York Times*, July 12, 2009.

84 *In a 2001 speech:* Sonya Sotomayor, "A Latina Judge's Voice." Address, University of California Berkeley School of Law Symposium: Raising the Bar, Berkeley, California, October 26, 2001.

85 *In this opinion: Krimstock v. Kelly*, 306 F.3d 40 (2d Cir. 2002).

86 *Sotomayor characterized the:* Savage, "A Nominee on Display, but Not Her Views."

86 *while the White House stated:* Joe Klein, "The Return of the Hot-Button Issues," *Time*, June 4, 2009.

86 *Sotomayor also insisted:* Michael Muskal, "Sotomayor, Senators Make Nice—For Now," *Los Angeles Times*, June 3, 2009.

86 *Asked whether being:* Chuck Raasch, "Sotomayor Speech at Center of Court Nomination," *USA Today*, June 4, 2009.

86 *In a 1994 case: J. E. B. v. Alabama ex rel.* T. B., 511 U.S. 127, 148–49 (1994) (O'Connor, J., concurring).

86 *She continued that:* Ibid.

87 *As some of the Democrats:* Senate Committee on the Judiciary, Confirmation Hearing on the Nomination of John G. Roberts, Jr., to be Chief Justice of the United States. S. Hrg. 109–158 sess., September 12–15, 2005.

87 *For instance, Roberts wrote: Parents Involved in Community Schools v. Seattle School Dist. No. 1*, 551 U.S. 701 (2007).

Chapter Four: The Factfinder: *Othello*

89 *The great eighteenth-century:* William Blackstone, *Commentaries on the Laws of England*, vol. 3 (1765–1769; Chicago: University of Chicago Press, 1979), 330.

89 *Through much of the Middle Ages:* J. H. Baker, *An Introduction to English Legal History*, 4th ed. (Oxford: Oxford University Press, 2007), 4–6.

91 *As legal historian George Fisher:* George Fisher, "The Jury's Rise as Lie De-

tector," *Yale Law Journal* 107 (1997): 578–79. See also Edson Sunderland, "Verdicts, General and Special," *Yale Law Journal* 29 (1920): 262.

92 *Critically, however:* Leonard W. Levy, *The Palladium of Justice: Origins of Trial by Jury* (Chicago: Ivan Dee Press, 1999), 4.

92 *Perhaps the most familiar:* Robert Bartlett, *Trial by Fire and Water: The Medieval Judicial Ordeal* (Oxford: Oxford University Press, 1986), 1–2; John H. Langbein, Renée Lettow Lerner, and Bruce P. Smith, *History of the Common Law: The Development of Anglo-American Legal Institutions* (New York: Aspen Publishers, 2009), 44–46.

92 *The pronouns here are deliberate:* Margaret H. Kerr, Richard D. Forsyth, and Michael J. Plyley, "Cold Water and Hot Iron: Trial by Ordeal in England," *Journal of Interdisciplinary History* 22 (1992): 582–83, 588–89.

93 *For less serious crimes:* Baker, *English Legal History*, 5.

93 *the accused could swear "in very general terms":* Ibid.

93 *The third supernatural proof:* Langbein, Lerner, and Smith, *History of the Common Law*, 29.

93 *"trial by battle as the presumptive":* Ibid.

93 *As medieval historian Robert Bartlett:* Bartlett, *Trial by Fire and Water*, 33.

93 *And, as Baker adds:* Baker, *English Legal History*, 72.

94 *On the one hand:* Fisher, "The Jury's Rise as Lie Detector," 587.

94 *On the other:* John Langbein, *Torture and the Law of Proof: Europe and England in the Ancien Régime* (1976; Chicago: University of Chicago Press, 2006), 6.

94 *The ordeal was:* Baker, *English Legal History*, 5.

94 *The Catholic Church:* Levy, *Palladium of Justice*, 16.

94 *Stripped of its divine:* Ibid.

94 *As historian Leonard Levy:* Ibid., 9–10.

94 *Compurgation was in decline:* Baker, *English Legal History*, 74.

94 *"Champions were hired":* Levy, *Palladium of Justice*, 10.

95 *Sovereigns also worried:* James Q. Whitman, *Origins of Reasonable Doubt* (New Haven: Yale University Press, 2007), 87.

95 *Astonishingly, the wager by battle:* Baker, *English Legal History*, 74.

95 *The decline of the:* Langbein, *Torture and the Law of Proof*, 6.

95 *While the confession:* Ibid., 7.

95 *The Fourth Lateran Council:* Christopher R. Fee and David A. Leeming,

Gods, Heroes, and Kings: The Battle for Mythic Britain (New York: Oxford University Press, 2001), 214.

95 *The Continent's inquisitorial:* Langbein, *Torture and the Law of Proof,* 9.

95 *In contrast, the English:* Ibid.

95 *Fisher draws a direct:* Fisher, "The Jury's Rise as Lie Detector," 585.

95 *Historian John Langbein suggests:* Langbein, *Torture and the Law of Proof,* 6.

95 *The question of how:* Barbara J. Shapiro, *A Culture of Fact: England, 1550–1720* (Ithaca, N.Y.: Cornell University Press, 2000).

96 *the historical Lear:* A. D. Nuttall, *Shakespeare the Thinker* (New Haven: Yale University Press, 2007), 300.

96 *Moreover, such trials:* Dunbar Plunket Barton and James Montgomery Beck, *Links Between Shakespeare and the Law* (London: Butler and Tanner, 1929), 95.

97 *Like* Measure, Othello *is largely based on a story from Giraldi Cinthio's* Hecatommithi: E. A. J. Honigmann, introduction to *Othello* by William Shakespeare (London: Arden Shakespeare, 2004), 2.

97 *Shakespeare's decision:* Marjorie Garber, *Shakespeare After All* (New York: Pantheon, 2004), 496.

98 *An "assay" was another: The Oxford English Dictionary* (Oxford: Clarendon Press, 1989), 703–704. The word "assay" is variously defined as "To make trial (of)," ibid., 703; "To practise by way of trial," ibid., 703; or "To challenge to a trial of strength, skill, etc.," ibid., 704.

99 *Interracial marriage was generally legal:* William D. Zabel, "Interracial Marriage and the Law," in *Interracialism: Black-White Intermarriage in American History, Literature and Law,* ed. Werner Sollors (New York: Oxford University Press, 2000), 56.

100 *This is consistent:* Shapiro, *Culture of Fact,* 17.

101 *"the Othello music":* G. Wilson Knight, *The Wheel of Fire* (1930; New York: Routledge Classics, 2001), 109–35.

103 *As E. A. J. Honigmann points:* Honigmann, introduction to *Othello,* 146.

104 *As the birthplace:* Irene Earls, *Renaissance Art: A Topical Dictionary* (Westport, Conn.: Greenwood Publishing, 1987), 45.

104 *As many have commented:* See, e.g., Harold Bloom, *Shakespeare: The Invention of the Human* (New York: Riverhead Books, 1998), 432–75; Nuttall, *Shakespeare the Thinker,* 280.

104 *The Turks have:* Winston Graham, *The Spanish Armadas* (New York: Doubleday, 1972), 221–22.

106   *The likely historical trigger:* Honigmann, introduction to *Othello*, 2.

106   *Leo, himself a Moor:* Ibid., 4 (quoting Pory's account of Leo).

106   *Critic Geoffrey Bullough's claim:* Ibid., 208 (quoting Bullough).

108   *Langbein describes how:* Langbein, *Torture and the Law of Proof,* 7.

108   *But, as he says, the jurists who devised:* Ibid.

108   *Those hard cases:* Ibid.

111   *Marjorie Garber:* Garber, *Shakespeare After All,* 496–97.

113   *The "O" is also:* Terry Eagleton, " 'Nothing': *Othello, Hamlet, Coriolanus,*" in *William Shakespeare* (Malden, Mass.: Blackwell, 1986), 64, n. 1.

115   *First, it is nonhierarchical:* During this period, the number of women bringing or otherwise participating in suits was exploding. See Tim Stretton, *Women Waging War in Elizabethan England* (Cambridge: Cambridge University Press, 1998).

116   *As a result, the paradigmatic factfinder in this country today is the jury:* See U.S. Const. art. III, § 2 ("The trial of all crimes, except in cases of impeachment, shall be by jury; and such trial shall be held in the state where the said crimes shall have been committed; but when not committed within any state, the trial shall be at such place or places as the Congress may by law have directed"); U.S. Const. amend. VI ("In all criminal prosecutions, the accused shall enjoy the right to a speedy and public trial, by an impartial jury of the State and district wherein the crime shall have been committed").

116   *and constitutionally available:* U.S. Const. amend. VII ("In suits at common law, where the value in controversy shall exceed twenty dollars, the right of trial by jury shall be preserved, and no fact tried by a jury, shall be otherwise reexamined in any Court of the United States, than according to the rules of the common law").

116   *though others have made this comparison:* Alan M. Dershowitz, *Reasonable Doubts* (New York: Simon & Schuster, 1996), 24.

117   *Nicole Brown Simpson bought two pairs of Aris Light gloves:* Jeffrey Toobin, *The Run of His Life: The People v. O. J. Simpson* (New York: Random House, 1996), 364.

117   *As* Newsweek *would comment:* Donna Foote, Mark Miller, and Tessa Namuth, "A Size Too Small," *Newsweek,* June 26, 1995.

118   *As the* New York Times: David Margolick, "O. J. Simpson Jury Revisits the Gloves, a Stitch at a Time," *New York Times,* September 13, 1995.

118 *"Glove expert":* Lawrence Schiller and James Willwerth, *American Tragedy: The Uncensored Story of the Simpson Case* (New York: Random House, 1996), 474, 478.

118 *But as the* Times: Margolick, "O. J. Simpson Jury Revisits the Gloves."

119 *In the Simpson case, a left-handed bloodstained glove:* Toobin, *Run of His Life,* 25.

119 *Its mate, also:* Ibid., 41–43.

119 *As prosecutor Marcia Clark:* Closing Argument by Ms. Clark and Closing Argument by Mr. Darden at *36, Simpson (No. BA097211), available in 1995 WL 672671 (closing argument by Clark).

120 *The prosecution argued:* Dershowitz, *Reasonable Doubts,* 81.

120 *Thomas Rymer criticized:* Thomas Rymer, *A Short View of Tragedy* (1693), reproduced in *Othello: A Sourcebook,* ed. Andrew Hadfield (New York: Routledge, 2003), 44.

121 *As legal commentator Vincent Bugliosi observes:* Vincent Bugliosi, *Outrage: The Five Reasons Why O. J. Simpson Got Away with Murder* (New York: W. W. Norton, 1996), 143. See also George Fisher, "The O. J. Simpson Corpus," *Stanford Law Review* 49 (1996–97): 998 (stating that "the point where the trial abandoned serious inquiry" was "the fateful moment when O. J. Simpson tried on the glove").

121 *In his closing arguments, defense attorney Johnnie Cochran:* "Excerpts from Closing Arguments on Murder Charges Against O. J. Simpson," *New York Times,* September 28, 1995.

122 *"In plain English":* Timothy Egan, "The Simpson Case: The Jury; With Spotlight Shifted to Them, Some Simpson Jurors Talk Freely," *New York Times,* October 5, 1995.

122 *Again, the emphasis on the glove was irrational:* Dershowitz, *Reasonable Doubts,* 30–31.

122 *As Cochran said: "I don't think he could 'act' the size of his hands":* Associated Press, "Expert: Shrinkage, Damage in Gloves," *Seattle Times,* June 15, 1995.

122 *Many misquoted Cochran's famous jingle:* Cochran used this phrase repeatedly in his final argument. Johnnie L. Cochran Jr. with Tim Rutten, *Journey to Justice* (New York: One World, 1996), 340, 342.

123 *Supporters of the* CSI *effect:* Simon A. Cole and Rachel Dioso-Villa, "Investigating the 'CSI Effect' Effect: Media and Litigation Crisis in Criminal Law," *Stanford Law Review* 61 (2009): 1351.

123 *Although empirical investigation:* Kimberlianne Podlas, "'The CSI Effect':

Exposing the Media Myth," *Fordham Intellectual Property Media and Entertainment Law Journal* 6 (2006): 429–65; Tom R. Tyler, "Viewing *CSI* and the Threshold of Guilt: Managing Truth and Justice in Reality and Fiction," *Yale Law Journal* 115 (2006): 1050–85.

123 *Nonetheless, some scholars:* Donald E. Shelton, Young S. Kim, and Gregg Barak, "A Study of Juror Expectations and Demands Concerning Scientific Evidence: Does the '*CSI* Effect' Exist?," *Vanderbilt Journal of Entertainment and Technology* 9 (Winter 2006): 331–68; Shelton, Kim, and Barak, "An Indirect-Effects Model of Mediated Adjudication: The *CSI* Myth, the Tech Effect, and Metropolitan Jurors' Expectations for Scientific Evidence," *Vanderbilt Journal of Entertainment and Technology* 12 (Fall 2009): 1–43.

124 *"double time" problem:* Honigmann, introduction to *Othello,* 68–72.

124 *As legal scholar Paul Butler:* Paul Butler, "Racially Based Jury Nullification: Black Power in the Criminal Justice System," *Yale Law Journal* 105 (1995): 721, n. 225.

124 *Fisher points out:* Fisher, "The Jury's Rise as Lie Detector," 579.

125 *Recall that Bartlett:* Bartlett, *Trial by Fire and Water,* 33.

Chapter Five: The Sovereign: The *Henriad*

127 *whose name draws on the* Iliad: Marjorie Garber, *Shakespeare After All* (New York: Pantheon, 2004), 314.

128 *Max Weber, who, in his 1919 lecture:* Max Weber, "Politics as a Vocation," in *The Vocation Lectures,* eds. David Owen and Tracy B. Strong, trans. Rodney Livingstone (Indianapolis, Ind.: Hackett, 2004): 32–94.

128 *First, there is feudal authority:* Ibid., 34.

128 *Second, there is the authority of charisma:* Ibid.

128 *Finally, there is legal authority:* Ibid.

129 *As literary scholar Stephen Greenblatt:* Stephen Greenblatt, "Invisible Bullets," in *Political Shakespeare: Essays in Cultural Materialism,* eds. Jonathan Dollimore and Alan Sinfield (Manchester: Manchester University Press, 1994), 31.

129 *Gallup poll:* Richard Benedetto, "Support for Bush, Military Action Remains Firm," *USA Today,* September 24, 2001.

132 *the historical Hotspur:* Garber, *Shakespeare After All,* 318.

133 *Harold Bloom, a famous devotee:* Harold Bloom, *Shakespeare: The Invention of the Human* (New York: Riverhead Books, 1998), 272.

133 *Queen Elizabeth's request:* Ibid., 315.

134 *He calls the travelers:* Edward J. White, *Commentaries on the Law in Shakespeare* (St. Louis, Mo.: F. H. Thomas Law Books Co., 1913), 255.

135 *as Freud observes:* Sigmund Freud, "Jokes and Their Relation to the Unconscious," in Sigmund Freud, *The Standard Edition of the Complete Psychological Works of Sigmund Freud,* ed. and trans. James Strachey (1905; London: Hogarth Press, 1955), 8: 231, n.1.

135 *Yet Bloom, whose identification with Falstaff is extreme:* Bloom, *Shakespeare: The Invention of the Human,* 285.

136 *most scythe-like comma:* I depart from the Arden edition here, which uses a semicolon. The First Quarto fragment does not include this exchange. The second Quarto has "I do, I will," and the Folio has "I doe, I will."

137 *Critics call Hal's jape:* David Scott Kastan, introduction to *The First Part of King Henry the Fourth* by William Shakespeare, ed. David Scott Kastan (London: Arden Shakespeare, 2007), 42.

137 *Daniel Kornstein observes:* Daniel J. Kornstein, *Kill All the Lawyers?: Shakespeare's Legal Appeal* (Lincoln: University of Nebraska Press, 2005), 135.

142 *the judiciary was not independent of the executive:* Jack Benoit Gohn, "Richard II: Shakespeare's Legal Brief on the Royal Prerogative and the Succession to the Throne," *Georgetown Law Journal* 70 (1982): 949. ("The King . . . was the chief magistrate and source of all judicial power.")

144 *As Ernst Kantorowicz demonstrates in his book:* Ernst Kantorowicz, *The King's Two Bodies: A Study in Mediaeval Political Theology* (Princeton: Princeton University Press, 1957), 7.

144 *One body was:* Ibid.

144 *The other was:* Ibid.

147 *As A. D. Nuttall:* A. D. Nuttall, *Shakespeare the Thinker* (New Haven: Yale University Press, 2007), 154.

147 *The relationship Hal has to Falstaff is similar to the relationship Plato's Socrates had to the poet:* Plato, *The Republic of Plato,* ed. and trans. Allan Bloom (New York: Basic Books, 1991), 397a–b.

147 *Aristotle did not:* Aristotle, *Poetics,* in *The Complete Works of Aristotle: The Revised Oxford Translation,* vol. 2, ed. Jonathan Barnes (Princeton: Princeton University Press, 1984), 2322–23.

147 *It was because Plato:* Socrates observes that if an imitative poet came to the city, we would "fall on our knees before him as a man sacred, wonderful, and pleasing." Plato, *Republic*, 398(a). Yet after doing so, "we would say that there is no such man among us in the city, nor is it lawful for such a man to be born there." Ibid.

151 *Kenneth Branagh's steely: Henry V*, DVD, directed by Kenneth Branagh (1989; Hollywood, Calif.: MGM, 2000).

151 *Law professor Theodor Meron:* Theodor Meron, *Henry's Wars and Shakespeare's Laws: Perspectives on the Law of War in the Later Middle Ages* (New York: Oxford University Press, 1993).

153 *father and son simply make different directorial decisions:* Kastan, introduction to *The First Part of King Henry the Fourth,* 32.

153 *The comparison dates back:* Julian Borger, "The Making of a Dynasty," *The Guardian* (U.K.), October 31, 1998.

154 *Yet the United States has long had political dynasties:* Richard Brookhiser, *America's First Dynasty* (New York: Free Press, 2002), 5.

154 *As historian Richard Brookhiser:* Ibid., 6.

154 *As Marjorie Garber observes:* Marjorie Garber, *Shakespeare and Modern Culture* (New York: Pantheon, 2008), 191.

154 *Ken Adelman, who runs:* Ken Adelman, "Not Lady Macbeth," *Washingtonian Magazine,* November 1, 1999.

154 *"misunderestimates":* George W. Bush, Campaign Speech, November 6, 2000, Bentonville, Ark., in Jacob Weisberg, *George W. Bushisms: The Slate Book of Accidental Wit and Wisdom of Our 43rd President* (New York: Fireside, 2001), 22.

154 *In his autobiography:* George W. Bush, *A Charge to Keep* (New York: Harper-Collins, 1999), 133; "Bush Faces New Round of Drug Questions," CNN, August 20, 1999, http://www.cnn.com/ALLPOLITICS/stories/1999/08/20/president.2000/bush.drug/ (accessed June 27, 2010).

154 *George H. W. Bush vested his political hopes in his son Jeb:* Bill Minutaglio, *First Son: George W. Bush and the Bush Family Dynasty* (New York: Three Rivers Press, 1999), 7.

154 *Joseph P. Kennedy Jr.:* Michael O'Brien, *John F. Kennedy* (New York: St. Martin's, 2005), 52.

155 *As English professor:* Scott Newstok, "'Step aside, I'll show thee a president': George W as Henry V?" (2003), www.poppolitics.com/archives/2003/05/George-W-as-Henry-V.

155 *As conservative editor Rich Lowry:* Rich Lowry, "Magnificent: This Was Not a Foggy Bottom Speech," *National Review Online,* September 21, 2001, http://www.nationalreview.com/lowry/lowry092101.shtml.

155 *Balint Vazsonyi agreed:* Balint Vazsonyi, "From Henry V to Bush II," *Washington Times,* October 12, 2001.

155 *Political commentator David Gergen:* Newstok, "'Step aside'" (quoting Gergen).

155 *Authorization for Use of Military Force:* "Authorization for Use of Military Force Against Terrorists 2001." (P. L. 107–40), *United States Statutes at Large,* 115 Stat. 224.

156 *"Shakespeare in Central Park":* Robert Dominguez, "Summer in the City 2003: One Thing's for Curtain, the Shows Go On," *New York Daily News,* May 23, 2003.

156 *London's* Observer *said:* Richard Ingrams, "Diary: Richard Ingrams' Week: Trial of King Tony: His Grounds for War Are Falling Apart, So Who Will Trust Blair on the Euro?," *The Observer* (London), May 18, 2003.

156 *Jack Lynch observes:* Jack Lynch, "The Politics of Shakespeare, the Shakespeare of Politics." Paper presented at the English Speaking Union of Monmouth County, Rumson, New Jersey, February 17, 2008.

156 *Columnist David Brooks:* Bob Thompson, "The King and We: Henry V's War Cabinet," *Washington Post,* May 18, 2004.

156 *Fallujah and Abu Ghraib:* "Picture Emerges of Fallujah Siege," *BBC News,* April 23, 2004, http://news.bbc.co.uk/2/hi/middle_east/3653223.stm (accessed June 27, 2010); Seymour M. Hersh, "Torture at Abu Ghraib," *The New Yorker,* May 10, 2004.

Chapter Six: The Natural World: *Macbeth*

159 *As stage historian:* Richard Huggett, *Supernatural on Stage* (New York: Taplinger, 1975), 153.

160 *If an actor speaks:* Ibid., 154.

160 *Merchant's general reputation:* Marjorie Garber, *Shakespeare After All* (New York: Pantheon, 2004), 537.

161 *I shall call this belief in the self-correcting universe "natural justice":* I stress that by "natural justice" I do not mean "natural law." Natural law theorist John Finnis makes the distinction with helpful force: "Theorists who

describe their theory of good and evil, right and wrong, as a 'natural law theory' are not committed to asserting that the normative propositions which they defend are 'derived from nature' or 'read off' or 'inspected in the nature of things'. Still less are natural law theorists committed to claiming that the normative propositions they defend stand in some definite relationship to, or are warranted by, the 'laws of nature' in the sense of the regularities observed, and explanatory factors adduced, by the 'natural sciences.'" John Finnis, "Natural Law," in *Routledge Encyclopedia of Philosophy*, ed. Edward Craig (London: Routledge, 1998), 1: 685.

161 *Shakespeare's main source:* David Bevington, "Shakespeare's Sources," in *Macbeth* by William Shakespeare, ed. David Bevington (New York: Random House, 1988).

162 *The fallacy led Susan Sontag:* Susan Sontag, *Illness as Metaphor* (New York: Farrar, Straus and Giroux, 1978).

162 *Harold Kushner's 1981 book:* Harold Kushner, *When Bad Things Happen to Good People* (New York: Random House, 1981).

162 *In 2001, Jerry Falwell:* http://archives.cnn.com/2001/US/09/14/Falwell.apology/. Falwell later apologized for his comment. Ibid.

167 *In an essay on:* Sigmund Freud, *Some Character-Types Met with in Psychoanalytic Work* (1916), reprinted in *The Standard Edition of the Complete Psychological Works of Sigmund Freud,* ed. and trans. James Strachey (London: Hogarth Press, 1955), 14: 316 (emphasis in original).

168 *Yet he offers:* Ibid., 14: 321–22.

168 *In the source materials:* Kenneth Muir, introduction to *Macbeth* by William Shakespeare, ed. Kenneth Muir (London: Arden Shakespeare, 1951), xxxviii.

169 *As Harold Bloom:* Harold Bloom, *Shakespeare: The Invention of the Human* (New York: Riverhead Books, 1998), 535.

171 *As literary scholar:* Jeff Dolven, "Spenser's Sense of Poetic Justice," *Raritan* 21, no. 1 (2001): 127–40.

172 *Holinshed describes Macbeth's bid:* Muir, introduction to *Macbeth*, xxxvi.

173 *E. M. Forster draws a distinction:* E. M. Forster, *Aspects of the Novel* (Orlando, Flor.: Harcourt, 1927), 67–78.

173 *Stephen Greenblatt's wonderful answer:* Stephen Greenblatt, *Will in the World: How Shakespeare Became Shakespeare* (New York: W. W. Norton, 2004), 337.

173 *As historian Alan Stewart:* Alan Stewart, *The Cradle King: The Life of James VI & I, the First Monarch of a United Great Britain* (New York: St. Martin's Press, 2007), 219.

175 *As Huggett (rather fancifully) puts it:* Huggett, *Supernatural on Stage*, 162–63.

176 *While performing the play:* Ibid., 192.

176 *why Diana Wynyard fell:* Ibid., 180.

176 *Incidentally, many do:* Dennis Coon and John Mitterer, *Introduction to Psychology: Gateways to Mind and Behavior* (Belmont, Calif.: Cengage Learning, 2008), 190.

177 *According to Huggett:* Huggett, *Supernatural on Stage*, 167.

177 *As Marjorie Garber observes:* Marjorie Garber, *Shakespeare and Modern Culture* (New York: Pantheon, 2008), 89–90.

178 *When he played the title role in 1937, Olivier:* Huggett, *Supernatural on Stage*, 172.

178 *Michael Knox Beran:* Michael Knox Beran, "Lincoln, *Macbeth,* and the Moral Imagination," *Humanitas* 2, no. 2 (1998): 13–14.

179 *Beran notes that Lincoln:* Ibid., 14.

179 *Some hypothesize that:* David Segal, "Macshush! Theater Superstition Warns of Double Trouble if the Name Is Spoken," *Washington Post,* June 13, 2006.

179 *Others have flatly:* Ibid.

179 *Still others argue:* Gabriel Egan, "Early Seventeenth-Century Origin of the Macbeth Superstition," *Notes and Queries* 49 (2002): 236.

180 *I know of only one "literary" prophecy:* I thank Robert Ferguson for bringing this instance to my attention. Jon. 3:10 (King James Version). ("And God saw their works, that they turned from their evil way; and God repented of the evil, that he had said that he would do unto them; and he did it not.")

182 *In an important 1996 essay:* Alan M. Dershowitz, "Life Is Not a Dramatic Narrative," in *Law's Stories: Narrative and Rhetoric in the Law,* eds. Peter Brooks and Paul Gewirtz (New Haven: Yale University Press, 1996), 99–105.

182 *begins by observing how Anton Chekhov:* Ibid., 99.

182 *In that universe:* Ibid., 100.

182 *But in our actual lives:* Ibid., 100–101.

182 *Dershowitz argues that the gap:* Ibid., 101.

183 *In honoring the anniversary of Martin Luther King Jr.'s death:* David Espo, "White House Hopefuls Pay Tribute to King," *Seattle Times,* April 6, 2008.

184 *As he put it:* Ibid.

Chapter Seven: The Intellectual: *Hamlet*

188 *A. C. Bradley states:* A. C. Bradley, *Shakespearean Tragedy* (1904; New York: Barnes and Noble, 2005), 69.

188 *The psychoanalyst Ernest Jones:* Ernest Jones, *Hamlet and Oedipus* (1949; New York: Norton, 1976), 22.

188 *Freud believes:* Sigmund Freud, *The Interpretation of Dreams* (1900), reprinted in the *Standard Edition of the Complete Psychological Works of Sigmund Freud,* ed. and trans. James Strachey (London: Hogarth Press, 1955), 4: 265.

188 *Goethe deems:* Johann Wolfgang von Goethe, *Wilhelm Meister's Apprenticeship,* trans. Thomas Carlyle (London: Oliver & Boyd, 1824), 2: 75.

188 *Nietzsche takes him:* Friedrich Nietzsche, *The Birth of Tragedy* (1871; Stilwell, Kans.: Digireads Publishing, 2007), 41.

188 *As Marjorie Garber observes:* Marjorie Garber, *Shakespeare and Modern Culture* (New York: Pantheon, 2008), 201.

189 *Stephen Greenblatt notes:* Stephen Greenblatt, *Hamlet in Purgatory* (Princeton: Princeton University Press, 2001), 4.

192 *Sir Thomas Browne:* Sir Thomas Browne, *Religio Medici* in *Religio Medici and Other Writings* (1643; New York: E. P. Dutton, 1951), 43.

194 *As legal scholar J. Anthony Burton:* J. Anthony Burton, "An Unrecognized Theme in *Hamlet*: Lost Inheritance and Claudius's Marriage to Gertrude," *The Shakespeare Newsletter* 50 (2000–2001): 71–82.

195 *Under prevailing ecclesiastical law:* Henry Ansgar Kelly, *The Matrimonial Trials of Henry VIII* (Palo Alto, Calif.: Stanford University Press, 1976), 276.

195 *As it states in Leviticus:* Lev. 18:16 (King James Version).

195 *And further:* Lev. 20:21 (King James Version).

195 *However, Deuteronomy states an exception:* Deut. 25:5–6 (King James Version).

196 *Jason Rosenblatt:* Jason Rosenblatt, "Aspects of the Incest Problem in *Hamlet*," *Shakespeare Quarterly* 29 (1978): 349–364.

197 *Literary critic Maynard Mack:* Maynard Mack, *Everybody's Shakespeare* (Lincoln: University of Nebraska Press, 1993), 107.

198 *Richard Posner observes:* Richard A. Posner, *Law and Literature,* 3rd ed. (Cambridge, Mass.: Harvard University Press, 2009), 112.

199 *The allusion is:* Genesis 4:11 (King James Version).

199 *The idea that there might be a right against self-incrimination:* John H. Langbein, Renée Lettow Lerner, and Bruce P. Smith, *History of the Common*

Law: The Development of Anglo-American Legal Institutions (New York: Aspen Publishers, 2009), 698–700.

201 *Samuel Johnson thought:* Ann Thompson and Neil Taylor, notes to *Hamlet* by William Shakespeare, eds. Ann Thompson and Neil Taylor (London: Arden Shakespeare, 2006), 331.

202 *Here is Bradley:* Bradley, *Shakespearean Tragedy,* 83.

204 *So Hazlitt is wrong:* William Hazlitt, *Hazlitt's Criticism of Shakespeare: A Selection,* ed. R. S. White (Lewiston, N.Y.: Edward Mellen Press, 1996), 122.

205 *In a 1931 essay:* Benjamin N. Cardozo, "Law and Literature," in *Law and Literature and Other Essays and Addresses* (New York: Harcourt, Brace, 1931).

205 *Cardozo observes:* Ibid., 36.

206 *Conversely, one of the costs:* Ibid., 34.

206 *The coercive force:* Ibid.

206 *In the 1857 case:* Dred Scott v. Sandford, 60 U.S. 393 (1857).

207 *the Fourteenth Amendment:* U.S. Const. amend. XIV.

207 *Sir Thomas More's* Utopia: Sir Thomas More, *Utopia,* trans. Clarence H. Miller (New Haven: Yale University Press, 2001).

207 *Étienne Cabet's* Travels in Icaria: Étienne Cabet, *Travels in Icaria,* trans. Leslie Roberts (1840; Syracuse, N.Y.: Syracuse University Press, 2003).

207 *B. F. Skinner's* Walden Two: B. F. Skinner, *Walden Two* (Indianapolis, Ind.: Hackett, 1948).

207 *French socialist readers:* Cabet, *Travels in Icaria,* xxviii–xlvii.

207 *disciples of Skinner:* Deborah E. Altus and Edward K. Morris, "B. F. Skinner's Utopian Vision: Behind and Beyond *Walden Two,*" *Contemporary Justice Review* 267 (2004): 272.

207 *As literary critic Northrop Frye:* Northrop Frye, "Varieties of Literary Utopias," in *Utopias and Utopian Thought,* ed. Frank E. Manuel (Boston: Beacon Press, 1965), 25–26.

Chapter Eight: The Madman: *King Lear*

209 *Yet as law professor:* Paul W. Kahn, *Law and Love: The Trials of King Lear* (New Haven: Yale University Press, 2000), x.

210 *In* Basilicon Doron: King James VI and I, *Basilicon Doron,* in *Political Writings,* ed. Johann P. Sommerville (1599; Cambridge: Cambridge University Press, 1994), 42.

213 *One common way to defend Lear is to demonize Cordelia:* In his review of the recent Broadway production starring Kevin Kline, Ben Brantley described Cordelia as a "smirky, spoiled, uh, princess . . . [she is] so smug that you can't blame Lear for disinheriting her." Ben Brantley, Theater Review, "Howl? Nay, Express His Lighter Purpose," *New York Times,* March 8, 2007.

215 *As A. C. Bradley:* A. C. Bradley, *Shakespearean Tragedy* (1905; New York: Barnes and Noble, 2005), 250.

222 *Under the common law:* B. J. Sokol and Mary Sokol, *Shakespeare, Law, and Marriage* (Cambridge: Cambridge University Press, 2003), 157.

227 *White first observes:* Edward J. White, *Commentaries on the Law in Shakespeare* (1913; Honolulu, Hawaii: University Press of the Pacific, 2002), 461.

227 *White continues:* Ibid.

227 *White further notes:* Ibid.

227 *Finally, he observes:* Ibid.

227 *So it is appropriate:* Ibid.

228 *R. A. Foakes:* R. A. Foakes, notes to *King Lear* by William Shakespeare, ed. R. A. Foakes (London: Arden Shakespeare, 1997), 322.

230 *In Holinshed, Cordelia saves Lear:* See generally David Bevington, "Shakespeare's Sources," in William Shakespeare, *King Lear* (New York: Bantam, 1988).

231 *Bradley argues we:* Bradley, *Shakespearean Tragedy,* 252–54.

Chapter Nine: The Magician: *The Tempest*

233 *The play tests Lord Acton's:* Lord John Emerich Edward Dalberg Acton, Letter to Bishop Mandell (1887).

233 *The play was almost certainly:* Virginia Mason Vaughan and Alden T. Vaughan, introduction to *The Tempest* by William Shakespeare (London: Arden Shakespeare, 1999), 41.

235 *The title page to a 1620 printing of Christopher Marlowe's* Doctor Faustus: Ibid., 65.

242 *Stephen Greenblatt:* Stephen Greenblatt, *Learning to Curse* (Chicago: University of Chicago Press, 1991), 33.

245 *Gonzalo's utopian vision:* Michel de Montaigne, "Of the Cannibals," in *The Essays of Montaigne,* trans. John Florio (1603).

248 *A self-styled expert on the occult, King James warned:* King James VI and I, *Daemonologie,* ed. G. B. Harrison (1597; San Diego: The Book Tree, 2002), 10.

250 *This speech echoes:* Ovid, *The Metamorphoses,* ed. and trans. Allen Mandelbaum (New York: Harcourt, 1993), 217.

252 *As James Madison:* Alexander Hamilton, James Madison, and John Jay, *The Federalist,* ed. Robert A. Ferguson (1787–88; New York: Barnes and Noble Classics, 2006), 288.

252 *As biographer Garry Wills:* Garry Wills, *Cincinnatus: George Washington and the Enlightenment* (New York: Doubleday, 1984), 13.

252 *The painter:* Ibid.

253 *As constitutional historian Akhil Reed Amar:* Akhil Reed Amar, *America's Constitution: A Biography* (New York: Random House, 2005), 146.

253 *President Jefferson invoked:* Ibid.

253 *In this way:* Ibid.

255 *Stephen Greenblatt speculates:* Stephen Greenblatt, *Will in the World: How Shakespeare Became Shakespeare* (New York: W. W. Norton, 2004), 389–90.

255 *Yeats said, "[t]he intellect of man":* William Butler Yeats, "The Choice," in *The Yeats Reader,* ed. Richard J. Finnerman. (New York: Scribner, 1997), 102.

256 *As Harold Bloom puts it:* Harold Bloom, *Shakespeare: The Invention of the Human* (New York: Riverhead Books, 1998), 671.

Epilogue

260 *Aristotle, for instance, characterized:* Aristotle, *Nichomachean Ethics,* in *The Complete Works of Aristotle: The Revised Oxford Translation,* vol. 2, ed. Jonathan Barnes (Princeton: Princeton University Press, 1984), 1739.

260 *And as present-day literary critic Elaine Scarry:* Elaine Scarry, *On Beauty and Being Just* (Princeton: Princeton University Press, 1999), 91–92.

260 *Plato banished the poet from the city:* Plato, *The Republic of Plato,* ed. and trans. Allan Bloom (New York: Basic Books, 1991), 397a–b.

260 *Modern-day skeptic Terry Eagleton:* Terry Eagleton, *Literary Theory: An Introduction* (Minneapolis: University of Minnesota Press, 2008), 30.

260 *Shakespeare's contemporary Sir Philip Sidney:* Sir Philip Sidney, *An Apology for Poetry,* ed. Geoffrey Shepherd (Manchester: Manchester University Press, 1973), 101.

260 *The poet, he said:* Ibid., 113.

260 *At some point:* Ibid.

Bibliography

Editions of Plays Used

Shakespeare, William. *Antony and Cleopatra*. Edited by John Wilders. Arden Shakespeare, 3rd ser. London: Thomson Learning, 1995.

———. *The Comedy of Errors*. Edited by R. A. Foakes. Arden Shakespeare, 2nd ser. London: Thomson Learning, 1962.

———. *Hamlet*. Edited by Ann Thompson and Neil Taylor. Arden Shakespeare, 3rd ser. London: Thomson Learning, 2006.

———. *King Henry IV, Part 1*. Edited by David Scott Kastan. Arden Shakespeare, 3rd ser. London: Thomson Learning, 2002.

———. *King Henry IV, Part 2*. Edited by A. R. Humphreys. Arden Shakespeare, 2nd ser. London: Thomson Learning, 1981.

———. *King Henry V*. Edited by T. W. Craik. Arden Shakespeare, 3rd ser. London: Thomson Learning, 1995.

———. *King Henry VI, Part 2*. Edited by Ronald Knowles. Arden Shakespeare, 3rd ser. London: Thomson Learning, 1999.

———. *King Henry VI, Part 3*. Edited by John D. Cox and Eric Rasmussen. Arden Shakespeare, 3rd ser. London: Thomson Learning, 2001.

———. *King Henry VIII*. Edited by Gordon McMullan. Arden Shakespeare, 3rd ser. London: Thomson Learning, 2000.

———. *King Lear*. Edited by R. A. Foakes. Arden Shakespeare, 3rd ser. London: Thomson Learning, 1997.

———. *Macbeth*. Edited by Kenneth Muir. Arden Shakespeare, 2nd ser. London: Thomson Learning, 1951.

———. *Measure for Measure*. Edited by J. W. Lever. Arden Shakespeare, 2nd ser. London: Thomson Learning, 1965.

——. *The Merchant of Venice.* Edited by John Russell Brown. Arden Shakespeare, 2nd ser. London: Thomson Learning, 1955.

——. *Othello.* Edited by E. A. J. Honigmann. Arden Shakespeare, 3rd ser. London: Thomson Learning, 1997.

——. *Richard II.* Edited by Charles R. Forker. Arden Shakespeare, 3rd ser. London: Thomson Learning, 2002.

——. *Shakespeare's Sonnets.* Edited by Katherine Duncan-Jones. Arden Shakespeare, 3rd ser. revised edition. London: Thomson Learning, 2010.

——. *The Tempest.* Edited by Virginia Mason Vaughan and Alden T. Vaughan. Arden Shakespeare, 3rd ser. London: Thomson Learning, 1999.

——. *Titus Andronicus.* Edited by Jonathan Bate. Arden Shakespeare, 3rd ser. London: Thomson Learning, 1995.

——. *The Winter's Tale.* Edited by John Pitcher. Arden Shakespeare, 3rd ser. London: Thomson Learning, 2010

Books

Amar, Akhil Reed. *America's Constitution: A Biography.* New York: Random House, 2005.

Andrews, Mark Edwin. *Law Versus Equity in* The Merchant of Venice. Boulder: University of Colorado Press, 1965.

Aristotle. *The Complete Works of Aristotle: The Revised Oxford Translation.* Edited by Jonathan Barnes. Princeton: Princeton University Press, 1984.

Bacon, Sir Francis. *The Essays or Counsels Moral and Civil.* 1597. Edited by Brian Vickers. Oxford: Oxford University Press, 1999.

Baker, J. H. *An Introduction to English Legal History.* 4th ed. Oxford: Oxford University Press, 2007.

Bartlett, Robert. *Trial by Fire and Water: The Medieval Judicial Ordeal.* Oxford: Oxford University Press, 1986.

Barton, Dunbar Plunket, and James Montgomery Beck. *Links Between Shakespeare and the Law.* London: Butler and Tanner, 1929.

Blackstone, William. *Commentaries on the Laws of England.* 1765–69. Chicago: University of Chicago Press, 1979.

Bloom, Harold. *Shakespeare: The Invention of the Human.* New York: Riverhead Books, 1998.

Bonfil, Robert. *Jewish Life in Renaissance Italy.* Translated by Anthony Oldcorn. Los Angeles: University of California Press, 1994.

Bowers, Fredson Thayer. *Elizabethan Revenge Tragedy 1587–1642.* Princeton: Princeton University Press, 1967.

Bradley, A. C. *Shakespearean Tragedy.* 1904. New York: Barnes and Noble, 2005.

Brookhiser, Richard. *America's First Dynasty.* New York: Free Press, 2002.

Brooks, Peter. *Troubling Confessions: Speaking Guilt in Law and Literature.* Chicago: University of Chicago Press, 2001.

Browne, Sir Thomas. *Religio Medici* in *Religio Medici and Other Writings.* 1643. New York: E. P. Dutton, 1951.

Browning, D. C., ed. *The Complete Dictionary of Shakespeare Quotations.* Poole, U.K.: New Orchard Editions, 1986.

Bugliosi, Vincent. *Outrage: The Five Reasons Why O. J. Simpson Got Away with Murder.* New York: W. W. Norton, 1996.

Bush, George W. *A Charge to Keep.* New York: HarperCollins, 1999.

Cabet, Étienne. *Travels in Icaria.* Translated by Leslie Roberts. 1840. Syracuse, N.Y.: Syracuse University Press, 2003.

Cardozo, Benjamin N. *Law and Literature and Other Essays and Addresses.* New York: Harcourt, Brace, 1931.

Cochran, Johnnie L., Jr., with Tim Rutten. *Journey to Justice.* New York: One World, 1996.

Coleridge, Samuel Taylor. *Lectures and Notes on Shakespe[a]re and Other English Poets.* Edited by T. Ashe. London: Bell, 1883.

Coon, Dennis, and John Mitterer. *Introduction to Psychology: Gateways to Mind and Behavior.* Belmont, Calif.: Cengage Learning, 2008.

Danson, Lawrence. *The Harmonies of* The Merchant of Venice. New Haven: Yale University Press, 1978.

Dershowitz, Alan M. *Reasonable Doubts.* New York: Simon & Schuster, 1996.

Dimont, Max I. *Jews, God, and History.* New York: Mentor, 1994.

Eagleton, Terry. *Literary Theory: An Introduction.* Minneapolis: University of Minnesota Press, 2008.

———. *William Shakespeare.* Malden, Mass.: Blackwell Publishing, 1986.

Earls, Irene. *Renaissance Art: A Topical Dictionary.* Westport, Conn.: Greenwood Publishing, 1987.

Einstein, Albert. *Ideas and Opinions*. 1954. Edited by Carl Seelig. Translated by Sonja Bargmann. New York: Wing Books, 1988.

Eliot, T. S. *Selected Essays*. 1932. New York: Harcourt Brace, 1964.

Ellis, Havelock. *The Psychology of Sex*. 1910. Philadelphia: F. A. Davis Company, 1913.

Fee, Christopher R., and David A. Leeming. *Gods, Heroes, and Kings: The Battle for Mythic Britain*. New York: Oxford University Press, 2001.

Forster, E. M. *Aspects of the Novel*. Orlando, Fla.: Harcourt, 1927.

Freud, Sigmund. *The Standard Edition of the Complete Psychological Works of Sigmund Freud*. Vol. 4, *The Interpretation of Dreams*. 1900. Vol. 8, *Jokes and Their Relation to the Unconscious*. 1905. Vol. 12, *The Theme of Three Caskets*. 1913. Vol. 14, *Some Character-Types Met with in Psychoanalytic Work*. 1916. Edited and translated by James Strachey. London: Hogarth Press, 1953–66.

Frye, Northrop. *Northrop Frye on Shakespeare*. Edited by Robert Sandler. New Haven: Yale University Press, 1986.

Galanter, Marc. *Lowering the Bar: Lawyer Jokes and Legal Culture*. Madison: University of Wisconsin Press, 2005.

Garber, Marjorie. *Shakespeare After All*. New York: Pantheon, 2004.

———. *Shakespeare and Modern Culture*. New York: Pantheon, 2008.

Gladwell, Malcolm. *The Tipping Point*. New York: Little, Brown, 2000.

Goethe, Johann Wolfgang von. *Wilhelm Meister's Apprenticeship*. Translated by Thomas Carlyle. London: Oliver & Boyd, 1824.

Graham, Winston. *The Spanish Armadas*. New York: Doubleday, 1972.

Greenblatt, Stephen. *Hamlet in Purgatory*. Princeton: Princeton University Press, 2001.

———. *Learning to Curse*. Chicago: University of Chicago Press, 1991.

———. *Will in the World: How Shakespeare Became Shakespeare*. New York: W. W. Norton, 2004.

Hall, Edith. *Inventing the Barbarian: Greek Self-Definition Through Tragedy*. Oxford: Oxford University Press, 1991.

Hamilton, Alexander, James Madison, and John Jay. *The Federalist*. 1787–88. Edited by Robert A. Ferguson. New York: Barnes and Noble Classics, 2006.

Haymes, Freeman Oliver. *Outlines of Equity: A Series of Elementary Lectures*. Philadelphia: T. and J. W. Johnson and Co., 1858.

Hazlitt, William. *Hazlitt's Criticism of Shakespeare: A Selection*. Edited by R. S. White. Lewiston, N.Y.: Edward Mellen Press, 1996.

Helmholz, R. H. *The Oxford History of the Laws of England*. Oxford: Oxford University Press, 2004.

Herodotus. *The Histories*. Translated by G. C. Macaulay. Revised throughout by Donald Lateiner. New York: Barnes and Noble, 2004.

Holden, William. *William Shakespeare: The Man Behind the Genius*. New York: Little, Brown, 2000.

Holmes, Oliver Wendell, Jr. *The Common Law*. 1938. New York: Dover Publications, 1991.

Holmes, Stephen. *The Matador's Cape: America's Reckless Response to Terror*. Cambridge: Cambridge University Press, 2007.

Huggett, Richard. *Supernatural on Stage*. New York: Taplinger, 1975.

Hutson, Lorna. *The Invention of Suspicion: Law and Mimesis in Shakespeare and Renaissance Drama*. Oxford and New York: Oxford University Press, 2007.

Ihering, Rudolph von. *The Struggle for Law*. N.P., 1872.

Jacob, P. L. *The Arts in the Middle Ages and the Renaissance*. New York: F. Ungar, 1964.

Jacoby, Susan. *Wild Justice: The Evolution of Revenge*. New York: Harper and Row, 1983.

King James VI and I. *Basilicon Doron*. In *Political Writings*. 1599. Edited by Johann P. Sommerville. Cambridge: Cambridge University Press, 1994.

——. *Daemonologie*. 1597. Edited by G. B. Harrison. San Diego: The Book Tree, 2002.

——. *The Political Works of James I*. Edited by Charles Howard McIlwain. Cambridge, Mass.: Harvard University Press, 1918.

Jones, Ernest. *Hamlet and Oedipus*. 1949. New York: W. W. Norton, 1976.

Joyce, James. *Ulysses*. 1925. New York: Random House, 1986.

Kahn, Paul W. *Law and Love: The Trials of King Lear*. New Haven: Yale University Press, 2000.

Kantorowicz, Ernst. *The King's Two Bodies: A Study in Mediaeval Political Theology*. Princeton: Princeton University Press, 1957.

Kelly, Henry Ansgar. *The Matrimonial Trials of Henry VIII*. Palo Alto, Calif.: Stanford University Press, 1976.

Kerferd, G. B. *The Sophistic Movement*. Cambridge: Cambridge University Press, 1981.

Knight, G. Wilson. *The Wheel of Fire*. 1930. New York: Routledge Classics, 2001.

Korda, Natasha. *Shakespeare's Domestic Economies: Gender and Property in Early Modern England.* Philadelphia: University of Pennsylvania Press, 2006.

Kornstein, Daniel J. *Kill All the Lawyers?: Shakespeare's Legal Appeal.* Lincoln: University of Nebraska Press, 2005.

Kushner, Harold. *When Bad Things Happen to Good People.* New York: Random House, 1981.

Langbein, John H. *Torture and the Law of Proof: Europe and England in the Ancien Régime.* 1976. Chicago: University of Chicago Press, 2006.

Langbein, John H., Renée Lettow Lerner, and Bruce P. Smith. *History of the Common Law: The Development of Anglo-American Legal Institutions.* New York: Aspen Publishers, 2009.

Levy, Leonard W. *The Palladium of Justice: Origins of Trial by Jury.* Chicago: Ivan Dee Press, 1999.

Machiavelli, Niccolò. *The Prince.* 1515. Edited by Quentin Skinner and Russell Price. Cambridge: Cambridge University Press, 1988.

Mack, Maynard. *Everybody's Shakespeare.* Lincoln: University of Nebraska Press, 1993.

Meron, Theodor. *Henry's Wars and Shakespeare's Laws: Perspectives on the Law of War in the Later Middle Ages.* New York: Oxford University Press, 1993.

Miller, William Ian. *Bloodtaking and Peacemaking: Feud, Law, and Society in Saga Iceland.* Chicago: University of Chicago, 1990.

Milton, John. *Paradise Lost.* 1667. Edited by David Scott Kastan. Indianapolis, Ind.: Hackett, 2005.

Minutaglio, Bill. *First Son: George W. Bush and the Bush Family Dynasty.* New York: Three Rivers Press, 1999.

Montaigne, Michel de. *The Essays of Montaigne.* 1580. Translated by M. A. Screech. London: Penguin, 1991.

More, Sir Thomas. *Utopia.* 1516. Translated by Clarence H. Miller. New Haven: Yale University Press, 2001.

Nietzsche, Friedrich. *The Birth of Tragedy.* 1871. Stilwell, Kans.: Digireads Publishing, 2007.

Nuttall, A. D. *Shakespeare the Thinker.* New Haven: Yale University Press, 2007.

O'Brien, Michael. *John F. Kennedy.* New York: St. Martin's, 2005.

Ovid. *The Metamorphoses.* Edited and translated by Allen Mandelbaum. New York: Harcourt, 1993.

Plato. *The Republic of Plato*. Edited and translated by Allan Bloom. New York: Basic Books, 1991.

Posner, Richard A. *Law and Literature: A Misunderstood Relation*. Cambridge, Mass.: Harvard University Press, 1988.

———. *Law and Literature*. Rev. ed. Cambridge, Mass.: Harvard University Press, 2002.

———. *Law and Literature*. 3rd ed. Cambridge, Mass.: Harvard University Press, 2009.

Rymer, Thomas. *A Short View of Tragedy*. 1693. Reproduced in *Othello: A Source-book*. Edited by Andrew Hadfield. New York: Routledge, 2003.

Scarry, Elaine. *On Beauty and Being Just*. Princeton: Princeton University Press, 1999.

Schiller, Lawrence, and James Willwerth. *American Tragedy: The Uncensored Story of the Simpson Case*. New York: Random House, 1996.

Seneca. *Thyestes*. Edited by Joost Daalder. Translated by Jasper Heywood. New York: W. W. Norton, 1982.

Shapiro, Barbara J. *A Culture of Fact: England, 1550–1720*. Ithaca, N.Y.: Cornell University Press, 2000.

Sidney, Sir Philip. *An Apology for Poetry*. Edited by Geoffrey Shepherd. Manchester: Manchester University Press, 1973.

Skinner, B. F. *Walden Two*. Indianapolis, Ind.: Hackett, 1948.

Sokol, B. J., and Mary Sokol. *Shakespeare, Law, and Marriage*. Cambridge: Cambridge University Press, 2003.

Sontag, Susan. *Illness as Metaphor*. New York: Farrar, Straus and Giroux, 1978.

Sophocles. *Antigone*. In *Antigone; Oedipus the King; Electra*. Edited by Edith Hall. Translated by Humphrey Davy Findley Kitto. Oxford: Oxford University Press, 1998.

The Starr Report: The Findings of Independent Counsel Kenneth W. Starr on President Clinton and the Lewinsky Affair. New York: Public Affairs, 1998.

Stewart, Alan. *The Cradle King: The Life of James V & I, the First Monarch of a United Great Britain*. New York: St. Martin's Press, 2007.

Stone, Lawrence. *The Crisis of the Aristocracy 1558–1641*. Oxford: Clarendon Press, 1965.

Stretton, Tim. *Women Waging War in Elizabethan England*. Cambridge: Cambridge University Press, 1998.

Toobin, Jeffrey. *The Run of His Life: The People v. O. J. Simpson*. New York: Random House, 1996.

Weber, Max. *The Vocation Lectures*. Edited by David Owen and Tracy B. Strong. Translated by Rodney Livingstone. Indianapolis, Ind.: Hackett, 2004.

Weisberg, Jacob. *George W. Bushisms: The Slate Book of Accidental Wit and Wisdom of Our 43rd President*. New York: Fireside, 2001.

White, Edward J. *Commentaries on the Law in Shakespeare*. St. Louis, Mo.: F. H. Thomas Law Books Co., 1913.

Whitman, James Q. *Origins of Reasonable Doubt*. New Haven: Yale University Press, 2007.

Wills, Garry. *Cincinnatus: George Washington and the Enlightenment*. New York: Doubleday, 1984.

Woodward, Bob. *State of Denial*. New York: Simon & Schuster, 2006.

Yeats, William Butler. *The Yeats Reader*. New York: Scribner, 1997.

Scholarly Articles

Altus, Deborah E., and Edward K. Morris. "B. F. Skinner's Utopian Vision: Behind and Beyond *Walden Two*." *Contemporary Justice Review* 267 (2004): 272.

Bate, Jonathan. "Introduction." In *The Most Lamentable Romaine Tragedie of Titus Andronicus*, by William Shakespeare. Edited by Jonathan Bate. London: Arden Shakespeare, 2006.

Beran, Michael Knox. "Lincoln, *Macbeth*, and the Moral Imagination." *Humanitas* 2, no. 2 (1998): 4–21.

Berger, Harry, Jr. "Marriage and Mercifixion in *The Merchant of Venice*: The Casket Scene Revisited." *Shakespeare Quarterly* 32, no. 2 (1981): 155–62.

Bevington, David. "Shakespeare's Sources." In *Macbeth*, by William Shakespeare. Edited by David Bevington. New York: Random House, 1988.

———. "Shakespeare's Sources." In *King Lear*, by William Shakespeare. Edited by David Bevington. New York: Bantam Books, 1988.

Boswell, Jackson Campbell. "Shylock's Turquoise Ring." *Shakespeare Quarterly* 14, no. 4 (1963): 481–83.

Burton, J. Anthony. "An Unrecognized Theme in *Hamlet*: Lost Inheritance and Claudius's Marriage to Gertrude." *The Shakespeare Newsletter* 50 (2000–2001): 71–82.

Butler, Paul. "Racially Based Jury Nullification: Black Power in the Criminal Justice System." *Yale Law Journal* 105 (1995): 677–725.

Cole, Simon A., and Rachel Dioso-Villa. "Investigating the 'CSI Effect' Effect: Media and Litigation Crisis in Criminal Law." *Stanford Law Review* 61 (2009): 1335–73.

Cover, Robert M. "Nomos and Narrative." *Harvard Law Review* 97 (1983): 4–68.

Dershowitz, Alan M. "Life Is Not a Dramatic Narrative." In *Law's Stories: Narrative and Rhetoric in the Law*. Edited by Peter Brooks and Paul Gewirtz. New Haven: Yale University Press, 1996, 99–105.

Dolven, Jeff. "Spenser's Sense of Poetic Justice." *Raritan* 21, no. 1 (2001): 127–40.

Egan, Gabriel. "The Early Seventeenth-Century Origin of the Macbeth Superstition." *Notes and Queries* 49 (2002): 236–37.

Elon, Menachem. "Law, Truth, and Peace: The Three Pillars of the World." *New York University Journal of International Law Politics* 29 (1996): 439–72.

Elster, Jon. "Norms of Revenge." *Ethics* 100 (1990): 862–85.

Finnis, John. "Natural Law." In *Routledge Encyclopedia of Philosophy*, vol. 6. Edited by Edward Craig. London: Routledge, 1998, 685.

Fish, Morris, J. "An Eye for an Eye: Proportionality as a Moral Principle of Punishment." *Oxford Journal of Legal Studies* 28 (2008): 57–71.

Fisher, George. "The Jury's Rise as Lie Detector." *Yale Law Journal* 107 (1997): 575–713.

———. "The O. J. Simpson Corpus." *Stanford Law Review* 49 (1996–97): 973–1019.

Frye, Northrop. "Varieties of Literary Utopias." In *Utopias and Utopian Thought*. Edited by Frank E. Manuel. Boston: Beacon Press, 1965, 25–49.

Gohn, Jack Benoit. "*Richard II*: Shakespeare's Legal Brief on the Royal Prerogative and the Succession to the Throne." *Georgetown Law Journal* 70 (1982): 943–73.

Greenblatt, Stephen. "Invisible Bullets." In *Political Shakespeare: Essays in Cultural Materialism*. Edited by Jonathan Dollimore and Alan Sinfield. Manchester: Manchester University Press, 1994, 18–47.

Henderson, Edith G. "Relief from Bonds in the English Chancery: Mid-Sixteenth Century." *American Journal of Legal History* 18, no. 4 (1974): 298–306.

Hughes, Alan. "Introduction." In *Titus Andronicus,* by William Shakespeare. Edited by Alan Hughes. New York: Cambridge University Press, 2006.

Kastan, David Scott. "Introduction." In *The First Part of King Henry the Fourth,* by William Shakespeare. Edited David Scott Kastan. London: Arden Shakespeare, 2007, 1–131.

Kerr, Margaret H., Richard D. Forsyth, and Michael J. Plyley. "Cold Water and Hot Iron: Trial by Ordeal in England." *Journal of Interdisciplinary History* 22, no. 4 (1992): 573–95.

Kerrigan, John. "Shakespeare's Poems." In *The Cambridge Companion to Shakespeare.* Edited by Margreta De Grazia and Stanley W. Wells. Cambridge: Cambridge University Press, 2001.

Kolin, Philip C. "*Titus Andronicus* and the Critical Legacy." In *Titus Andronicus: Critical Essays.* Edited by Philip C. Kolin. New York: Garland, 1995.

Lynch, Jack. "The Politics of Shakespeare, the Shakespeare of Politics." Paper presented at the English Speaking Union of Monmouth County, Rumson, New Jersey, February 17, 2008.

Midgley, G. "The Merchant of Venice: A Reconsideration." *Essays in Criticism* 10, no. 2 (1960): 119–33.

Morgan, Edmund. "The Puritans and Sex." *The New England Quarterly* 15, no. 4 (1942): 591–607.

Muir, Kenneth. "Introduction." In *Macbeth,* by William Shakespeare. Edited by Kenneth Muir. London: Arden Shakespeare, 2005, xiii–lxv.

Podlas, Kimberlianne. "'The *CSI* Effect': Exposing the Media Myth." *Fordham Intellectual Property Media and Entertainment Law Journal* 6 (2006): 429–65.

Posner, Richard. "The Ethical Significance of Free Choice: A Reply to Professor West," *Harvard Law Review* 99 (1986): 1433.

Raffield, Paul "'Terras Astraea reliquit': *Titus Andronicus* and the Loss of Justice." In *Shakespeare and the Law.* Edited by Paul Raffield and Gary Watt. Oxford: Hart Publishing, 2008, 203–20.

Ravid, Benjamin. "From Yellow to Red: On the Distinguishing Head-Covering of the Jews of Venice." *Jewish History* 6, no. 1 (1992): 179–210.

Rosenblatt, Jason P. "Aspects of the Incest Problem in *Hamlet*." *Shakespeare Quarterly* 29 (1978): 349–64.

Shelton, Donald E., Young S. Kim, and Gregg Barak. "A Study of Juror Expectations and Demands Concerning Scientific Evidence: Does the '*CSI*

Effect' Exist?" *Vanderbilt Journal of Entertainment and Technology* 9 (Winter 2006): 331–68.

———. "An Indirect-Effects Model of Mediated Adjudication: The CSI Myth, the Tech Effect, and Metropolitan Jurors' Expectations for Scientific Evidence." *Vanderbilt Journal of Entertainment and Technology* 12 (Fall 2009): 1–43.

Stevens, John Paul. "The Shakespeare Canon of Statutory Construction." *University of Pennsylvania Law Review* 140 (1992): 1372–87.

Sunderland, Edson. "Verdicts, General and Special." *Yale Law Journal* 29 (1920): 253–67.

Thompson, Ann, and Neil Taylor. "Notes." In *Hamlet*, by William Shakespeare. Edited by Ann Thompson and Neil Taylor. London: Arden Shakespeare, 2006.

Tyler, Tom R. "Viewing CSI and the Threshold of Guilt: Managing Truth and Justice in Reality and Fiction." *Yale Law Journal* 115 (2006): 1050–85.

Vaughan, Virginia Mason, and Alden T. Vaughan. "Introduction." In *The Tempest*, by William Shakespeare. London: Arden Shakespeare, 1999, 1–138.

Zabel, William D. "Interracial Marriage and the Law." In *Interracialism: Black-White Intermarriage in American History, Literature and Law*. Edited by Werner Sollors. New York: Oxford University Press, 2000, 54–61.

Magazine, Newspaper, and Weblog Articles

"9/11 by the Numbers." *New York Magazine*, September 16, 2002, http://nymag.com/news/articles/wtc/1year/numbers.htm (accessed June 26, 2010).

Adelman, Ken. "Not Lady Macbeth." *Washingtonian Magazine*, November 1, 1999.

Althouse, Ann. "When is it considered socially acceptable to joke to a stranger that people like you should all be dead?" Althouse blog, posted December 21, 2004, http://althouse.blogspot.com/2004/12/when-is-it-considered-socially.html (accessed June 26, 2010).

Associated Press. "Expert: Shrinkage, Damage in Gloves." *Seattle Times*, June 15, 1995.

Benedetto, Richard. "Support for Bush, Military Action Remains Firm." *USA Today*, September 24, 2001.

Bergman, Barry. "'Who's going to believe us?' Richard Clarke faults Bush team's post–9/11 policies." *U.C. Berkeley News,* September 8, 2004, http://berkeley.edu/news/media/releases/2004/09/08_clarke.shtml (accessed June 26, 2010).

Borger, Julian. "The Making of a Dynasty." *The Guardian* (U.K.), October 31, 1998.

Brantley, Ben. "Howl? Nay, Express His Lighter Purpose." *New York Times,* March 8, 2007.

"Bush Faces New Round of Drug Questions." CNN, August 20, 1999, http://www.cnn.com/ALLPOLITICS/stories/1999/08/20/president.2000/bush.drug/ (accessed June 27, 2010).

"Bush Rejects Taliban Offer to Hand Bin Laden Over." *The Guardian* (U.K.), October 14, 2001, http://www.guardian.co.uk/world/2001/oct/14/afghanistan.terrorism5 (accessed June 26, 2010).

Dominguez, Robert. "Summer in the City 2003: One Thing's for Curtain, the Shows Go On." *New York Daily News,* May 23, 2003.

Egan, Timothy. "The Simpson Case: The Jury: With Spotlight Shifted to Them, Some Simpson Jurors Talk Freely." *New York Times,* October 5, 1995.

Espo, David. "White House Hopefuls Pay Tribute to King." *Seattle Times,* April 6, 2008.

Foote, Donna, Mark Miller, and Tessa Namuth. "A Size Too Small." *Newsweek,* June 26, 1995.

Hakim, Danny, and William K. Rashbaum. "Spitzer Is Linked to Prostitution Ring." *New York Times,* March 10, 2008.

Hersh, Seymour M. "Torture at Abu Ghraib." *The New Yorker,* May 10, 2004.

Holden, Stephen. "It's a Sort of Family Dinner, Your Majesty." *New York Times,* December 24, 1999.

Ifill, Gwen. "The 1992 Campaign: New York; Clinton Admits Experiment with Marijuana in 1960's." *New York Times,* March 30, 1992.

Ingrams, Richard. "Diary: Richard Ingrams' Week: Trial of King Tony: His Grounds for War Are Falling Apart, So Who Will Trust Blair on the Euro?" *The Observer* (London), May 18, 2003.

Kane, Paul, and Chris Cillizza. "Sen. Ensign Acknowledges an Extramarital Affair." *Washington Post,* June 17, 2009.

Kiely, Kathy, and Joan Biskupic. "Sotomayor's Remarks Cap Emotional Day." *USA Today,* July 13, 2009.

Klein, Joe. "The Return of the Hot-Button Issues." *Time,* June 4, 2009.

LaSalle, Mick. "Taymor's *Titus* Twisted and Terrific." *San Francisco Chronicle,* January 28, 2000.

Lipkin, Michael. "Justice Breyer Speaks on Shakespeare and Law." *Chicago Maroon,* May 19, 2009, http://www.chicagomaroon.com/2009/5/19/justice-breyer-speaks-on-shakespeare-and-law.

Lowry, Rich. "Magnificent: This Was Not a Foggy Bottom Speech." *National Review Online,* September 21, 2001, http://www.nationalreview.com/lowry/lowry092101.shtml.

Margolick, David. "O. J. Simpson Jury Revisits the Gloves, a Stitch at a Time." *New York Times,* September 13, 1995.

Muskal, Michael. "Sotomayor, Senators Make Nice—For Now." *Los Angeles Times,* June 3, 2009.

Newstok, Scott. "'Step aside, I'll show thee a president': George W as Henry V?" (2003), www.poppolitics.com/archives/2003/05/George-W-as-Henry-V.

"Obama's Remarks on the Resignation of Justice Souter." *New York Times,* May 1, 2009.

O'Brian, John F. "Opportunity for All." New England School of Law History Project, http://www.nesl.edu/historyProject/ (accessed June 26, 2010).

Office of the Independent Counsel, Transcript of Testimony of William Jefferson Clinton, President of the United States, Before the Grand Jury Empanelled for Independent Counsel Kenneth Starr. August 17, 1998, http://jurist.law.pitt.edu/transcr.htm (accessed June 26, 2010).

"Picture Emerges of Fallujah Siege." *BBC News,* April 23, 2004, http://news.bbc.co.uk/2/hi/middle_east/3653223.stm (accessed June 27, 2010).

Raasch, Chuck. "Sotomayor Speech at Center of Court Nomination." *USA Today,* June 4, 2009.

Rove, Karl. "'Empathy' Is Code for Judicial Activism." *Wall Street Journal,* May 28, 2009.

Savage, Charlie. "A Nominee on Display, but Not Her Views." *New York Times,* July 16, 2009.

Segal, David. "Macshush! Theater Superstition Warns of Double Trouble if the Name Is Spoken." *Washington Post,* June 13, 2006.

Sontag, Susan. "Regarding the Torture of Others." *New York Times,* May 23, 2004.

Sotomayor, Sonya. "A Latina Judge's Voice." Address, University of California Berkeley School of Law Symposium: Raising the Bar, Berkeley, California, October 26, 2001.

Statement of Senator Obama, *Congressional Record* 151 (September 22, 2005): S10365.

Thompson, Bob. "The King and We: Henry V's War Cabinet." *Washington Post,* May 18, 2004.

Vazsonyi, Balint. "From Henry V to Bush II." *Washington Times,* October 12, 2001.

Weber, Bruce. "Umpires v. Judges." *New York Times,* July 12, 2009.

Weigant, Chris. "Is the Media Misinterpreting Obama's 'Empathy' Dog Whistle?," *Huffington Post,* May 7, 2009, http://www.huffingtonpost.com/chris-weigant/is-the-media-misinterpret_b_198389.html

Will, George F. "In 'Forgiveness Mode.'" *Washington Post,* September 16, 1998.

Cases

AT & T Corporation v. Hulteen, 129 S. Ct. 1962, 1980 (2009).

Boumediene v. Bush, 553 U.S. 723 (2008).

Dred Scott v. Sandford, 60 U.S. 393 (1857).

Hamdan v. Rumsfeld, 548 U.S. 557 (2006).

Hamdi v. Rumsfeld, 542 U.S. 507 (2004).

J. E. B. v. Alabama ex rel. T. B., 511 U.S. 127 (1994).

Krimstock v. Kelly, 306 F.3d 40 (2d Cir. 2002).

Marbury v. Madison, 5 U.S. (1 Cranch) 137, 163 (1803).

Parents Involved in Community Schools v. Seattle School Dist. No. 1, 551 U.S. 701 (2007).

Rasul v. Bush, 542 U.S. 466 (2004).

Constitutions, Statutes, and Regulations

Acte Against Usurie, 13 Eliz. I, c. 8 (1571).

"Authorization for Use of Military Force Against Terrorists 2001." (P. L. 107–40), *United States Statutes at Large,* 115 Stat. 224.

Statute of Marlbridge, 52 Hen. 3, c.6 (1257).

U.S. Constitution, art. III; amends. VI, VII, XIV.

Other Legal Materials

Closing Argument by Ms. Clark and Closing Argument by Mr. Darden at *36, Simpson (No. BA097211), available in 1995 WL 672671 (closing argument by Clark).

"Excerpts from Closing Arguments on Murder Charges Against O. J. Simpson," *New York Times,* September 28, 1995.

Senate Committee on the Judiciary, Confirmation Hearing on the Nomination of John G. Roberts, Jr., to be Chief Justice of the United States. S. Hrg. 109–158 sess., September 12–15, 2005.

Miscellaneous

Acton, Lord. Letter to Bishop Mandell, 1887.

Falwell, Jerry. Interview, CNN, September 14, 2001, http://archives.cnn.com/2001/US/09/14/Falwell.apology/.

Henry V, DVD, directed by Kenneth Branagh (1989; Hollywood, Calif.: MGM, 2000).

The Merchant of Venice, DVD, directed by Michael Radford (2004; Sony Pictures Classics, 2005).

Obama, Barack. Interview by Wolf Blitzer, *The Situation Room,* CNN, May 8, 2008.

Stewart, Patrick. *Shylock: Shakespeare's Alien.* Leeds, England: 2001.

Titus, DVD, directed by Julie Taymor (1999; Century City, Calif.: 20th Century Fox, 2006).